Feature Enginee
Easy

MW00581069

Identify unique features from your dataset in order to build
powerful machine learning systems

Sinan Ozdemir
Divya Susarla

BIRMINGHAM - MUMBAI

Feature Engineering Made Easy

Commissioning Editor: Veena Pagare
Acquisition Editor: Varsha Shetty
Content Development Editor: Tejas Limkar
Technical Editor: Sayli Nikalje
Copy Editor: Safis Editing
Project Coordinator: Manthan Patel
Proofreader: Safis Editing
Indexer: Tejal Daruwale Soni
Graphics: Tania Datta
Production Coordinator: Shantanu Zagade

First published: January 2018

Production reference: 1190118

Published by Packt Publishing Ltd.
Livery Place
35 Livery Street
Birmingham
B3 2PB, UK.

ISBN 978-1-78728-760-0

www.packtpub.com

`mapt.io`

Mapt is an online digital library that gives you full access to over 5,000 books and videos, as well as industry leading tools to help you plan your personal development and advance your career. For more information, please visit our website.

Why subscribe?

- Spend less time learning and more time coding with practical eBooks and Videos from over 4,000 industry professionals

- Improve your learning with Skill Plans built especially for you

- Get a free eBook or video every month

- Mapt is fully searchable

- Copy and paste, print, and bookmark content

PacktPub.com

Did you know that Packt offers eBook versions of every book published, with PDF and ePub files available? You can upgrade to the eBook version at `www.PacktPub.com` and as a print book customer, you are entitled to a discount on the eBook copy. Get in touch with us at `service@packtpub.com` for more details.

At `www.PacktPub.com`, you can also read a collection of free technical articles, sign up for a range of free newsletters, and receive exclusive discounts and offers on Packt books and eBooks.

Contributors

About the authors

Sinan Ozdemir is a data scientist, start-up founder, and educator living in the San Francisco Bay Area. He studied pure mathematics at Johns Hopkins University. He then spent several years conducting lectures on data science at Johns Hopkins University before founding his own start-up, Kylie.ai, which uses artificial intelligence to clone brand personalities and automate customer service communications.

Sinan is also the author of *Principles of Data Science*, available through Packt.

> *I would like to thank my parents and sister for supporting me throughout my life, and also my partner, Elizabeth Beutel. I also would like to thank my co-author, Divya Susarla, and Packt Publishing for all of their support.*

Divya Susarla is an experienced leader in data methods, implementing and applying tactics across a range of industries and fields, such as investment management, social enterprise consulting, and wine marketing. She studied business economics and political science at the University of California, Irvine, USA.

Divya is currently focused on natural language processing and generation techniques at Kylie.ai, a start-up helping clients automate their customer support conversations.

> *I would like to thank my parents for their unwavering support and guidance, and also my partner, Neil Trivedi, for his patience and encouragement. Also, a shoutout to DSI-SF2; this book wouldn't be a reality without you all. Thanks to my co-author, Sinan Ozdemir, and to Packt Publishing for making this book possible.*

About the reviewer

Michael Smith uses big data and machine learning to learn about how people behave. His experience includes IBM Watson and consulting for the US government. Michael actively publishes at and attends several prominent conferences as he engineers systems using text data and AI. He enjoys discussing technology and learning new ways to tackle problems.

Packt is searching for authors like you

If you're interested in becoming an author for Packt, please visit `authors.packtpub.com` and apply today. We have worked with thousands of developers and tech professionals, just like you, to help them share their insight with the global tech community. You can make a general application, apply for a specific hot topic that we are recruiting an author for, or submit your own idea.

Table of Contents

Preface

This book will cover the topic of feature engineering. A huge part of the data science and machine learning pipeline, feature engineering includes the ability to identify, clean, construct, and discover new characteristics of data for the purpose of interpretation and predictive analysis.

In this book, we will be covering the entire process of feature engineering, from inspection to visualization, transformation, and beyond. We will be using both basic and advanced mathematical measures to transform our data into a form that's much more digestible by machines and machine learning pipelines.

By discovering and transforming, we, as data scientists, will be able to gain a whole new perspective on our data, enhancing not only our algorithms but also our insights.

Who this book is for

This book is for people who are looking to understand and utilize the practices of feature engineering for machine learning and data exploration.

The reader should be fairly well acquainted with machine learning and coding in Python to feel comfortable diving into new topics with a step-by-step explanation of the basics.

What this book covers

Chapter 1, *Introduction to Feature Engineering*, is an introduction to the basic terminology of feature engineering and a quick look at the types of problems we will be solving throughout this book.

Chapter 2, *Feature Understanding – What's in My Dataset?*, looks at the types of data we will encounter in the wild and how to deal with each one separately or together.

Chapter 3, *Feature Improvement - Cleaning Datasets*, explains various ways to fill in missing data and how different techniques lead to different structural changes in data that may lead to poorer machine learning performance.

Chapter 4, *Feature Construction*, is a look at how we can create new features based on what was already given to us in an effort to inflate the structure of data.

Chapter 5, *Feature Selection*, shows quantitative measures to decide which features are worthy of being kept in our data pipeline.

Chapter 6, *Feature Transformations*, uses advanced linear algebra and mathematical techniques to impose a rigid structure on data for the purpose of enhancing performance of our pipelines.

Chapter 7, *Feature Learning*, covers the use of state-of-the-art machine learning and artificial intelligence learning algorithms to discover latent features of our data that few humans could fathom.

Chapter 8, *Case Studies*, is an array of case studies shown in order to solidify the ideas of feature engineering.

To get the most out of this book

What do we require for this book:

1. This book uses Python to complete all of its code examples. A machine (Linux/Mac/Windows is OK) with access to a Unix-style terminal and Python 2.7 installed is required.
2. Installing the Anaconda distribution is also recommended as it comes with most of the packages used in the examples.

Download the example code files

You can download the example code files for this book from your account at www.packtpub.com. If you purchased this book elsewhere, you can visit www.packtpub.com/support and register to have the files emailed directly to you.

You can download the code files by following these steps:

1. Log in or register at www.packtpub.com.
2. Select the **SUPPORT** tab.
3. Click on **Code Downloads & Errata**.
4. Enter the name of the book in the **Search** box and follow the onscreen instructions.

Once the file is downloaded, please make sure that you unzip or extract the folder using the latest version of:

- WinRAR/7-Zip for Windows
- Zipeg/iZip/UnRarX for Mac
- 7-Zip/PeaZip for Linux

The code bundle for the book is also hosted on GitHub at `https://github.com/PacktPublishing/Feature-Engineering-Made-Easy`. We also have other code bundles from our rich catalog of books and videos available at `https://github.com/PacktPublishing/`. Check them out!

Download the color images

We also provide a PDF file that has color images of the screenshots/diagrams used in this book. You can download it here: `https://www.packtpub.com/sites/default/files/downloads/FeatureEngineeringMadeEasy_ColorImages.pdf`.

Conventions used

There are a number of text conventions used throughout this book.

`CodeInText`: Indicates code words in text, database table names, folder names, filenames, file extensions, pathnames, dummy URLs, user input, and Twitter handles. Here is an example: "Suppose further that given this dataset, our task is to be able to take in three of the attributes (`datetime`, `protocol`, and `urgent`) and to be able to accurately predict the value of `malicious`. In layman's terms, we want a system that can map the values of `datetime`, `protocol`, and `urgent` to the values in `malicious`."

A block of code is set as follows:

```
Network_features = pd.DataFrame({'datetime': ['6/2/2018', '6/2/2018',
'6/2/2018', '6/3/2018'], 'protocol': ['tcp', 'http', 'http', 'http'],
'urgent': [False, True, True, False]})
Network_response = pd.Series([True, True, False, True])
Network_features
>>
 datetime protocol  urgent
0  6/2/2018      tcp   False
1  6/2/2018     http    True
2  6/2/2018     http    True
3  6/3/2018     http   False
Network_response
```

```
>>
  0      True
  1      True
  2     False
  3      True
dtype: bool
```

When we wish to draw your attention to a particular part of a code block, the relevant lines or items are set in bold:

```
times_pregnant                    0.221898
plasma_glucose_concentration      0.466581
diastolic_blood_pressure          0.065068
triceps_thickness                 0.074752
serum_insulin                     0.130548
bmi                               0.292695
pedigree_function                 0.173844
age                               0.238356
onset_diabetes                    1.000000
Name: onset_diabetes, dtype: float64
```

Bold: Indicates a new term, an important word, or words that you see onscreen.

 Warnings or important notes appear like this.

 Tips and tricks appear like this.

Get in touch

Feedback from our readers is always welcome.

General feedback: Email feedback@packtpub.com and mention the book title in the subject of your message. If you have questions about any aspect of this book, please email us at questions@packtpub.com.

Errata: Although we have taken every care to ensure the accuracy of our content, mistakes do happen. If you have found a mistake in this book, we would be grateful if you would report this to us. Please visit www.packtpub.com/submit-errata, selecting your book, clicking on the Errata Submission Form link, and entering the details.

Piracy: If you come across any illegal copies of our works in any form on the Internet, we would be grateful if you would provide us with the location address or website name. Please contact us at copyright@packtpub.com with a link to the material.

If you are interested in becoming an author: If there is a topic that you have expertise in and you are interested in either writing or contributing to a book, please visit authors.packtpub.com.

Reviews

Please leave a review. Once you have read and used this book, why not leave a review on the site that you purchased it from? Potential readers can then see and use your unbiased opinion to make purchase decisions, we at Packt can understand what you think about our products, and our authors can see your feedback on their book. Thank you!

For more information about Packt, please visit packtpub.com.

1
Introduction to Feature Engineering

In recent years, engineers and executives have been attempting to implement **machine learning (ML)** and **artificial intelligence (AI)** to solve problems that, for the most part, have been solved using fairly manual methodologies. A great example would have to be advancements in **natural language processing (NLP)** and more specifically in natural language generation and understanding. Even more specifically, we point to AI systems that are able to read in raw text from a user (perhaps a disgruntled user of the latest smartphone) and can articulately and accurately respond with the prose of a human and the speed of a machine. In this chapter, we will be introducing topics of feature engineering, such as:

- Motivating examples of why feature engineering matters
- Basic understanding of machine learning, including performance, evaluation
- A detailed list of the chapters included in this book

Motivating example – AI-powered communications

Meet Arty, our AI chat system that is able to handle and respond to incoming customer support requests, just as any of our human employees would. Arty is endowed with the knowledge of our company and is ready to go at a moment's notice.

Here is how a sample dialogue between a human and an AI customer support system would transpire:

Human	AI
Hello, my phone is broken.	Sorry to hear that, how is it broken?
It's frozen and I can't reset it.	What kind of phone is it?
The new iDroid 28	Ahh, I see. Hold the power and volume down button for 20 seconds and it should reset.
It worked, thanks!	No problem, have a great day.

The reason that these types of systems are exciting and are disrupting major markets is the simplicity of such a complicated system. Let us break it down. On the surface, you might think, *what an easy problem!* The person has a simple problem with a simple solution. A request comes in and a response comes out. *Hello, my phone froze, what should I do?* Easy, just reset it. And sure, on the surface, that is what is happening here:

```
from Arty import AI
AI.respond_to("my phone froze, what should I do?")
>> "reset it."
```

The tough part comes in when you look at it from the AI's perspective. It hasn't had the entire human experience that we have had. It hasn't had the privilege to read *The Illiad* or even *Clifford the Big Red Dog* and learn to internalize their messages. The point is, the AI hasn't had a lot of experience in reading things. This AI has probably been given a few hundred thousand (maybe even millions) of previous chat dialogues of people in the past and was told to figure it out.

The following is a sample of data given to our AI system based on previous chat logs:

Request	Response
Helllo	Hi, what seems to be the problem?
My phone doesn't work!!!!	Oh noo!!!! What's going on with it?
>Hold on, I have to go walk my dog. BRB.	OK. I will wait.
Hey.	Hello. My name is Mark, how can I help?

The data is organized into two columns where the `Request` column represents what the end user types into a chat support dialogue. The next column, `Response`, represents the customer support agent's response to the incoming message.

While reading over the thousands of typos, angry messages, and disconnected chats, the AI starts to think that it has this customer support thing down. Once this happens, the humans set the AI loose on new chats coming in. The humans, not realizing their mistake, start to notice that the AI hasn't fully gotten the hang of this yet. The AI can't seem to recognize even simple messages and keeps returning nonsensical responses. It's easy to think that the AI just needs more time or more data, but these solutions are just band-aids to the bigger problem, and often do not even solve the issue in the first place.

The underlying problem is likely that the data given to the AI in the form of raw text wasn't good enough and the AI wasn't able to pick up on the nuances of the English language. For example, some of the problems would likely include:

- Typos artificially expand the AI's vocabulary without cause. *Helllo* and *hello* are two different words that are not related to each other.
- Synonyms mean nothing to the AI. Words such as *hello* and *hey* have no similarity and therefore make the problem artificially harder.

Why feature engineering matters

Data scientists and machine learning engineers frequently gather data in order to solve a problem. Because the problem they are attempting to solve is often highly relevant and exists and occurs naturally in this messy world, the data that is meant to represent the problem can also end up being quite messy and unfiltered, and often incomplete.

This is why in the past several years, positions with titles such as *Data Engineer* have been popping up. These engineers have the unique job of engineering pipelines and architectures designed to handle and transform raw data into something usable by the rest of the company, particularly the data scientists and machine learning engineers. This job is not only as important as the machine learning experts' job of creating machine learning pipelines, it is often overlooked and undervalued.

A survey conducted by data scientists in the field revealed that over 80% of their time was spent capturing, cleaning, and organizing data. The remaining less than 20% of their time was spent creating these machine learning pipelines that end up dominating the conversation. Moreover, these data scientists are spending most of their time preparing the data; more than 75% of them also reported that preparing data was the least enjoyable part of their process.

Here are the findings of the survey mentioned earlier:

Following is the graph of the what Data Scientist spend the most time doing:

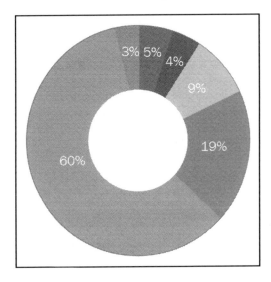

As seen from the preceding graph, we breakup the Data Scientists's task in the following percentage :

- **Building training sets**: 3%
- **Cleaning and organizing data**: 60%
- **Collecting data for sets**: 19%
- **Mining data for patterns**: 9%
- **Refining algorithms**: 5%

A similar pie diagram for what is the least enjoyable part of data science:

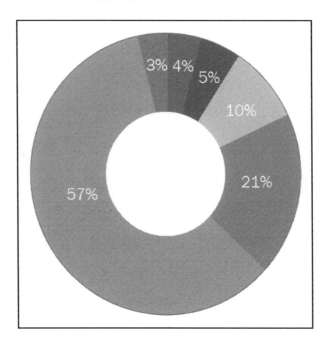

From the graph a similar poll for the least enjoyable part of data science revealed:

- **Building training sets**: 10 %
- **Cleaning and organizing data**: 57%
- **Collecting data sets**: 21%
- **Mining for data patterns**: 3%
- **Refining algorithms**: 4%
- **Others**: 5%

The uppermost chart represents the percentage of time that data scientists spend on different parts of the process. Over 80% of a data scientists' time is spent preparing data for further use. The lower chart represents the percentage of those surveyed reporting their least enjoyable part of the process of data science. Over 75% of them report that preparing data is their least enjoyable part.

Source of the data:
https://whatsthebigdata.com/2016/05/01/data-scientists-spend-most-of-their-time-cleaning-data/.

A stellar data scientist knows that preparing data is not only so important that it takes up most of their time, they also know that it is an arduous process and can be unenjoyable. Far too often, we take for granted clean data given to us by machine learning competitions and academic sources. More than 90% of data, the data that is interesting, and the most useful, exists in this raw format, like in the AI chat system described earlier.

Preparing data can be a vague phrase. Preparing takes into account capturing data, storing data, cleaning data, and so on. As seen in the charts shown earlier, a smaller, but still majority chunk of a data scientist's time is spent on cleaning and organizing data. It is in this process that our Data Engineers are the most useful to us. Cleaning refers to the process of transforming data into a format that can be easily interpreted by our cloud systems and databases. Organizing generally refers to a more radical transformation. Organizing tends to involve changing the entire format of the dataset into a much neater format, such as transforming raw chat logs into a tabular row/column structure.

Here is an illustration of **Cleaning** and **Organizing**:

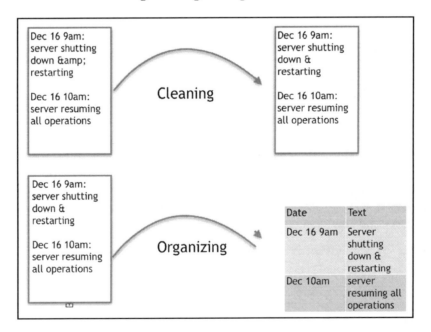

The top transformation represents cleaning up a sample of server logs that include both the data and a text explanation of what is occurring on the servers. Notice that while cleaning, the **&** character, which is a Unicode character, was transformed into a more readable ampersand (**&**). The cleaning phase left the document pretty much in the same exact format as before. The bottom organizing transformation was a much more radical one. It turned the raw document into a row/column structure, in which each row represents a single action taken by the server and the columns represent attributes of the server action. In this case, the two attributes are **Date** and **Text**.

Both cleaning and organizing fall under a larger category of data science, which just so happens to be the topic of this book, feature engineering.

What is feature engineering?

Finally, the title of the book.

Yes, folks, feature engineering will be the topic of this book. We will be focusing on the process of cleaning and organizing data for the purposes of machine learning pipelines. We will also go beyond these concepts and look at more complex transformations of data in the forms of mathematical formulas and neural understanding, but we are getting ahead of ourselves. Let's start a high level.

 Feature engineering is the process of transforming data into features that better represent the underlying problem, resulting in improved machine learning performance.

To break this definition down a bit further, let's look at precisely what feature engineering entails:

- **Process of transforming data**: Note that we are not specifying raw data, unfiltered data, and so on. Feature engineering can be applied to data at any stage. Oftentimes, we will be applying feature engineering techniques to data that is already *processed* in the eyes of the data distributor. It is also important to mention that the data that we will be working with will usually be in a tabular format. The data will be organized into rows (observations) and columns (attributes). There will be times when we will start with data at its most raw form, such as in the examples of the server logs mentioned previously, but for the most part, we will deal with data already somewhat cleaned and organized.

- **Features**: The word features will obviously be used a lot in this book. At its most basic level, a feature is an attribute of data that is meaningful to the machine learning process. Many times we will be diagnosing tabular data and identifying which columns are features and which are merely attributes.

- **Better represent the underlying problem**: The data that we will be working with will always serve to represent a specific problem in a specific domain. It is important to ensure that while we are performing these techniques, we do not lose sight of the bigger picture. We want to transform data so that it better represents the bigger problem at hand.

- **Resulting in improved machine learning performance**: Feature engineering exists as a single part of the process of data science. As we saw, it is an important and oftentimes undervalued part. The eventual goal of feature engineering is to obtain data that our learning algorithms will be able to extract patterns from and use in order to obtain better results. We will talk in depth about machine learning metrics and results later on in this book, but for now, know that we perform feature engineering not only to obtain cleaner data, but to eventually use that data in our machine learning pipelines.

We know what you're thinking, *why should I spend my time reading about a process that people say they do not enjoy doing?* We believe that many people do not enjoy the process of feature engineering because they often do not have the benefits of understanding the results of the work that they do.

Most companies employ both data engineers and machine learning engineers. The data engineers are primarily concerned with the preparation and transformation of the data, while the machine learning engineers usually have a working knowledge of learning algorithms and how to mine patterns from already cleaned data.

Their jobs are often separate but intertwined and iterative. The data engineers will present a dataset for the machine learning engineers, which they will claim they cannot get good results from, and ask the Data Engineers to try to transform the data further, and so on, and so forth. This process can not only be monotonous and repetitive, it can also hurt the bigger picture.

Without having knowledge of both feature and machine learning engineering, the entire process might not be as effective as it could be. That's where this book comes in. We will be talking about feature engineering and how it relates directly to machine learning. It will be a results-driven approach where we will deem techniques as helpful if, and only if, they can lead to a boost in performance. It is worth now diving a bit into the basics of data, the structure of data, and machine learning, to ensure standardization of terminology.

Understanding the basics of data and machine learning

When we talk about data, we are generally dealing with tabular data, that is, data that is organized into rows and columns. Think of this as being able to be opened in a spreadsheet technology such as Microsoft Excel. Each row of data, otherwise known as an **observation**, represents a single instance/example of a problem. If our data belongs to the domain of day-trading in the stock market, an observation might represent an hour's worth of changes in the overall market and price.

For example, when dealing with the domain of network security, an observation could represent a possible attack or a packet of data sent over a wireless system.

The following shows sample tabular data in the domain of cyber security and more specifically, network intrusion:

DateTime	Protocol	Urgent	Malicious
June 2nd, 2018	TCP	FALSE	TRUE
June 2nd, 2018	HTTP	TRUE	TRUE
June 2nd, 2018	HTTP	TRUE	FALSE
June 3rd, 2018	HTTP	FALSE	TRUE

We see that each row or observation consists of a network connection and we have four attributes of the observation: `DateTime`, `Protocol`, `Urgent`, and `Malicious`. While we will not dive into these specific attributes, we will simply notice the structure of the data given to us in a tabular format.

Because we will, for the most part, consider our data to be tabular, we can also look at specific instances where the matrix of data has only one column/attribute. For example, if we are building a piece of software that is able to take in a single image of a room and output whether or not there is a human in that room. The data for the input might be represented as a matrix of a single column where the single column is simply a URL to a photo of a room and nothing else.

For example, considering the following table of table that has only a single column titled, `Photo URL`. The values of the table are URLs (these are fake and do not lead anywhere and are purely for example) of photos that are relevant to the data scientist:

Photo URL
`http://photo-storage.io/room/1`
`http://photo-storage.io/room/2`
`http://photo-storage.io/room/3`
`http://photo-storage.io/room/4`

The data that is inputted into the system might only be a single column, such as in this case. In our ability to create a system that can analyze images, the input might simply be a URL to the image in question. It would be up to us as data scientists to engineer features from the URL.

As data scientists, we must be ready to ingest and handle data that might be large, small, wide, narrow (in terms of attributes), sparse in completion (there might be missing values), and be ready to utilize this data for the purposes of machine learning. Now's a good time to talk more about that. Machine learning algorithms belong to a class of algorithms that are defined by their ability to extract and exploit patterns in data to accomplish a task based on historical training data. Vague, right? machine learning can handle many types of tasks, and therefore we will leave the definition of machine learning as is and dive a bit deeper.

We generally separate machine learning into two main types, supervised and unsupervised learning. Each type of machine learning algorithm can benefit from feature engineering, and therefore it is important that we understand each type.

Supervised learning

Oftentimes, we hear about feature engineering in the specific context of supervised learning, otherwise known as predictive analytics. Supervised learning algorithms specifically deal with the task of predicting a value, usually one of the attributes of the data, using the other attributes of the data. Take, for example, the dataset representing the network intrusion:

DateTime	Protocol	Urgent	Malicious
June 2nd, 2018	TCP	FALSE	TRUE
June 2nd, 2018	HTTP	TRUE	TRUE
June 2nd, 2018	HTTP	TRUE	FALSE
June 3rd, 2018	HTTP	FALSE	TRUE

This is the same dataset as before, but let's dissect it further in the context of predictive analytics.

Notice that we have four attributes of this dataset: `DateTime`, `Protocol`, `Urgent`, and `Malicious`. Suppose now that the malicious attribute contains values that represent whether or not the observation was a malicious intrusion attempt. So in our very small dataset of four network connections, the first, second, and fourth connection were malicious attempts to intrude a network.

Suppose further that given this dataset, our task is to be able to take in three of the attributes (`datetime`, `protocol`, and `urgent`) and be able to accurately predict the value of malicious. In laymen's terms, we want a system that can map the values of `datetime`, `protocol`, and `urgent` to the values in malicious. This is exactly how a supervised learning problem is set up:

```
Network_features = pd.DataFrame({'datetime': ['6/2/2018', '6/2/2018',
'6/2/2018', '6/3/2018'], 'protocol': ['tcp', 'http', 'http', 'http'],
'urgent': [False, True, True, False]})
Network_response = pd.Series([True, True, False, True])
Network_features
>>
  datetime protocol   urgent
0  6/2/2018      tcp    False
1  6/2/2018     http     True
2  6/2/2018     http     True
3  6/3/2018     http    False
Network_response
```

```
>>
  0       True
  1       True
  2      False
  3       True
dtype: bool
```

When we are working with supervised learning, we generally call the attribute (usually only one of them, but that is not necessary) of the dataset that we are attempting to predict the response of. The remaining attributes of the dataset are then called the **features**.

Supervised learning can also be considered the class of algorithms attempting to exploit the structure in data. By this, we mean that the machine learning algorithms try to extract patterns in usually very nice and neat data. As discussed earlier, we should not always expect data to come in tidy; this is where feature engineering comes in.

But if we are not predicting something, what good is machine learning you may ask? I'm glad you did. Before machine learning can exploit the structure of data, sometimes we have to alter or even create structure. That's where unsupervised learning becomes a valuable tool.

Unsupervised learning

Supervised learning is all about making predictions. We utilize features of the data and use them to make informative predictions about the response of the data. If we aren't making predictions by exploring structure, we are attempting to extract structure from our data. We generally do so by applying mathematical transformations to numerical matrix representations of data or iterative procedures to obtain new sets of features.

This concept can be a bit more difficult to grasp than supervised learning, and so I will present a motivating example to help elucidate how this all works.

Unsupervised learning example – marketing segments

Suppose we are given a large (one million rows) dataset where each row/observation is a single person with basic demographic information (age, gender, and so on) as well as the number of items purchased, which represents how many items this person has bought from a particular store:

Age	Gender	Number of items purchased
25	F	1
28	F	23
61	F	3
54	M	17
51	M	8
47	F	3
27	M	22
31	F	14

This is a sample of our marketing dataset where each row represents a single customer with three basic attributes about each person. Our goal will be to segment this dataset into types or **clusters** of people so that the company performing the analysis can understand the customer profiles much better.

Now, of course, We've only shown 8 out of one million rows, which can be daunting. Of course, we can perform basic descriptive statistics on this dataset and get averages, standard deviations, and so on of our numerical columns; however, what if we wished to segment these one million people into different **types** so that the marketing department can have a much better sense of the types of people who shop and create more appropriate advertisements for each segment?

Each type of customer would exhibit particular qualities that make that segment unique. For example, they may find that 20% of their customers fall into a category they like to call young and wealthy that are generally younger and purchase several items.

This type of analysis and the creation of these types can fall under a specific type of unsupervised learning called **clustering**. We will discuss this machine learning algorithm in further detail later on in this book, but for now, clustering will create a new feature that separates out the people into distinct types or clusters:

Age	Gender	Number of items purchased	Cluster
25	F	1	6
28	F	23	1
61	F	3	3
54	M	17	2
51	M	8	3
47	F	3	8
27	M	22	5
31	F	14	1

This shows our customer dataset after a clustering algorithm has been applied. Note the new column at the end called `cluster` that represents the types of people that the algorithm has identified. The idea is that the people who belong to similar clusters *behave* similarly in regards to the data (have similar ages, genders, purchase behaviors). Perhaps cluster six might be renamed as *young buyers*.

This example of clustering shows us why sometimes we aren't concerned with predicting anything, but instead wish to understand our data on a deeper level by adding new and interesting features, or even removing irrelevant features.

 Note that we are referring to every column as a feature because there is no response in unsupervised learning since there is no prediction occurring.

It's all starting to make sense now, isn't it? These features that we talk about repeatedly are what this book is primarily concerned with. Feature engineering involves the understanding and transforming of features in relation to both unsupervised and supervised learning.

Evaluation of machine learning algorithms and feature engineering procedures

It is important to note that in literature, oftentimes there is a stark contrast between the terms *features* and *attributes*. The term **attribute** is generally given to columns in tabular data, while the term **feature** is generally given only to attributes that contribute to the success of machine learning algorithms. That is to say, some attributes can be unhelpful or even hurtful to our machine learning systems. For example, when predicting how long a used car will last before requiring servicing, the color of the car will probably not very indicative of this value.

In this book, we will generally refer to all columns as features until they are proven to be unhelpful or hurtful. When this happens, we will usually cast those attributes aside in the code. It is extremely important, then, to consider the basis for this decision. How does one evaluate a machine learning system and then use this evaluation to perform feature engineering?

Example of feature engineering procedures – can anyone really predict the weather?

Consider a machine learning pipeline that was built to predict the weather. For the sake of simplicity in our introduction chapter, assume that our algorithm takes in atmospheric data directly from sensors and is set up to predict between one of two values, *sun* or *rain*. This pipeline is then, clearly, a classification pipeline that can only spit out one of two answers. We will run this algorithm at the beginning of every day. If the algorithm outputs *sun* and the day is mostly sunny, the algorithm was correct, likewise, if the algorithm predicts *rain* and the day is mostly rainy, the algorithm was correct. In any other instance, the algorithm would be considered incorrect. If we run the algorithm every day for a month, we would obtain nearly 30 values of the predicted weather and the actual, observed weather. We can calculate an accuracy of the algorithm. Perhaps the algorithm predicted correctly for 20 out of the 30 days, leading us to label the algorithm with a two out of three or about 67% accuracy. Using this standardized value or accuracy, we could tweak our algorithm and see if the accuracy goes up or down.

Of course, this is an oversimplification, but the idea is that for any machine learning pipeline, it is essentially useless if we cannot evaluate its performance using a set of standard metrics and therefore, feature engineering as applied to the bettering of machine learning, is impossible without said evaluation procedure. Throughout this book, we will revisit this idea of evaluation; however, let's talk briefly about how, in general, we will approach this idea.

When presented with a topic in feature engineering, it will usually involve transforming our dataset (as per the definition of feature engineering). In order to definitely say whether or not a particular feature engineering procedure has helped our machine learning algorithm, we will follow the steps detailed in the following section.

Steps to evaluate a feature engineering procedure

Here are the steps to evaluate a feature engineering procedure:

1. Obtain a baseline performance of the machine learning model before applying any feature engineering procedures
2. Apply feature engineering and combinations of feature engineering procedures
3. For each application of feature engineering, obtain a performance measure and compare it to our baseline performance
4. If the delta (change in) performance precedes a threshold (usually defined by the human), we deem that procedure helpful and apply it to our machine learning pipeline
5. This change in performance will usually be measured as a percentage (if the baseline went from 40% accuracy to 76% accuracy, that is a 90% improvement)

In terms of performance, this idea varies between machine learning algorithms. Most good primers on machine learning will tell you that there are dozens of accepted metrics when practicing data science.

In our case, because the focus of this book is not necessarily on machine learning and rather on the understanding and transformation of features, we will use baseline machine learning algorithms and associated baseline metrics in order to evaluate the feature engineering procedures.

Evaluating supervised learning algorithms

When performing predictive modeling, otherwise known as **supervised learning,** performance is directly tied to the model's ability to exploit structure in the data and use that structure to make appropriate predictions. In general, we can further break down supervised learning into two more specific types, **classification** (predicting qualitative responses) and **regression** (predicting quantitative responses).

When we are evaluating classification problems, we will directly calculate the accuracy of a logistic regression model using a five-fold cross-validation:

```
# Example code for evaluating a classification problem
from sklearn.linear_model import LogisticRegression
from sklearn.model_selection import cross_val_score
X = some_data_in_tabular_format
y = response_variable
lr = LinearRegression()
scores = cross_val_score(lr, X, y, cv=5, scoring='accuracy')
scores
>> [.765, .67, .8, .62, .99]
```

Similarly, when evaluating a regression problem, we will use the **mean squared error (MSE)** of a linear regression using a five-fold cross-validation:

```
# Example code for evaluating a regression problem
from sklearn.linear_model import LinearRegression
from sklearn.model_selection import cross_val_score
X = some_data_in_tabular_format
y = response_variable
lr = LinearRegression()
scores = cross_val_score(lr, X, y, cv=5, scoring='mean_squared_error')
scores
>> [31.543, 29.5433, 32.543, 32.43, 27.5432]
```

We will use these two linear models instead of newer, more advanced models for their speed and their low variance. This way, we can be surer that any increase in performance is directly related to the feature engineering procedure and not to the model's ability to pick up on obscure and hidden patterns.

Evaluating unsupervised learning algorithms

This is a bit trickier. Because unsupervised learning is not concerned with predictions, we cannot directly evaluate performance based on how well the model can predict a value. That being said, if we are performing a cluster analysis, such as in the previous marketing segmentation example, then we will usually utilize the **silhouette coefficient** (a measure of separation and cohesion of clusters between -1 and 1) and some human-driven analysis to decide if a feature engineering procedure has improved model performance or if we are merely wasting our time.

Here is an example of using Python and scikit-learn to import and calculate the silhouette coefficient for some fake data:

```
attributes = tabular_data
cluster_labels = outputted_labels_from_clustering

from sklearn.metrics import silhouette_score
silhouette_score(attributes, cluster_labels)
```

We will spend much more time on unsupervised learning later on in this book as it becomes more relevant. Most of our examples will revolve around predictive analytics/supervised learning.

 It is important to remember that the reason we are standardizing algorithms and metrics is so that we may showcase the power of feature engineering and so that you may repeat our procedures with success. Practically, it is conceivable that you are optimizing for something other than accuracy (such as a true positive rate, for example) and wish to use decision trees instead of logistic regression. This is not only fine but encouraged. You should always remember though to follow the steps to evaluating a feature engineering procedure and compare baseline and post-engineering performance.

It is possible that you are not reading this book for the purposes of improving machine learning performance. Feature engineering is useful in other domains such as hypothesis testing and general statistics. In a few examples in this book, we will be taking a look at feature engineering and data transformations as applied to a statistical significance of various statistical tests. We will be exploring metrics such as R^2 and p-values in order to make judgements about how our procedures are helping.

In general, we will quantify the benefits of feature engineering in the context of three categories:

- **Supervised learning**: Otherwise known as **predictive analytics**
  - Regression analysis—predicting a *quantitative* variable:
    - Will utilize MSE as our primary metric of measurement
  - Classification analysis—predicting a *qualitative* variable
    - Will utilize accuracy as our primary metric of measurement
- **Unsupervised learning**: Clustering—the assigning of meta-attributes as denoted by the behavior of data:
  - Will utilize the silhouette coefficient as our primary metric of measurement
- **Statistical testing**: Using correlation coefficients, t-tests, chi-squared tests, and others to evaluate and quantify the usefulness of our raw and transformed data

In the following few sections, we will look at what will be covered throughout this book.

Feature understanding – what's in my dataset?

In our first subtopic, we will start to build our fundamentals in dealing with data. By understanding the data in front of us, we can start to have a better idea of where to go next. We will begin to explore the different types of data out there as well as how to recognize the type of data inside datasets. We will look at datasets from several domains and identify how they are different from each other and how they are similar to each other. Once we are able to comfortably examine data and identify the characteristics of different attributes, we can start to understand the types of transformations that are allowed and that promise to improve our machine learning algorithms.

Among the different methods of understanding, we will be looking at:

- Structured versus unstructured data
- The four levels of data
- Identifying missing data values
- Exploratory data analysis
- Descriptive statistics
- Data visualizations

We will begin at a basic level by identifying the structure of, and then the types of data in front of us. Once we are able to understand what the data is, we can start to fix problems with the data. As an example, we must know how much of our data is missing and what to do when we have missing data.

Make no mistake, data visualizations, descriptive statistics, and exploratory data analysis are all a part of feature engineering. We will be exploring each of these procedures from the perspective of the machine learning engineer. Each of these procedures has the ability to enhance our machine learning pipelines and we will test and alter hypotheses about our data using them.

Feature improvement – cleaning datasets

In this topic, we take the results of our understanding of the data and use them in order to clean the dataset. Much of this book will flow in such a way, using results from previous sections to be able to work on current sections. In feature improvement, our understanding will allow us to begin our first manipulations of datasets. We will be using mathematical transformations to enhance the given data, but not remove or insert any new attributes (this is for the next chapters).

We will explore several topics in this section, including:

- Structuring unstructured data
- Data imputing—inserting data where there was not a data before (missing data)
- Normalization of data:
    - Standardization (known as z-score normalization)
    - Min-max scaling
    - L1 and L2 normalization (projecting into different spaces, fun stuff)

By this point in the book, we will be able to identify whether our data has a *structure* or not. That is, whether our data is in a nice, tabular format. If it is not, this chapter will give us the tools to transform that data into a more tabular format. This is imperative when attempting to create machine learning pipelines.

Data imputing is a particularly interesting topic. The ability to fill in data where data was missing previously is trickier than it sounds. We will be proposing all kinds of solutions from the very, very easy, merely removing the column altogether, boom no more missing data, to the interestingly complex, using machine learning on the rest of the features to fill in missing spots. Once we have filled in a bulk of our missing data, we can then measure how that affected our machine learning algorithms.

Normalization uses (generally simple) mathematical tools used to change the scaling of our data. Again, this ranges from the easy, turning miles into feet or pounds into kilograms, to the more difficult, such as projecting our data onto the unit sphere (more on that to come).

This chapter and remaining chapters will be much more heavily focused on our quantitative feature engineering procedure evaluation flow. Nearly every single time we look at a new dataset or feature engineering procedure, we will put it to the test. We will be grading the performance of various feature engineering methods on the merits of machine learning performance, speed, and other metrics. This text should only be used as a reference and not as a guide to select with feature engineering the procedures you are allowed to **ignore** based on difficulty and change in performance. Every new data task comes with its own caveats and may require different procedures than the previous data task.

Feature selection – say no to bad attributes

By this chapter, we will have a level of comfort when dealing with new datasets. We will have under our belt the abilities to understand and clean the data in front of us. Once we are able to work with the data given to us, we can start to make big decisions such as, *at what point is a feature actually an attribute*. Recall that by this distinction, feature versus attribute, the question really is, *which columns are not helping my ML pipeline and therefore are hurting my pipeline and should be removed?* This chapter focuses on techniques used to make the decision of which attributes to get rid of in our dataset. We will explore several statistical and iterative processes that will aid us in this decision.

Among these processes are:

- Correlation coefficients
- Identifying and removing multicollinearity
- Chi-squared tests
- Anova tests
- Interpretation of p-values
- Iterative feature selection
- Using machine learning to measure entropy and information gain

All of these procedures will attempt to suggest the removal of features and will give different reasons for doing so. Ultimately, it will be up to us, the data scientists, to make the final call over which features will be allowed to remain and contribute to our machine learning algorithms.

Feature construction – can we build it?

While in previous chapters we focused heavily on removing features that were not helping us with our machine learning pipelines, this chapter will look at techniques in creating brand new features and placing them correctly within our dataset. These new features will ideally hold new information and generate new patterns that ML pipelines will be able to exploit and use to increase performance.

These created features can come from many places. Oftentimes, we will create new features out of existing features given to us. We can create new features by applying transformations to existing features and placing the resulting vectors alongside their previous counterparts. We will also look at adding new features from separate party systems. As an example, if we are working with data attempting to cluster people based on shopping behaviors, then we might benefit from adding in census data that is separate from the corporation and their purchasing data. However, this will present a few problems:

- If the census is aware of 1,700 Jon does and the corporation only knows 13, how do we know which of the 1,700 people match up to the 13? This is called *entity matching*
- The census data would be quite large and entity matching would take a very long time

These problems and more make for a fairly difficult procedure but oftentimes create a very dense and data-rich environment.

In this chapter, we will take some time to talk about the manual creation of features through highly unstructured data. Two big examples are text and images. These pieces of data by themselves are incomprehensible to machine learning and artificial intelligence pipelines, so it is up to us to manually create features that represent the images/pieces of text. As a simple example, imagine that we are making the basics of a self-driving car and to start, we want to make a model that can take in an image of what the car is seeing in front of it and decide whether or not it should stop. The raw image is not good enough because a machine learning algorithm would have no idea what to do with it. We have to manually construct features out of it. Given this raw image, we can split it up in a few ways:

- We could consider the color intensity of each pixel and consider each pixel an attribute:
  - For example, if the camera of the car produces images of 2,048 x 1,536 pixels, we would have 3,145,728 columns
- We could consider each row of pixels as an attribute and the average color of each row being the value:
  - In this case, there would only be 1,536 rows
- We could project this image into space where features represent objects within the image. This is the hardest of the three and would look something like this:

Stop sign	Cat	Sky	Road	Patches of grass	Submarine
1	0	1	1	4	0

Where each feature is an object that may or may not be within the image and the value represents the number of times that object appears in the image. If a model were given this information, it would be a fairly good idea to stop!

Feature transformation – enter math-man

This chapter is where things get mathematical and interesting. We'll have talked about understating features and cleaning them. We'll also have looked at how to remove and add new features. In our feature construction chapter, we had to manually create these new features. We, the human, had to use our brains and come up with those three ways of decomposing that image of a stop sign. Sure, we can create code that makes the features automatically, but we ultimately chose what features we wanted to use.

This chapter will start to look at the automatic creation of these features as it applies to mathematical dimensionality. If we regard our data as vectors in an n-space (n being the number of columns), we will ask ourselves, *can we create a new dataset in a k-space (where k < n) that fully or nearly represents the original data, but might give us speed boosts or performance enhancements in machine learning?* The goal here is to create a dataset of smaller dimensionality that performs better than our original dataset at a larger dimensionality.

The first question here is, *weren't we creating data in smaller dimensionality before when we were feature selecting? If we start with 17 features and remove five, we've reduced the dimensionality to 12, right?* Yes, of course! However, we aren't talking simply about removing columns here, we are talking about using complex mathematical transformations (usually taken from our studies in linear algebra) and applying them to our datasets.

One notable example we will spend some time on is called **Principal Components Analysis (PCA)**. It is a transformation that breaks down our data into three different datasets, and we can use these results to create brand new datasets that can outperform our original!

Here is a visual example is taken from a Princeton University research experiment that used PCA to exploit patterns in gene expressions. This is a great application of dimensionality reduction as there are so many genes and combinations of genes, it would take even the most sophisticated algorithms in the world plenty of time to process them:

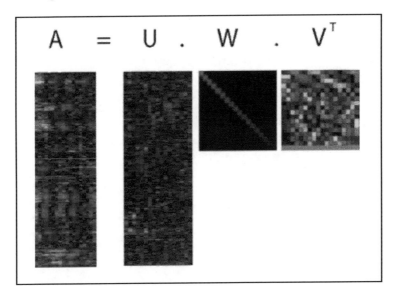

In the preceding screenshot, **A** represents the original dataset, where **U**, **W**, and **V**$^\mathrm{T}$ represent the results of a singular value decomposition. The results are then put together to make a brand new dataset that can replace **A** to a certain extent.

Feature learning – using AI to better our AI

The cherry on top, a cherry powered by the most sophisticated algorithms used today in the automatic construction of features for the betterment of machine learning and AI pipelines.

The previous chapter dealt with automatic feature creation using mathematical formulas, but once again, in the end, it is us, the humans, that choose the formulas and reap the benefits of them. This chapter will outline algorithms that are not in and of themselves a mathematical formula, but an architecture attempting to understand and model data in such a way that it will exploit patterns in data in order to create new data. This may sound vague at the moment, but we hope to get you excited about it!

We will focus mainly on neural algorithms that are specially designed to use a neural network design (nodes and weights). These algorithms will then impose features onto the data in such a way that can sometimes be unintelligible to humans, but extremely useful for machines. Some of the topics we'll look at are:

- Restricted Boltzmann machines
- Word2Vec/GLoVe for word embedding

Word2Vec and GLoVe are two ways of adding large dimensionality data to seemingly word tokens in the text. For example, if we look at a visual representation of the results of a Word2Vec algorithm, we might see the following:

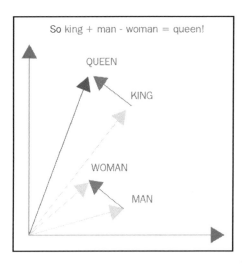

By representing words as vectors in Euclidean space, we can achieve mathematical-esque results. In the previous example, by adding these automatically generated features we can *add* and *subtract* words by adding and subtracting their vector representations as given to us by Word2Vec. We can then generate interesting conclusions, such as **king+man-woman=queen**. Cool!

Summary

Feature engineering is a massive task to be undertaken by data scientists and machine learning engineers. It is a task that is imperative to having successful and production-ready machine learning pipelines. In the coming seven chapters, we are going to explore six major aspects of feature engineering:

- Feature understanding: learning how to identify data based on its qualities and quantitative state
- Feature improvement: cleaning and imputing missing data values in order to maximize the dataset's value
- Feature selection -statistically selecting and subsetting feature sets in order to reduce the noise in our data
- Feature construction - building new features with the intention of exploiting feature interactions

- Feature transformation - extracting latent (hidden) structure within datasets in order to mathematically transform our datasets into something new (and usually better)
- Feature learning - harnessing the power of deep learning to view data in a whole new light that will open up new problems to be solved.

In this book, we will be exploring feature engineering as it relates to our machine learning endeavors. By breaking down this large topic into our subtopics and diving deep into each one in separate chapters, we will be able to get a much broader and more useful understanding of how these procedures work and how to apply each one in Python.

In our next chapter, we will dive straight into our first subsection, *Feature understanding*. We will finally be getting our hands on some real data, so let's begin!

2
Feature Understanding – What's in My Dataset?

Finally! We can start to jump into some real data, some real code, and some real results. Specifically, we will be diving deeper into the following ideas:

- Structured versus unstructured data
- Quantitative versus qualitative data
- The four levels of data
- Exploratory data analysis and data visualizations
- Descriptive statistics

Each of these topics will give us a better sense of the data given to us, what is present within the dataset, what is not present within the dataset, and some basic notions on how to proceed from there.

If you're familiar with, *Principles of Data Science*, much of this echoes *Chapter 2, Types of Data* of that book. That being said, in this chapter, we will specifically look at our data less from a holistic standpoint, and more from a machine-learning standpoint.

The structure, or lack thereof, of data

When given a new dataset, it is first important to recognize whether or not your data is structured or unstructured:

- **Structured (organized) data**: Data that can be broken down into observations and characteristics. They are generally organized using a tabular method (where rows are observations and columns are characteristics).

- **Unstructured (unorganized) data**: Data that exists as a free-flowing entity and does not follow standard organizational hierarchy such as tabularity. Often, unstructured data appears to us as a *blob* of data, or as a single characteristic (column).

A few examples that highlight the difference between structured and unstructured data are as follows:

- Data that exists in a raw free-text form, including server logs and tweets, are unstructured

- Meteorological data, as reported by scientific instruments in precise movements, would be considered highly structured as they exist in a tabular row/column structure

An example of unstructured data – server logs

As an example of unstructured data, we have pulled some sample server logs from a public source and included them in a text document. We can take a glimpse of what this unstructured data looks like, so we can recognize it in the future:

```
# Import our data manipulation tool, Pandas
import pandas as pd
# Create a pandas DataFrame from some unstructured Server Logs
logs = pd.read_table('../data/server_logs.txt', header=None,
names=['Info'])

# header=None, specifies that the first line of data is the first data
point, not a column name
```

```
# names=['Info] is me setting the column name in our DataFrame for easier
access
```

We created a DataFrame in pandas called `logs` that hold our server logs. To take a look, let's call the `.head()` method to look at the first few rows:

```
# Look at the first 5 rows
logs.head()
```

This will show us a table of the first 5 rows in our logs DataFrame as follows:

Info	
0	64.242.88.10 - - [07/Mar/2004:16:05:49 -0800] ...
1	64.242.88.10 - - [07/Mar/2004:16:06:51 -0800] ...
2	64.242.88.10 - - [07/Mar/2004:16:10:02 -0800] ...
3	64.242.88.10 - - [07/Mar/2004:16:11:58 -0800] ...
4	64.242.88.10 - - [07/Mar/2004:16:20:55 -0800] ...

We can see in our logs that each row represents a single log and there is only a single column, the text of the log itself. Not exactly a characteristic or anything, just the raw log is taken directly from the server. This is a great example of unstructured data. Most often, data in the form of text is usually unstructured.

It is important to recognize that most unstructured data can be transformed into structured data through a few manipulations, but this is something that we will tackle in the next chapter.

Most of the data that we will be working on the book will be structured. That means that there will be a sense of rows and columns. Given this, we can start to look at the types of values in the cells of our tabular data.

Quantitative versus qualitative data

To accomplish our diagnoses of the various types of data, we will begin with the highest order of separation. When dealing with structured, tabular data (which we usually will be doing), the first question we generally ask ourselves is whether the values are of a numeric or categorical nature.

Quantitative data are data that are numerical in nature. They should be measuring the quantity of something.

Qualitative data are data that are categorical in nature. They should be describing the quality of something.

Basic examples:

- Weather measured as temperature in Fahrenheit or Celsius would be quantitative
- Weather measured as cloudy or sunny would be qualitative
- The name of a person visiting the White House would be qualitative
- The amount of blood you donate at a blood drive is quantitative

The first two examples show that we can describe similar systems using data from both the qualitative and quantitative side. In fact, in most datasets, we will be working with both qualitative and quantitative data.

Sometimes, data can, arguably, be either quantitative or qualitative. The ranking you would give a restaurant (one through five stars) could be considered quantitative or qualitative, for example. While they are numbers, the numbers themselves might also represent categories. For example, if the restaurant rating app asked you to rate the restaurant using a quantitative star system, then feasibly the restaurant's average ranking might be a decimal, like 4.71 stars, making the data quantitative. At the same time, if the app asked you if you *hated it, thought it was OK, liked it, loved it,* or *really loved it,* then these are now categories. As a result of these ambiguities between quantitative and qualitative data, we employ an even deeper method called the four levels of data. Before we do that, let's introduce our first dataset for the chapter and really solidify some examples of qualitative and quantitative data.

Salary ranges by job classification

Let's first do some import statements:

```
# import packages we need for exploratory data analysis (EDA)
# to store tabular data
import pandas as pd
# to do some math
import numpy as np
# a popular data visualization tool
import matplotlib.pyplot as plt
# another popular data visualization tool
import seaborn as sns
# allows the notebook to render graphics
%matplotlib inline
# a popular data visualization theme
plt.style.use('fivethirtyeight')
```

And then, let's import our first dataset, which will explore salaries of different job titles in San Francisco. This dataset is available publicly and so you are encouraged to play around with it as much as you want:

```
# load in the data set
#
https://data.sfgov.org/City-Management-and-Ethics/Salary-Ranges-by-Job-Clas
sification/7h4w-reyq
salary_ranges =
pd.read_csv('../data/Salary_Ranges_by_Job_Classification.csv')

# view the first few rows and the headers
salary_ranges.head()
```

Let us have a look at the following table to understand better:

	SetID	Job Code	Eff Date	Sal End Date	Salary SetID	Sal Plan	Grade	Step	Biweekly High Rate	Biweekly Low Rate	Union Code	Extended Step	Pay Type
0	COMMN	0109	07/01/2009 12:00:00 AM	06/30/2010 12:00:00 AM	COMMN	SFM	00000	1	$0.00	$0.00	330	0	C
1	COMMN	0110	07/01/2009 12:00:00 AM	06/30/2010 12:00:00 AM	COMMN	SFM	00000	1	$15.00	$15.00	323	0	D
2	COMMN	0111	07/01/2009 12:00:00 AM	06/30/2010 12:00:00 AM	COMMN	SFM	00000	1	$25.00	$25.00	323	0	D

| 3 | COMMN | 0112 | 07/01/2009 12:00:00 AM | 06/30/2010 12:00:00 AM | COMMN | SFM | 00000 | 1 | $50.00 | $50.00 | 323 | 0 | D |
| 4 | COMMN | 0114 | 07/01/2009 12:00:00 AM | 06/30/2010 12:00:00 AM | COMMN | SFM | 00000 | 1 | $100.00 | $100.00 | 323 | 0 | M |

We can see that we have a bunch of columns, and some already start to jump out at us as being quantitative or qualitative. Let's get a sense of how many rows of data there are using the .info() command:

```
# get a sense of how many rows of data there are, if there are any missing
values, and what data type each column has
salary_ranges.info()
```

```
<class 'pandas.core.frame.DataFrame'>
RangeIndex: 1356 entries, 0 to 1355
Data columns (total 13 columns):
SetID                   1356 non-null object
Job Code                1356 non-null object
Eff Date                1356 non-null object
Sal End Date            1356 non-null object
Salary SetID            1356 non-null object
Sal Plan                1356 non-null object
Grade                   1356 non-null object
Step                    1356 non-null int64
Biweekly High Rate      1356 non-null object
Biweekly Low Rate       1356 non-null object
Union Code              1356 non-null int64
Extended Step           1356 non-null int64
Pay Type                1356 non-null object
dtypes: int64(3), object(10)
memory usage: 137.8+ KB
```

So, we have 1356 entries (rows) and 13 columns. The .info() command also tells us the number of non-null items in each column. This is important because missing data is by far one of the most common issues in feature engineering. Sometimes, we are working with datasets that are just incomplete. In pandas, we have many ways of figuring out if we are working with missing data, and many ways of dealing with them. A very quick and common way to count the number of missing values is to run:

```
# another method to check for missing values
salary_ranges.isnull().sum()
```

```
SetID                   0
```

```
Job Code                0
Eff Date                0
Sal End Date            0
Salary SetID            0
Sal Plan                0
Grade                   0
Step                    0
Biweekly High Rate      0
Biweekly Low Rate       0
Union Code              0
Extended Step           0
Pay Type                0
dtype: int64
```

So, we see we are not missing any pieces of data in this one, phew (for now). Moving on, let's run the `describe` method to check out some descriptive statistics of our quantitative columns (which we should have). Note that the `describe` method will default to describing quantitative columns, but will describe qualitative columns if there are no quantitative columns:

```
# show descriptive stats:
salary_ranges.describe()
```

Let us have a look at the following table for a better understanding here:

	Step	Union Code	Extended Step
count	1356.000000	1356.000000	1356.000000
mean	1.294985	392.676991	0.150442
std	1.045816	338.100562	1.006734
min	1.000000	1.000000	0.000000
25%	1.000000	21.000000	0.000000
50%	1.000000	351.000000	0.000000
75%	1.000000	790.000000	0.000000
max	5.000000	990.000000	11.000000

According to pandas, we only have three quantitative columns: `Step`, `Union Code`, and `Extended Step`. Let's ignore `Step` and `Extended Step` for now, and also notice that `Union Code` isn't really quantitative. While it is a number, it doesn't really represent a quantity of something, it's merely describing the union through a unique coding. So, we have some work to do here to even understand the features that we are more interested in. Most notably, let's say we wish to pull out a single quantitative column, the `Biweekly High Rate`, and a single qualitative column, `Grade` (the type of job):

```
salary_ranges = salary_ranges[['Biweekly High Rate', 'Grade']]
salary_ranges.head()
```

The following is the result of the preceding code:

	Biweekly High Rate	Grade
0	$0.00	00000
1	$15.00	00000
2	$25.00	00000
3	$50.00	00000
4	$100.00	00000

To do some cleaning up on these columns, let's remove those dollar signs ($) from the salary rate and ensure that the columns are of the correct type. When working with quantitative columns, we generally want them to be integer or floats (floats are preferred), while qualitative columns are usually strings or Unicode objects:

```
# Rate has dollar signs in a few of them, we need to clean that up..
salary_ranges['Biweekly High Rate'].describe()

count              1356
unique              593
top            $3460.00
freq                 12
Name: Biweekly High Rate, dtype: object
```

To clean up this column, let's use the map feature in pandas to efficiently map a function to an entire series of data:

```
# need to clean our Biweekly High columns to remove the dollar sign in
order to visualize
salary_ranges['Biweekly High Rate'] = salary_ranges['Biweekly High
Rate'].map(lambda value: value.replace('$',''))

# Check to see the '$' has been removed
salary_ranges.head()
```

The following table gives us a better understanding here:

	Biweekly High Rate	Grade
0	0.00	00000
1	15.00	00000
2	25.00	00000
3	50.00	00000
4	100.00	00000

To finish our transformation of the `Biweekly High Rate` column, we will cast the whole thing as a `float`:

```
# Convert the Biweeky columns to float
salary_ranges['Biweekly High Rate'] = salary_ranges['Biweekly High
Rate'].astype(float)
```

While we are casting, let's also cast the `Grade` column as a string:

```
# Convert the Grade columns to str
salary_ranges['Grade'] = salary_ranges['Grade'].astype(str)

# check to see if converting the data types worked
salary_ranges.info()
```

```
<class 'pandas.core.frame.DataFrame'>
RangeIndex: 1356 entries, 0 to 1355
Data columns (total 2 columns):
Biweekly High Rate    1356 non-null float64
Grade                 1356 non-null object
dtypes: float64(1), object(1)
memory usage: 21.3+ KB
```

We see that we now have a total of:

- 1,356 rows (like we started with)
- Two columns (that we selected):
    - **Biweekly High Rate**: A quantitative column that refers to the average high weekly salary for a specified department:
        - This column is quantitative because the the values are numerical in nature and describe the quantity of money that the person earns weekly
        - It is of type float, which we cast it to
    - **Grade**: The department that the salary is in reference to:
        - This column is definitely qualitative because the codes refer to a department and not a quantity of any kind
        - It is of type object, which is the type pandas will stipulate if it is a string

To break quantitative and qualitative data even further, let's dive into the four levels of data.

The four levels of data

We already know that we can identify data as being either qualitative or quantitative. But, from there, we can go further. The four levels of data are:

- The nominal level
- The ordinal level
- The interval level
- The ratio level

Each level comes with a varying level of control and mathematical possibilities. It is crucial to know which level data lives on because it will dictate the types of visualizations and operations you are allowed to perform.

The nominal level

The first level of data, the nominal level, has the weakest structure. It consists of data that are purely described by name. Basic examples include blood type (A, O, AB), species of animal, or names of people. These types of data are all qualitative.

Some other examples include:

- In the SF Job Salary dataset, the Grade column would be nominal
- Given visitor logs of a company, the first and last names of the visitors would be nominal
- Species of animals in a lab experiment would be nominal

Mathematical operations allowed

At each level, we will describe briefly the type of math that is allowed, and more importantly, not allowed. At this level, we cannot perform any quantitative mathematical operations, such as addition or division. These would not make any sense. Due to the lack of addition and division, we obviously cannot find an average value at the nominal level. There is no average name or average job department.

We can, however, do basic counts using pandas' value_counts methods:

```
# Basic Value Counts of the Grade column
salary_ranges['Grade'].value_counts().head()
```

```
00000    61
07450    12
06870     9
07170     9
07420     9
Name: Grade, dtype: int64
```

The most commonly occurring `Grade` is `00000`, meaning that that is our **mode** or most commonly occurring category. Because of our ability to count at the nominal level, graphs, like bar charts, are available to us:

```
# Bar Chart of the Grade column
salary_ranges['Grade'].value_counts().sort_values(ascending=False).head(20)
.plot(kind='bar')
```

The following is the result of the preceding code:

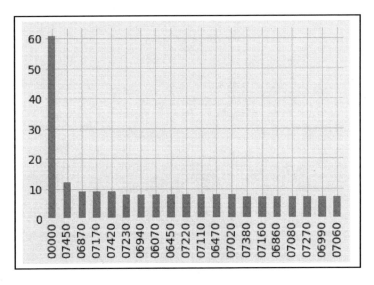

At the nominal level, we may also utilize pie charts:

```
# Bar Chart of the Grade column as a pie chart (top 5 values only)
salary_ranges['Grade'].value_counts().sort_values(ascending=False).head(5).
plot(kind='pie')
```

The following is the output of the preceding code:

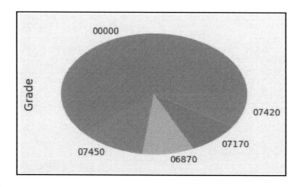

The ordinal level

The nominal level provided us with much in the way of capabilities for further exploration. Moving one level up, we are now on the ordinal scale. The ordinal scale inherits all of the properties of the nominal level, but has important additional properties:

- Data at the ordinal level can be **naturally ordered**
- This implies that some data values in the column can be considered better than or greater than others

As with the nominal level, data at the ordinal level is still categorical in nature, even if numbers are used to represent the categories.

Mathematical operations allowed

We have a few new abilities to work with at the ordinal level compared to the nominal level. At the ordinal level, we may still do basic counts as we did at the nominal level, but we can also introduce comparisons and orderings into the mix. For this reason, we may utilize new graphs at this level. We may use bar and pie charts like we did at the nominal level, but because we now have ordering and comparisons, we can calculate medians and percentiles. With medians and percentiles, stem-and-leaf plots, as well as box plots, are possible.

Some examples of data at the ordinal level include:

- Using a Likert scale (rating something on a scale from one to ten, for example)

- Grade levels on an exam (F, D, C, B, A)

For a real-world example of data at the ordinal scale, let's bring in a new dataset. This dataset holds key insights into how much people enjoy the San Francisco International Airport or SFO. This dataset is also publicly available on SF's open database (`https://data.sfgov.org/Transportation/2013-SFO-Customer-Survey/mjr8-p6m5`):

```
# load in the data set
customer = pd.read_csv('../data/2013_SFO_Customer_survey.csv')
```

This CSV has many, many columns:

```
customer.shape

(3535, 95)
```

95 columns, to be exact. For more information on the columns available for this dataset, check out the data dictionary on the website (`https://data.sfgov.org/api/views/mjr8-p6m5/files/FHnAUtMCD0C8CyLD3jqZ1-Xd1aap8L086KLWQ9SKZ_8?download=truefilename=AIR_DataDictionary_2013-SFO-Customer-Survey.pdf`)

For now, let's focus on a single column, `Q7A_ART`. As described by the publicly available data dictionary, `Q7A_ART` is about artwork and exhibitions. The possible choices are 0, 1, 2, 3, 4, 5, 6 and each number has a meaning:

- **1**: Unacceptable
- **2**: Below Average
- **3**: Average
- **4**: Good
- **5**: Outstanding
- **6**: Have Never Used or Visited
- **0**: Blank

We can represent it as follows:

```
art_ratings = customer['Q7A_ART']
art_ratings.describe()
```

```
count    3535.000000
mean        4.300707
std         1.341445
min         0.000000
25%         3.000000
50%         4.000000
75%         5.000000
max         6.000000
Name: Q7A_ART, dtype: float64
```

The pandas is considering the column numerical because it is full of numbers, however, we must remember that even though the cells' values are numbers, those numbers represent a category, and therefore this data belongs to the qualitative side, and more specifically, ordinal. If we remove the 0 and 6 category, we are left with five ordinal categories which basically resemble the star rating of restaurant ratings:

```
# only consider ratings 1-5
art_ratings = art_ratings[(art_ratings >=1) & (art_ratings <=5)]
```

We will then cast the values as strings:

```
# cast the values as strings
art_ratings = art_ratings.astype(str)

art_ratings.describe()
```

```
count     2656
unique       5
top          4
freq      1066
Name: Q7A_ART, dtype: object
```

Now that we have our ordinal data in the right format, let's look at some visualizations:

```
# Can use pie charts, just like in nominal level
art_ratings.value_counts().plot(kind='pie')
```

The following is the result of the preceding code:

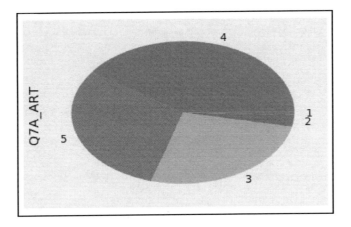

We can also visualize this as a bar chart as follows:

```
# Can use bar charts, just like in nominal level
art_ratings.value_counts().plot(kind='bar')
```

The following is the output of the preceding code:

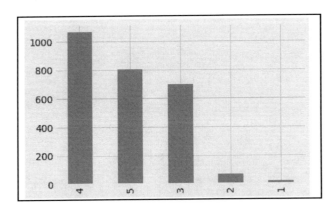

However, now we can also introduce box plots since we are at the ordinal level:

```
# Boxplots are available at the ordinal level
art_ratings.value_counts().plot(kind='box')
```

The following is the output of the preceding code:

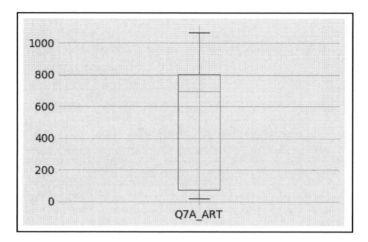

This box plot would not be possible for the `Grade` column in the salary data, as finding a median would not be possible.

The interval level

We are starting to cook with gas now. At the nominal and ordinal level, we were working with data that was qualitative in nature. There was data that did not describe a true quantity. At the interval level, we move away from this notion and move into quantitative data. At the interval data level, we are working with numerical data that not only has ordering like at the ordinal level, but also has meaningful differences between values. This means that at the interval level, not only may we order and compare values, we may also **add** and **subtract** values.

Example:

A classic example of data at the interval level is temperature. If it is 90 degrees in Texas, and 40 degrees in Alaska, then we may calculate a 90-40 = 50 degrees difference between the locations. This may seem like a very simple example, but thinking back on the last two levels, we have never had this amount of control over our data before.

Non-example:

A classic non-example of data that is not at the interval level are Likert scales. We have identified Likert at the ordinal levels for their ability to be ordered, but it is important to notice that subtractions do not have a true consistent meaning. If we subtract a 5-3 on a Likert scale, the resulting 2 doesn't actually mean the number 2, nor does it represent the category 2. Thus, subtraction in a Likert scale is difficult.

Mathematical operations allowed

Remember, at the interval level, we have addition and subtraction to work with. This is a real game-changer. With the ability to add values together, we may introduce two familiar concepts, the **arithmetic mean** (referred to simply as the mean) and **standard deviation**. At the interval level, both of these are available to us. To see a great example of this, let's pull in a new dataset, one about climate change:

```
# load in the data set
climate = pd.read_csv('../data/GlobalLandTemperaturesByCity.csv')
climate.head()
```

Let us have a look at the following table for a better understanding:

dt	AverageTemperature	AverageTemperatureUncertainty	City	Country	Latitude	Longitude	
0	1743-11-01	6.068	1.737	Århus	Denmark	57.05N	10.33E
1	1743-12-01	NaN	NaN	Århus	Denmark	57.05N	10.33E
2	1744-01-01	NaN	NaN	Århus	Denmark	57.05N	10.33E
3	1744-02-01	NaN	NaN	Århus	Denmark	57.05N	10.33E
4	1744-03-01	NaN	NaN	Århus	Denmark	57.05N	10.33E

This dataset has 8.6 million rows, where each row quantifies the average temperature of cities around the world by the month, going back to the 18th century. Note that just by looking at the first five rows, we already have some missing values. Let's remove them for now in order to get a better look:

```
# remove missing values
climate.dropna(axis=0, inplace=True)

climate.head() . # check to see that missing values are gone
```

The following table gives us a better understanding here:

dt	AverageTemperature	AverageTemperatureUncertainty	City	Country	Latitude	Longitude	
0	1743-11-01	6.068	1.737	Århus	Denmark	57.05N	10.33E
5	1744-04-01	5.788	3.624	Århus	Denmark	57.05N	10.33E
6	1744-05-01	10.644	1.283	Århus	Denmark	57.05N	10.33E
7	1744-06-01	14.051	1.347	Århus	Denmark	57.05N	10.33E
8	1744-07-01	16.082	1.396	Århus	Denmark	57.05N	10.33E

Let's see if we have any missing values with the following line of code:

```
climate.isnull().sum()

dt                                0
AverageTemperature                0
AverageTemperatureUncertainty     0
City                              0
Country                           0
Latitude                          0
Longitude                         0
year                              0
dtype: int64

# All good
```

The column in question is called `AverageTemperature`. One quality of data at the interval level, which temperature is, is that we cannot use a bar/pie chart here because we have too many values:

```
# show us the number of unique items
climate['AverageTemperature'].nunique()

111994
```

111,994 values is absurd to plot, and also absurd because we know that the data is quantitative. Likely, the most common graph to utilize starting at this level would be the **histogram**. This graph is a cousin of the bar graph, and visualizes buckets of quantities and shows frequencies of these buckets.

Let's see a histogram for the AverageTemperature around the world, to see the distribution of temperatures in a very holistic view:

```
climate['AverageTemperature'].hist()
```

The following is the output of the preceding code:

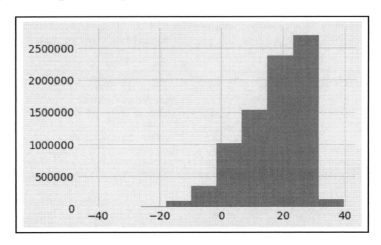

Here, we can see that we have an average value of 20°C. Let's confirm this:

```
climate['AverageTemperature'].describe()
```

```
count 8.235082e+06 mean 1.672743e+01 std 1.035344e+01 min -4.270400e+01
25% 1.029900e+01 50% 1.883100e+01 75% 2.521000e+01 max 3.965100e+01 Name:
AverageTemperature, dtype: float64
```

We were close. The mean seems to be around 17°. Let's make this a bit more fun and add new columns called year and century, and also subset the data to only be the temperatures recorded in the US:

```
# Convert the dt column to datetime and extract the year
climate['dt'] = pd.to_datetime(climate['dt'])
climate['year'] = climate['dt'].map(lambda value: value.year)

climate_sub_us['century'] = climate_sub_us['year'].map(lambda x: x/100+1)
# 1983 would become 20
# 1750 would become 18

# A subset the data to just the US
climate_sub_us = climate.loc[climate['Country'] == 'United States']
```

With the new column `century`, let's plot four histograms of temperature, one for each century:

```
climate_sub_us['AverageTemperature'].hist(by=climate_sub_us['century'],
  sharex=True, sharey=True,
  figsize=(10, 10),
  bins=20)
```

The following is the output of the preceding code:

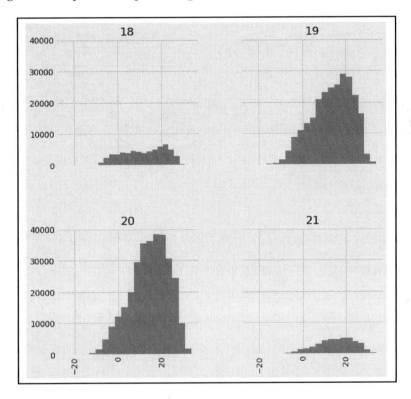

Here, we have our four histograms, showing that the `AverageTemperature` is going up slightly. Let's confirm this:

```
climate_sub_us.groupby('century')['AverageTemperature'].mean().plot(kind='l
ine')
```

The following is the output of the preceding code:

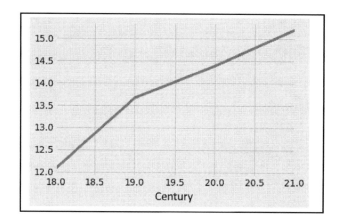

Interesting! And because differences are significant at this level, we can answer the question of how much, on average, the temperature has risen since the 18th century in the US. Let's store the changes over the centuries as its own pandas Series object first:

```
century_changes =
climate_sub_us.groupby('century')['AverageTemperature'].mean()

century_changes

century 18 12.073243 19 13.662870 20 14.386622 21 15.197692 Name:
AverageTemperature, dtype: float64
```

And now, let's use the indices in the Series to subtract the value in the 21st century minus the value in the 18th century, to get the difference in temperature:

```
# 21st century average temp in US minus 18th century average temp in US
century_changes[21] - century_changes[18]

# average difference in monthly recorded temperature in the US since the
18th century
3.12444911546
```

Plotting two columns at the interval level

One large advantage of having two columns of data at the interval level, or higher, is that it opens us up to using scatter plots where we can graph two columns of data on our axes and visualize data-points as literal points on the graph. The `year` and `averageTemperature` column of our `climate change` dataset are both at the interval level, as they both have meaning differences, so let's take a crack at plotting all of the monthly recorded US temperatures as a scatter plot, where the *x* axis will be the year and the *y* axis will be the temperature. We hope to notice a trending increase in temperature, as the line graph previously suggested:

```
x = climate_sub_us['year']
y = climate_sub_us['AverageTemperature']
fig, ax = plt.subplots(figsize=(10,5))
ax.scatter(x, y)
plt.show()
```

The following is the output of the preceding code:

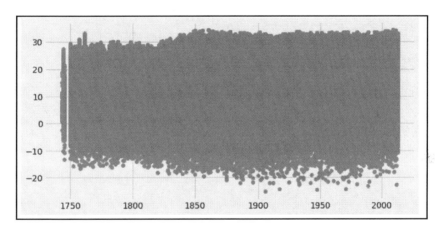

Oof, that's not pretty. There seems to be a lot of noise, and that is to be expected. Every year has multiple towns reporting multiple average temperatures, so it makes sense that we see many vertical points at each year.

Let's employ a `groupby` the year column to remove much of this noise:

```
# Let's use a groupby to reduce the amount of noise in the US
climate_sub_us.groupby('year').mean()['AverageTemperature'].plot()
```

The following is the output of the preceding code:

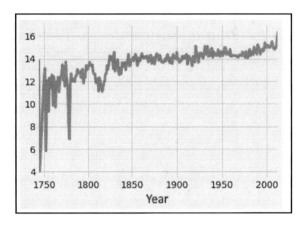

Better! We can definitely see the increase over the years, but let's smooth it out slightly by taking a rolling mean over the years:

```
# A moving average to smooth it all out:
climate_sub_us.groupby('year').mean()['AverageTemperature'].rolling(10).mea
n().plot()
```

The following is the output of the preceding code:

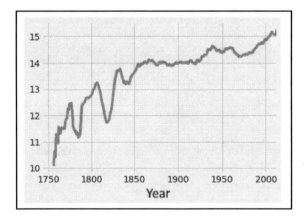

So, our ability to plot two columns of data at the interval level has re-confirmed what the previous line graph suggested; that there does seem to be a general trend upwards in average temperature across the US.

The interval level of data provides a whole new level of understanding of our data, but we aren't done yet.

The ratio level

Finally, we move up to the highest level, the ratio level. At this level, we arguably have the highest degree of control and mathematics at our disposal. At the ratio level, like the interval level, we are still working with quantitative data. We inherit addition and subtraction from the interval level, but now we have a notion of *true zero* which gives us the ability to multiply and divide values.

Mathematical operations allowed

At the ratio level, we may multiply and divide values together. This may not seem like a big deal, but it does allow us to make unique observations about data at this level that we cannot do at lower levels. Let's jump into a few examples to see exactly what this means.

Example:

When working with financial data, we almost always have to work with some monetary value. Money is at the ratio level because we have a concept of having "zero money". For this reason, we may make statements such as:

- $100 is *twice* as much as $50 because 100/50 = 2

- 10mg of penicillin is *half* as much as 20mg of penicillin because 10/20 = .5

It is because of the existence of zero that ratios have meaning at this level.

Non-example:

We generally consider temperature to be at the interval level and not the ratio level, because it doesn't make sense to say something like 100 degree is twice as hot as 50 degree. That doesn't quite make sense. Temperature is quite subjective and this is not objectively correct.

It can be argued that Celsius and Fahrenheit have a starting point mainly because we can convert them into Kelvin, which does boast a true zero. In reality, because Celsius and Fahrenheit allow negative values, while Kelvin does not; both Celsius and Fahrenheit do not have a real *true zero*, while Kelvin does.

Going back to the salary data from San Francisco, we now see that the salary weekly rate is at the ratio level, and there we can start making new observations. Let's begin by looking at the highest paid salaries:

```
# Which Grade has the highest Biweekly high rate
# What is the average rate across all of the Grades
fig = plt.figure(figsize=(15,5))
ax = fig.gca()

salary_ranges.groupby('Grade')[['Biweekly High Rate']].mean().sort_values(
  'Biweekly High Rate', ascending=False).head(20).plot.bar(stacked=False,
ax=ax, color='darkorange')
ax.set_title('Top 20 Grade by Mean Biweekly High Rate')
```

The following is the output of the preceding code:

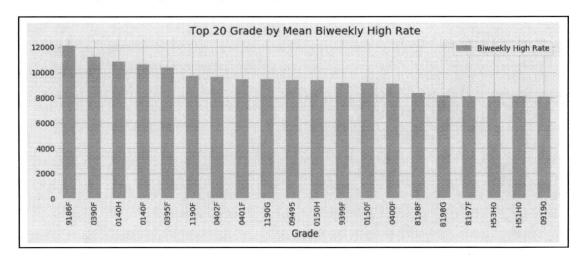

If we look up the highest-paid salary in a San Francisco public record found at:

```
http://sfdhr.org/sites/default/files/documents/
Classification%20and%20Compensation/Archives/Compensation-Manual-FY09-10.pdf
```

We see that it is the **General Manager, Public Transportation Dept.**. Let's take a look at the lowest-paid jobs by employing a similar strategy:

```
# Which Grade has the lowest Biweekly high rate
fig = plt.figure(figsize=(15,5))
ax = fig.gca()

salary_ranges.groupby('Grade')[['Biweekly High Rate']].mean().sort_values(
  'Biweekly High Rate', ascending=False).tail(20).plot.bar(stacked=False,
ax=ax, color='darkorange')
ax.set_title('Bottom 20 Grade by Mean Biweekly High Rate')
```

The following is the output of the preceding code:

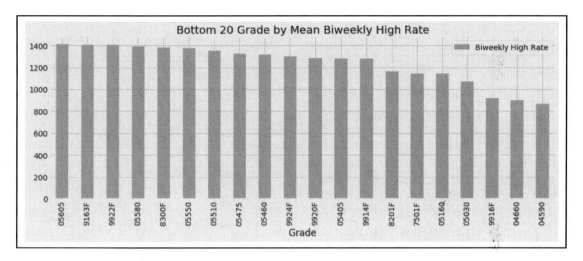

Again, looking up the lowest-paid job, we see that it is a **Camp Assistant**.

Because money is at the ratio level, we can also find the ratio of the highest-paid employee to the lowest-paid employee:

```
sorted_df = salary_ranges.groupby('Grade')[['Biweekly High
Rate']].mean().sort_values(
  'Biweekly High Rate', ascending=False)
  sorted_df.iloc[0][0] / sorted_df.iloc[-1][0]

13.931919540229886
```

The highest-paid employee makes 14x the lowest city employee. Thanks, ratio level!

Recap of the levels of data

Understanding the various levels of data is necessary to perform feature engineering. When it comes time to build new features, or fix old ones, we must have ways of identifying how to work with every column.

Here is a quick table to summarize what is and isn't possible at every level:

Level of Measurement	Properties	Examples	Descriptive statistics	Graphs
Nominal	Discrete Orderless	Binary Responses (True or False) Names of People Colors of paint	Frequencies/Percentages Mode	Bar Pie
Ordinal	Ordered categories Comparisons	Likert Scales Grades on an exam	Frequencies Mode Median Percentiles	Bar Pie Stem and leaf
Interval	Differences between ordered values have meaning	Deg. C or F Some Likert Scales (must be specific)	Frequencies Mode Median Mean Standard Deviation	Bar Pie Stem and leaf Box plot Histogram
Ratio	Continuous True 0 allows ratio statements (for example, $100 is twice as much as $50)	Money Weight	Mean Standard Deviation	Histogram Box plot

The following is a table showing the types of statistics allowed at each level:

Statistic	Nominal	Ordinal	Interval	Ratio
Mode	√	√	√	Sometimes
Median	X	√	√	√
Range, Min. Max	X	√	√	√
Mean	X	X	√	√
SD	X	X	√	√

And finally, the following is a table showing purely the graphs that are and are not possible at each level:

Graph	Nominal	Ordinal	Interval	Ratio
Bar/Pie	√	√	Sometimes	X
Stem and Leaf	X	√	√	√
Boxplot	X	√	√	√
Histogram	X	X	Sometimes	√

Whenever you are faced with a new dataset, here is a basic workflow to follow:

1. Is the data organized or unorganized? Does our data exist in a tabular format with distinct rows and columns, or does it exist as a mess of text in an unstructured format?
2. Is each column quantitative or qualitative? Are the values in the cells numbers that represent quantity, or strings that do not?
3. At what level of data is each column? Are the values at the nominal, ordinal, interval, or ratio level?
4. What graphs can I utilize to visualize my data—bar, pie, box, histogram, and so on?

Here is a visualization of this flow:

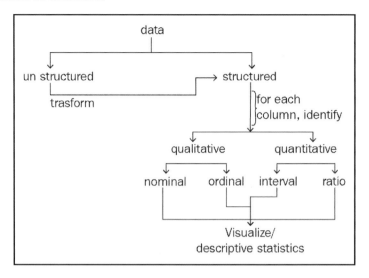

Summary

Understanding the features that we are working with is step zero of feature engineering. If we cannot understand the data given to us, we will never hope to fix, create, and utilize features in order to create well-performing, machine-learning pipelines. In this chapter, we were able to recognize, and extract the levels of data from our datasets and use that information to create useful and meaningful visuals that shine new lights on our data.

In the next chapter, we will use all of this new-found knowledge of the levels of data to start improving our features, and we will start to use machine-learning to effectively measure the impact of our feature engineering pipelines.

3
Feature Improvement - Cleaning Datasets

In the last two chapters, we have gone from talking about a basic understanding of feature engineering and how it can be used to enhance our machine learning pipelines to getting our hands dirty with datasets and evaluating and understanding the different types of data that we can encounter in the wild.

In this chapter, we will be using what we learned and taking things a step further and begin to change the datasets that we work with. Specifically, we will be starting to *clean* and *augment* our datasets. By cleaning, we will generally be referring to the process of altering columns and rows already given to us. By augmenting, we will generally refer to the processes of removing columns and adding columns to datasets. As always, our goal in all of these processes is to enhance our machine learning pipelines.

In the following chapters, we will be:

- Identifying missing values in data
- Removing harmful data
- Imputing (filling in) these missing values
- Normalizing/standardizing data
- Constructing brand new features
- Selecting (removing) features manually and automatically
- Using mathematical matrix computations to transform datasets to different dimensions

These methods will help us develop a better sense of which features are important within our data. In this chapter, we will be diving deeper into the first four methods, and leave the other three for future chapters.

Identifying missing values in data

Our first method of identifying missing values is to give us a better understanding of how to work with real-world data. Often, data can have missing values due to a variety of reasons, for example with survey data, some observations may not have been recorded. It is important for us to analyze our data, and get a sense of what the missing values are so we can decide how we want to handle missing values for our machine learning. To start, let's dive into a dataset that we will be interested in for the duration of this chapter, the Pima Indian Diabetes Prediction dataset.

The Pima Indian Diabetes Prediction dataset

This dataset is available on the UCI Machine Learning Repository at:

https://archive.ics.uci.edu/ml/datasets/pima+indians+diabetes.

From the main website, we can learn a few things about this publicly available dataset. We have nine columns and 768 instances (rows). The dataset is primarily used for predicting the onset of diabetes within five years in females of Pima Indian heritage over the age of 21 given medical details about their bodies.

The dataset is meant to correspond with a binary (2-class) classification machine learning problem. Namely, the answer to the question, *will this person develop diabetes within five years?* The column names are provided as follows (in order):

1. Number of times pregnant
2. Plasma glucose concentration a 2 hours in an oral glucose tolerance test
3. Diastolic blood pressure (mm Hg)
4. Triceps skinfold thickness (mm)
5. 2-Hour serum insulin measurement (mu U/ml)
6. Body mass index (weight in kg/(height in m)^2)

7. Diabetes pedigree function
8. Age (years)
9. Class variable (zero or one)

The goal of the dataset is to be able to predict the final column of `class` variable, which predicts if the patient has developed diabetes, using the other eight features as inputs to a machine learning function.

There are two very important reasons we will be working with this dataset:

- We will have to work with missing values
- All of the features we will be working with will be quantitative

The first point makes more sense for now as a reason, because the point of this chapter is to deal with missing values. As far as only choosing to work with quantitative data, this will only be the case for this chapter. We do not have enough tools to deal with missing values in categorical columns. In the next chapter, when we talk about feature construction, we will deal with this procedure.

The exploratory data analysis (EDA)

To identify our missing values we will begin with an EDA of our dataset. We will be using some useful python packages, pandas and numpy, to store our data and make some simple calculations as well as some popular visualization tools to see what the distribution of our data looks like. Let's begin and dive into some code. First, we will do some imports:

```
# import packages we need for exploratory data analysis (EDA)
import pandas as pd # to store tabular data
import numpy as np # to do some math
import matplotlib.pyplot as plt # a popular data visualization tool
import seaborn as sns  # another popular data visualization tool
%matplotlib inline
plt.style.use('fivethirtyeight') # a popular data visualization theme
```

We will import our tabular data through a CSV, as follows:

```
# load in our dataset using pandas
pima = pd.read_csv('../data/pima.data')

pima.head()
```

The `head` method allows us to see the first few rows in our dataset. The output is as follows:

	6	148	72	35	0	33.6	0.627	50	1
0	1	85	66	29	0	26.6	0.351	31	0
1	8	183	64	0	0	23.3	0.627	32	1
2	1	89	66	23	94	28.1	0.167	21	0
3	0	137	40	35	168	43.1	2.288	33	1
4	5	116	74	0	0	25.6	0.201	30	0

Something's not right here, there's no column names. The CSV must not have the names for the columns built into the file. No matter, we can use the data source's website to fill this in, as shown in the following code:

```
pima_column_names = ['times_pregnant', 'plasma_glucose_concentration',
'diastolic_blood_pressure', 'triceps_thickness', 'serum_insulin', 'bmi',
'pedigree_function', 'age', 'onset_diabetes']

pima = pd.read_csv('../data/pima.data', names=pima_column_names)

pima.head()
```

Now, using the `head` method again, we can see our columns with the appropriate headers. The output of the preceding code is as follows:

	times_pregnant	plasma_glucose_concentration	diastolic_blood_pressure	triceps_thickness	serum_insulin	bmi	pedigree_function	age	onset_diabetes
0	6	148	72	35	0	33.6	0.627	50	1
1	1	85	66	29	0	26.6	0.351	31	0
2	8	183	64	0	0	23.3	0.672	32	1
3	1	89	66	23	94	28.1	0.167	21	0
4	0	137	40	35	168	43.1	2.288	33	1

Much better, now we can use the column names to do some basic stats, selecting, and visualizations. Let's first get our null accuracy as follows:

```
pima['onset_diabetes'].value_counts(normalize=True)
# get null accuracy, 65% did not develop diabetes

0    0.651042
1    0.348958
Name: onset_diabetes, dtype: float64
```

If our eventual goal is to exploit patterns in our data in order to predict the onset of diabetes, let us try to visualize some of the differences between those that developed diabetes and those that did not. Our hope is that the histogram will reveal some sort of pattern, or obvious difference in values between the classes of prediction:

```
# get a histogram of the plasma_glucose_concentration column for
# both classes

col = 'plasma_glucose_concentration'
plt.hist(pima[pima['onset_diabetes']==0][col], 10, alpha=0.5, label='non-
diabetes')
plt.hist(pima[pima['onset_diabetes']==1][col], 10, alpha=0.5,
label='diabetes')
plt.legend(loc='upper right')
plt.xlabel(col)
plt.ylabel('Frequency')
plt.title('Histogram of {}'.format(col))
plt.show()
```

The output of the preceding code is as follows:

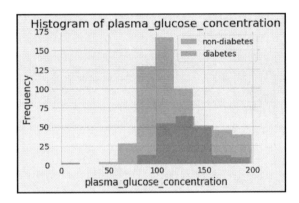

It seems that this histogram is showing us a pretty big difference between `plasma_glucose_concentration` between the two prediction classes. Let's show the same histogram style for multiple columns as follows:

```
for col in ['bmi', 'diastolic_blood_pressure',
'plasma_glucose_concentration']:
    plt.hist(pima[pima['onset_diabetes']==0][col], 10, alpha=0.5,
label='non-diabetes')
    plt.hist(pima[pima['onset_diabetes']==1][col], 10, alpha=0.5,
label='diabetes')
    plt.legend(loc='upper right')
    plt.xlabel(col)
```

```
plt.ylabel('Frequency')
plt.title('Histogram of {}'.format(col))
plt.show()
```

The output of the preceding code will give us the following three histograms. The first one is show us the distributions of **bmi** for the two class variables (non-diabetes and diabetes):

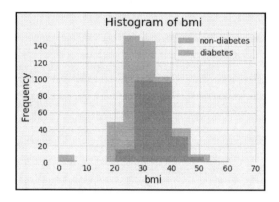

The next histogram to appear will shows us again contrastingly different distributions between a feature across our two class variables. This time we are looking at **diastolic_blood_pressure**:

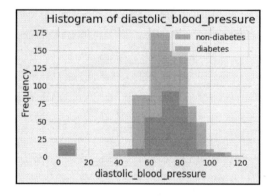

The final graph will show **plasma_glucose_concentration** differences between our two class variables:

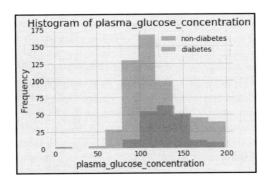

We can definitely see some major differences simply by looking at just a few histograms. For example, there seems to be a large jump in `plasma_glucose_concentration` for those who will eventually develop diabetes. To solidify this, perhaps we can visualize a linear correlation matrix in an attempt to quantify the relationship between these variables. We will use the visualization tool, seaborn, which we imported at the beginning of this chapter for our correlation matrix as follows:

```
# look at the heatmap of the correlation matrix of our dataset
sns.heatmap(pima.corr())
# plasma_glucose_concentration definitely seems to be an interesting
feature here
```

Following is the correlation matrix of our dataset. This is showing us the correlation amongst the different columns in our `Pima` dataset. The output is as follows:

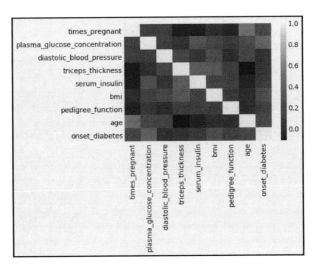

This correlation matrix is showing a strong correlation between `plasma_glucose_concentration` and `onset_diabetes`. Let's take a further look at the numerical correlations for the `onset_diabetes` column, with the following code:

```
pima.corr()['onset_diabetes'] # numerical correlation matrix
# plasma_glucose_concentration definitely seems to be an interesting
feature here
```

```
times_pregnant                   0.221898
plasma_glucose_concentration     0.466581
diastolic_blood_pressure         0.065068
triceps_thickness                0.074752
serum_insulin                    0.130548
bmi                              0.292695
pedigree_function                0.173844
age                              0.238356
onset_diabetes                   1.000000
Name: onset_diabetes, dtype: float64
```

We will explore the powers of correlation in a later Chapter 4, *Feature Construction*, but for now we are using **exploratory data analysis** (EDA) to hint at the fact that the `plasma_glucose_concentration` column will be an important factor in our prediction of the onset of diabetes.

Moving on to more important matters at hand, let's see if we are missing any values in our dataset by invoking the built-in `isnull()` method of the pandas DataFrame:

```
pima.isnull().sum()
>>>>
times_pregnant                   0
plasma_glucose_concentration     0
diastolic_blood_pressure         0
triceps_thickness                0
serum_insulin                    0
bmi                              0
pedigree_function                0
age                              0
onset_diabetes                   0
dtype: int64
```

Great! We don't have any missing values. Let's go on to do some more EDA, first using the `shape` method to see the number of rows and columns we are working with:

```
pima.shape . # (# rows, # cols)
(768, 9)
```

Confirming we have 9 columns (including our response variable) and 768 data observations (rows). Now, let's take a peak at the percentage of patients who developed diabetes, using the following code:

```
pima['onset_diabetes'].value_counts(normalize=True)
# get null accuracy, 65% did not develop diabetes


0     0.651042
1     0.348958
Name: onset_diabetes, dtype: float64
```

This shows us that `65%` of the patients did not develop diabetes, while about 35% did. We can use a nifty built-in method of a pandas DataFrame called `describe` to look at some basic descriptive statistics:

```
pima.describe()    # get some basic descriptive statistics
```

We get the output as follows:

	times_pregnant	plasma_glucose _concentration	diastolic_ blood_pressure	triceps _thickness	serum _insulin	bmi	pedigree _function	age	onset _diabetes
count	768.000000	768.000000	768.000000	768.000000	768.000000	768.000000	768.000000	768.000000	768.000000
mean	3.845052	120.894531	69.105469	20.536458	79.799479	31.992578	0.471876	33.240885	0.348958
std	3.369578	31.972618	19.355807	15.952218	115.244002	7.884160	0.331329	11.760232	0.476951
min	0.000000	0.000000	0.000000	0.000000	0.000000	0.000000	0.078000	21.000000	0.000000
25%	1.000000	99.000000	62.000000	0.000000	0.000000	27.300000	0.243750	24.000000	0.000000
50%	3.000000	117.000000	72.000000	23.000000	30.500000	32.000000	0.372500	29.000000	0.000000
75%	6.000000	140.250000	80.000000	32.000000	127.250000	36.600000	0.626250	41.000000	1.000000
max	17.000000	199.000000	122.000000	99.000000	846.000000	67.100000	2.420000	81.000000	1.000000

This shows us quite quickly some basic stats such as mean, standard deviation, and some different percentile measurements of our data. But, notice that the minimum value of the `BMI` column is 0. That is medically impossible; there must be a reason for this to happen. Perhaps the number zero has been encoded as a missing value instead of the None value or a missing cell. Upon closer inspection, we see that the value 0 appears as a minimum value for the following columns:

- `times_pregnant`

- `plasma_glucose_concentration`
- `diastolic_blood_pressure`
- `triceps_thickness`
- `serum_insulin`
- `bmi`
- `onset_diabetes`

Because zero is a class for `onset_diabetes` and 0 is actually a viable number for `times_pregnant`, we may conclude that the number 0 is encoding missing values for:

- `plasma_glucose_concentration`
- `diastolic_blood_pressure`
- `triceps_thickness`
- `serum_insulin`
- `bmi`

So, we actually do having missing values! It was obviously not luck that we happened upon the zeros as missing values, we knew it beforehand. As a data scientist, you must be ever vigilant and make sure that you know as much about the dataset as possible in order to find missing values encoded as other symbols. Be sure to read any and all documentation that comes with open datasets in case they mention any missing values.

If no documentation is available, some common values used instead of missing values are:

- **0** (for numerical values)
- **unknown** or **Unknown** (for categorical variables)
- **?** (for categorical variables)

So, we have five columns in which missing values exist, so now we get to talk about how to deal with them, in depth.

Dealing with missing values in a dataset

When working with data, one of the most common issues a data scientist will run into is the problem of missing data. Most commonly, this refers to empty cells (row/column intersections) where the data just was not acquired for whatever reason. This can become a problem for many reasons; notably, when applying learning algorithms to data with missing values, most (not all) algorithms are not able to cope with missing values.

For this reason, data scientists and machine learning engineers have many tricks and tips on how to deal with this problem. Although there are many variations of methodologies, the two major ways in which we can deal with missing data are:

- Remove rows with missing values in them
- Impute (fill in) missing values

Each method will **clean** our dataset to a point where a learning algorithm can handle it, but each method will have its pros and cons.

First off, before we go too far, let's get rid of the zeros and replace them all with the value None in Python. This way, our `fillna` and `dropna` methods will work correctly. We could manually replace all zeros with None, each column at a time, like so:

```
# Our number of missing values is (incorrectly) 0
pima['serum_insulin'].isnull().sum()
```

```
0
```

```
pima['serum_insulin'] = pima['serum_insulin'].map(lambda x:x if x != 0 else
None)
# manually replace all 0's with a None value

pima['serum_insulin'].isnull().sum()
# check the number of missing values again
```

```
374
```

We could repeat this procedure for every column with incorrectly labeled missing values, or we could use a `for` loop and a built-in `replace` method to speed things up, as shown in the following code:

```
# A little faster now for all columns

columns = ['serum_insulin', 'bmi', 'plasma_glucose_concentration',
'diastolic_blood_pressure', 'triceps_thickness']

for col in columns:
    pima[col].replace([0], [None], inplace=True)
```

So, now if we try to count the number of missing values using the `isnull` method, we should start to see missing values being counted as follows:

```
pima.isnull().sum()   # this makes more sense now!

times_pregnant                   0
plasma_glucose_concentration     5
diastolic_blood_pressure        35
triceps_thickness              227
serum_insulin                  374
bmi                             11
pedigree_function                0
age                              0
onset_diabetes                   0
dtype: int64
```

```
pima.head()
```

Now, looking at the first few rows of our dataset, we get the output as follows:

	times_pregnant	plasma_glucose_concentration	diastolic_blood_pressure	triceps_thickness	serum_insulin	bmi	pedigree_function	age	onset_diabetes
0	6	148	72	35	NaN	33.6	0.627	50	1
1	1	85	66	29	NaN	26.6	0.351	31	0
2	8	183	64	None	NaN	23.3	0.672	32	1
3	1	89	66	23	NaN	28.1	0.167	21	0
4	0	137	40	35	NaN	43.1	2.288	33	1

OK, this is starting to make much more sense. We can now see that five columns have missing values, and the degree to which data is missing is staggering. Some columns, such as `plasma_glucose_concentration`, are only missing five values, but look at `serum_insulin`; that column is missing almost half of its values.

Now that we have missing values properly injected into our dataset instead of the 0 placeholders that the dataset originally came with, our exploratory data analysis will be more accurate:

```
pima.describe()   # grab some descriptive statistics
```

The preceding code produces the following output:

	times_pregnant	serum_insulin	pedigree_function	age	onset_diabetes
count	768.000000	394.000000	768.000000	768.000000	768.000000
mean	3.845052	155.548223	0.471876	33.240885	0.348958
std	3.369578	118.775855	0.331329	11.760232	0.476951
min	0.000000	14.000000	0.078000	21.000000	0.000000
25%	1.000000	76.250000	0.243750	24.000000	0.000000
50%	3.000000	125.000000	0.372500	29.000000	0.000000
75%	6.000000	190.000000	0.626250	41.000000	1.000000
max	17.000000	846.000000	2.420000	81.000000	1.000000

Notice that the describe method doesn't include columns with missing values, which while not ideal, doesn't mean that we cannot obtain them by computing the mean and standard deviation of the specific columns, like so:

```
pima['plasma_glucose_concentration'].mean(),
pima['plasma_glucose_concentration'].std()

(121.68676277850589, 30.53564107280403)
```

Let us move on to our two ways of dealing with missing data.

Removing harmful rows of data

Probably the most common and easiest of our two options for dealing with missing data is to simply remove the observations that have any missing values. By doing so, we will be left with only the **complete** data points with all data filled in. We can obtain a new DataFrame by invoking the dropna method in pandas, as shown in the following code:

```
# drop the rows with missing values
pima_dropped = pima.dropna()
```

Now, of course, the obvious problem here is that we lost a few rows. To check how many exactly, use the following code:

```
num_rows_lost = round(100*(pima.shape[0] -
pima_dropped.shape[0])/float(pima.shape[0]))

print "retained {}% of rows".format(num_rows_lost)
# lost over half of the rows!

retained 49.0% of rows
```

Wow! We lost about 51% of the rows from the original dataset, and if we think about this from a machine learning perspective, even though now we have clean data with everything filled in, we aren't really learning as much as we possibly could be by ignoring over half of the data's observations. That's like a doctor trying to understand how heart attacks happen, ignoring over half of their patients coming in for check-ups.

Let's perform some more EDA on the dataset and compare the statistics about the data from before and after dropping the missing-values rows:

```
# some EDA of the dataset before it was dropped and after

# split of trues and falses before rows dropped
pima['onset_diabetes'].value_counts(normalize=True)

0    0.651042
1    0.348958
Name: onset_diabetes, dtype: float64
```

Now, let's look at the same split after we dropped the rows, using the following code:

```
pima_dropped['onset_diabetes'].value_counts(normalize=True)

0    0.668367
1    0.331633
Name: onset_diabetes, dtype: float64

# the split of trues and falses stay relatively the same
```

It seems that the binary response stayed relatively the same during the drastic transformation of our dataset. Let's take a look at the *shape* of our data by comparing the average values of columns before and after the transformation, using the `pima.mean` function, as follows:

```
# the mean values of each column (excluding missing values)
pima.mean()

times_pregnant                    3.845052
plasma_glucose_concentration    121.686763
diastolic_blood_pressure         72.405184
triceps_thickness                29.153420
serum_insulin                   155.548223
bmi                              32.457464
pedigree_function                 0.471876
age                              33.240885
onset_diabetes                    0.348958
dtype: float64
```

And now for the same averages after dropping the rows, using the `pima_dropped.mean()` function, as follows:

```
# the mean values of each column (with missing values rows dropped)
pima_dropped.mean()

times_pregnant                    3.301020
plasma_glucose_concentration    122.627551
diastolic_blood_pressure         70.663265
triceps_thickness                29.145408
serum_insulin                   156.056122
bmi                              33.086224
pedigree_function                 0.523046
age                              30.864796
onset_diabetes                    0.331633
dtype: float64
```

To get a better look at how these numbers changed, let's create a new chart that visualizes the percentages changed on average for each column. First, let's create a table of the percent changes in the average values of each column, as shown in the following code:

```
# % change in means
(pima_dropped.mean() - pima.mean()) / pima.mean()

times_pregnant                  -0.141489
plasma_glucose_concentration     0.007731
diastolic_blood_pressure        -0.024058
triceps_thickness               -0.000275
```

```
serum_insulin            0.003265
bmi                      0.019372
pedigree_function        0.108439
age                     -0.071481
onset_diabetes          -0.049650
dtype: float64
```

And now let's visualize these changes as a bar chart, using the following code:

```
# % change in means as a bar chart
ax = ((pima_dropped.mean() - pima.mean()) / pima.mean()).plot(kind='bar',
title='% change in average column values')
ax.set_ylabel('% change')
```

The preceding code produces the following output:

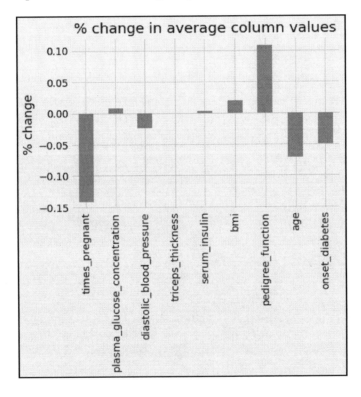

We can see that the number of `times_pregnant` variable average fell 14% after dropping missing values, which is a big change! The `pedigree_function` also rose 11%, another big leap. We can see how dropping rows (observations) severely affects the shape of the data and we should try to retain as much data as possible. Before moving on to the next method of dealing with missing values, let's introduce some actual machine learning into the mix.

The following code block (which we will go over line by line in a moment) will become a very familiar code block in this book. It describes and achieves a single fitting of a machine learning model over a variety of parameters in the hope of obtaining the best possible model, given the features at hand:

```
# now lets do some machine learning

# note we are using the dataset with the dropped rows

from sklearn.neighbors import KNeighborsClassifier
from sklearn.model_selection import GridSearchCV

X_dropped = pima_dropped.drop('onset_diabetes', axis=1)
# create our feature matrix by removing the response variable
print "learning from {} rows".format(X_dropped.shape[0])
y_dropped = pima_dropped['onset_diabetes']


# our grid search variables and instances

# KNN parameters to try
knn_params = {'n_neighbors':[1, 2, 3, 4, 5, 6, 7]}

knn = KNeighborsClassifier() . # instantiate a KNN model

grid = GridSearchCV(knn, knn_params)
grid.fit(X_dropped, y_dropped)

print grid.best_score_, grid.best_params_
# but we are learning from way fewer rows..
```

OK, let's go through this line by line. First, we have two new import statements:

```
from sklearn.neighbors import KNeighborsClassifier
from sklearn.model_selection import GridSearchCV
```

We will be utilizing scikit-learn's **K-Nearest Neighbors (KNN)** classification model, as well as a grid search module that will automatically find the best combo of parameters (using brute force) for the KNN model that best fits our data with respect to cross-validated accuracy. Next, let's take our dropped dataset (with the missing-valued rows removed) and create an X and a y variable for our predictive model. Let's start with our X (our feature matrix):

```
X_dropped = pima_dropped.drop('onset_diabetes', axis=1)
# create our feature matrix by removing the response variable
print "learning from {} rows".format(X_dropped.shape[0])

learning from 392 rows
```

Ouch, it's already obvious that there's a major problem with this approach. Our machine learning algorithm is going to be fitting and learning from far fewer data observations than which we started with. Let's now create our y (response series):

```
y_dropped = pima_dropped['onset_diabetes']
```

Now that we have our X and our y variable, we can introduce the variables and instances we need to successfully run a **grid search**. We will set the number of `params` to try at seven to keep things simple in this chapter. For every data cleaning and feature engineering method we try (dropping rows, filling in data), we will try to fit the best KNN as having somewhere between one and seven neighbors complexity. We can set this model up as follows:

```
# our grid search variables and instances

# KNN parameters to try

knn_params = {'n_neighbors':[1, 2, 3, 4, 5, 6, 7]}
```

Next, we will instantiate a grid search module, as shown in the following code, and fit it to our feature matrix and response variable. Once we do so, we will print out the best accuracy as well as the best parameter used to learn:

```
grid = GridSearchCV(knn, knn_params)
grid.fit(X_dropped, y_dropped)

print grid.best_score_, grid.best_params_
# but we are learning from way fewer rows..

0.744897959184 {'n_neighbors': 7}
```

So, it seems that using seven neighbors as its parameter, our KNN model was able to achieve a `74.4%` accuracy (better than our null accuracy of around 65%), but keep in mind that it is only learning from 49% of the original data, so who knows how it could have done on the rest of the data.

 This is our first real look into using machine learning in this book. We will be assuming that the reader does have basic familiarity with machine learning as well as statistical procedures such as cross-validation.

It's probably pretty clear that while dropping the *dirty* rows may not exactly be feature engineering, it is still a data cleaning technique we can utilize to help sanitize our machine learning pipeline inputs. Let's try for a slightly harder method.

Imputing the missing values in data

Imputing is the more involved method of dealing with missing values. By *imputing*, we refer to the act of filling in missing data values with numerical quantities that are somehow ascertained from existing knowledge/data. We have a few options on how we can fill in these missing values, the most common of them being filling in missing values with the average value for the rest of the column, as shown in the following code:

```
pima.isnull().sum()   # let's fill in the plasma column

times_pregnant                    0
plasma_glucose_concentration      5
diastolic_blood_pressure         35
triceps_thickness               227
serum_insulin                   374
bmi                              11
pedigree_function                 0
age                               0
onset_diabetes                    0
dtype: int64
```

Let's look at the five rows where `plasma_glucose_concentration` is missing:

```
empty_plasma_index =
pima[pima['plasma_glucose_concentration'].isnull()].index
pima.loc[empty_plasma_index]['plasma_glucose_concentration']


75      None
```

```
182      None
342      None
349      None
502      None
Name: plasma_glucose_concentration, dtype: object
```

Now, let's use the built-in `fillna` method to replace all of the `None` values with the mean value of the rest of the `plasma_glucose_concentration` column:

```
pima['plasma_glucose_concentration'].fillna(pima['plasma_glucose_concentrat
ion'].mean(), inplace=True)
# fill the column's missing values with the mean of the rest of the column

pima.isnull().sum()   # the column should now have 0 missing values
```

```
times_pregnant                   0
plasma_glucose_concentration     0
diastolic_blood_pressure        35
triceps_thickness              227
serum_insulin                  374
bmi                             11
pedigree_function                0
age                              0
onset_diabetes                   0
dtype: int64
```

And if we check out the column, we should see that the `None` values have been replaced by `121.68`, the mean value we obtained earlier for this column:

```
pima.loc[empty_plasma_index]['plasma_glucose_concentration']
```

```
75     121.686763
182    121.686763
342    121.686763
349    121.686763
502    121.686763
Name: plasma_glucose_concentration, dtype: float64
```

Great! But this can be cumbersome. Let's use a module in the scikit-learn preprocessing class (the documentation can be found at `http://scikit-learn.org/stable/modules/classes.html#module-sklearn.preprocessing`) called the `Imputer` (aptly named). We can import it as follows:

```
from sklearn.preprocessing import Imputer
```

As with most scikit-learn modules, we have a few new parameters to play with, but I will focus on the major one, called the `strategy`. We can define how we want to impute values into our dataset by setting this parameter. For quantitative values, we can use the built-in mean and median strategies to fill in values with either quantity. To use the `Imputer`, we must first instantiate the object, as shown in the following code:

```
imputer = Imputer(strategy='mean')
```

Then, we can call the `fit_transform` method to create a new object, as shown in the following code:

```
pima_imputed = imputer.fit_transform(pima)
```

We do have a small issue to deal with. The output of the Imputer is not a pandas DataFrame, but rather the output is of type **NumPy** array:

```
type(pima_imputed)   # comes out as an array

numpy.ndarray
```

This can be easily dealt with, as we could just cast the array as a DataFrame, as shown in the following code:

```
pima_imputed = pd.DataFrame(pima_imputed, columns=pima_column_names)
# turn our numpy array back into a pandas DataFrame object
```

Let's take a look at our new DataFrame:

```
pima_imputed.head()   # notice for example the triceps_thickness missing
values were replaced with 29.15342
```

The preceding code produces the following output:

	times_pregnant	plasma_glucose_concentration	diastolic_blood_pressure	triceps_thickness	serum_insulin	bmi	pedigree_function	age	onset_diabetes
0	6.0	148.0	72.0	35.00000	155.548223	33.6	0.627	50.0	1.0
1	1.0	85.0	66.0	29.00000	155.548223	26.6	0.351	31.0	0.0
2	8.0	183.0	64.0	29.15342	155.548223	23.3	0.672	32.0	1.0
3	1.0	89.0	66.0	23.00000	94.000000	28.1	0.167	21.0	0.0
4	0.0	137.0	40.0	35.00000	168.000000	43.1	2.288	33.0	1.0

Let's check in on our `plasma_glucose_concentration` column to make sure that the values are still filled in with the same mean we calculated manually earlier:

```
pima_imputed.loc[empty_plasma_index]['plasma_glucose_concentration']
# same values as we obtained with fillna

75      121.686763
182     121.686763
342     121.686763
349     121.686763
502     121.686763
Name: plasma_glucose_concentration, dtype: float64
```

As a final check, our imputed DataFrame should have no missing values, as shown in the following code:

```
pima_imputed.isnull().sum()   # no missing values

times_pregnant                    0
plasma_glucose_concentration      0
diastolic_blood_pressure          0
triceps_thickness                 0
serum_insulin                     0
bmi                               0
pedigree_function                 0
age                               0
onset_diabetes                    0
dtype: int64
```

Great! The `Imputer` helps a great deal with the menial task of imputing data values into missing slots. Let's try imputing a few types of values and seeings its effect on our KNN model for classification. Let's first try an even simpler imputing method. Let's re-fill in the empty values with zeros:

```
pima_zero = pima.fillna(0) # impute values with 0

X_zero = pima_zero.drop('onset_diabetes', axis=1)
print "learning from {} rows".format(X_zero.shape[0])
y_zero = pima_zero['onset_diabetes']

knn_params = {'n_neighbors':[1, 2, 3, 4, 5, 6, 7]}
grid = GridSearchCV(knn, knn_params)
grid.fit(X_zero, y_zero)

print grid.best_score_, grid.best_params_
# if the values stayed at 0, our accuracy goes down
```

```
learning from 768 rows
0.73046875 {'n_neighbors': 6}
```

If we had left the values as 0, our accuracy would have been lower than dropping the rows with missing values. Our goal now is to obtain a machine learning pipeline that can learn from all 768 rows, but can perform better than the model that learned from only 392 rows. This means that the accuracy to beat is 0.745, or 74.5%.

Imputing values in a machine learning pipeline

If we wish to transfer the Imputer over to a production-ready machine learning pipeline, we will need to talk briefly about the topic of pipelines.

Pipelines in machine learning

When we talk about *pipelines* in machine learning, we are usually talking about the fact that data is only passed through a learning algorithm raw, but also through a variety of preprocessing steps and even multiple learning algorithms before the final output is interpreted. Because it is so common to have several steps and transformation and prediction within a single machine learning pipeline, scikit-learn has a built-in module for building these pipelines.

Pipelines are especially important because it is actually *improper* to not use a pipeline when imputing values using the Imputer class. This is because the goal of the learning algorithm is to generalize the patterns in the training set in order to apply those patterns to the testing set. If we impute values for the entire dataset before splitting the set and applying learning algorithms, then we are cheating and our models are not actually learning any patterns. To visualize this concept, let's take a single train test split, a potential one of many during a cross-validation training phase.

Let's take a copy of a single column of the Pima dataset in order to emphasize our point a bit more drastically, and also import a single train test split module from scikit-learn:

```
from sklearn.model_selection import train_test_split

X = pima[['serum_insulin']].copy()
y = pima['onset_diabetes'].copy()

X.isnull().sum()

serum_insulin    374
dtype: int64
```

Now, let's take a single split. But before doing so, we will impute the average value of X in the entire dataset, using the following code:

```
# the improper way.. imputing values BEFORE splitting

entire_data_set_mean = X.mean()     # take the entire datasets mean
X = X.fillna(entire_data_set_mean) # and use it to fill in the missing
spots
print entire_data_set_mean

serum_insulin    155.548223
dtype: float64

# Take the split using a random state so that we can examine the same
split.
X_train, X_test, y_train, y_test = train_test_split(X, y, random_state=99)
```

Now, let's fit a KNN model to the training and testing sets:

```
knn = KNeighborsClassifier()

knn.fit(X_train, y_train)

knn.score(X_test, y_test)

0.65625  # the accuracy of the improper split
```

Note that we aren't implementing any grid searching here, just a plain fit. We see that our model boasts a 66% accuracy rate (not great, but that's not the point). The important thing to note here is that both the training and the testing set of X were imputed using the mean of the entire X matrix. This is in direct violation of a core tenet of the machine learning procedure. We cannot assume that we know the mean of the entire dataset when predicting the test set's response values. Simply put, our KNN model is using information gained from the testing set to fit to the training set. This is a big red flag.

For more information on pipelines and why we need to use them, check out *The Principles of Data Science* (available from Packt Publishing) at https://www.packtpub.com/big-data-and-business-intelligence/ principles-data-science

Now, let's do it properly by first taking the mean of the training set and then using the mean of the training set to fill in values of the testing set. Again, this procedure tests the model's ability to use the average value of training data to predict unseen test cases:

```
# the proper way.. imputing values AFTER splitting
from sklearn.model_selection import train_test_split

X = pima[['serum_insulin']].copy()
y = pima['onset_diabetes'].copy()

# using the same random state to obtain the same split
X_train, X_test, y_train, y_test = train_test_split(X, y, random_state=99)

X.isnull().sum()

serum_insulin    374
dtype: int64
```

Now, instead of taking the mean of the entire X matrix, we will properly only do so for the training set and use that value to fill in missing cells in **both** the training and test set:

```
training_mean = X_train.mean()
X_train = X_train.fillna(training_mean)
X_test = X_test.fillna(training_mean)

print training_mean

serum_insulin    158.546053
dtype: float64

# not the entire dataset's mean, it's much higher!!
```

Finally, let's score a KNN model on the *same* dataset, but imputed correctly, as shown in the following code:

```
knn = KNeighborsClassifier()

knn.fit(X_train, y_train)

print knn.score(X_test, y_test)

0.4895

# lower accuracy, but much more honest in the mode's ability to generalize
a pattern to outside data
```

This is of course a much lower accuracy, but at least it is a more honest representation of the model's ability to learn from the training set's features and apply what it learned to unseen and withheld testing data. Scikit-learn's pipelines make this entire process much easier by giving structure and order to the steps of our machine learning pipelines. Let's take a look at a code block of how to use the scikit-learn `Pipeline` with the `Imputer`:

```
from sklearn.pipeline import Pipeline

knn_params = {'classify__n_neighbors':[1, 2, 3, 4, 5, 6, 7]}
# must redefine params to fit the pipeline

knn = KNeighborsClassifier() . # instantiate a KNN model

mean_impute = Pipeline([('imputer', Imputer(strategy='mean')), ('classify',
knn)])

X = pima.drop('onset_diabetes', axis=1)
y = pima['onset_diabetes']

grid = GridSearchCV(mean_impute, knn_params)
grid.fit(X, y)

print grid.best_score_, grid.best_params_

0.731770833333 {'classify__n_neighbors': 6}
mean_impute = Pipeline([('imputer', Imputer(strategy='mean')), ('classify',
knn)])
```

A few new things to note. First off, our `Pipeline` has two steps:

- An `Imputer` with `strategy=` mean
- A classifier of type KNN

Secondly, we had to redefine our `param` dict for the grid search as we have to specify exactly to which step of the pipeline the n_neighbors parameter belongs:

```
knn_params = {'classify__n_neighbors':[1, 2, 3, 4, 5, 6, 7]}
```

Other than that, everything is normal and proper. The Pipeline class will handle most of the procedure for us. It will handle properly imputing values from several training sets and using them to fill in missing values in the test set, properly testing the KNN's ability to generalize patterns in the data and finally outputting the best performing model, having an accuracy of 73%, just beneath our goal to beat of .745. Now that we have this syntax down, let's try the entire procedure again, but with a slight modification, as shown in the following code:

```
knn_params = {'classify__n_neighbors':[1, 2, 3, 4, 5, 6, 7]}

knn = KNeighborsClassifier() . # instantiate a KNN model

median_impute = Pipeline([('imputer', Imputer(strategy='median')),
('classify', knn)])
X = pima.drop('onset_diabetes', axis=1)
y = pima['onset_diabetes']

grid = GridSearchCV(median_impute, knn_params)
grid.fit(X, y)

print grid.best_score_, grid.best_params_

0.735677083333 {'classify__n_neighbors': 6}
```

Here, the only difference is that our pipeline will try a different strategy of imputing **median**, wherein the missing values will be filled in the median of the remaining values. It is important to reiterate that our accuracies may be lower than the model's fit on the dropped rows, but they were made on more than twice the size of the dataset with missing values! And they were still better than leaving them all at 0, as the data was originally presented to us.

Let's take a minute to recap the scores we have gotten so far using our proper pipelines:

Pipeline description	# rows model learned from	Cross-validated accuracy
drop missing-valued rows	**392**	**.74489**
Impute values with 0	768	.7304
Impute values with mean of column	768	.7318
Impute values with median of column	768	.7357

If we go by accuracy alone, it appears the best procedure is to drop the missing-values rows. Perhaps using the `Pipeline` and `Imputer` features alone in scikit-learn is not enough. We still would like to see comparable (if not better) performance coming from all 768 rows if possible. In order to achieve this, let's try introducing a brand new feature engineering trick, standardization and normalization.

Standardization and normalization

Up until now, we have dealt with identifying the types of data as well as the ways data can be missing and finally, the ways we can fill in missing data. Now, let's talk about how we can manipulate our data (and our features) in order to enhance our machine pipelines further. So far, we have tried four different ways of manipulating our dataset, and the best cross-validated accuracy we have achieved with a KNN model is .745. If we look back at some of the EDA we have previously done, we will notice something about our features:

```
impute = Imputer(strategy='mean')
# we will want to fill in missing values to see all 9 columns

pima_imputed_mean = pd.DataFrame(impute.fit_transform(pima),
columns=pima_column_names)
```

Now, let's use a standard histogram to see the distribution across all nine columns, as follows, specifying a figure size:

```
pima_imputed_mean.hist(figsize=(15, 15))
```

The preceding code produces the following output:

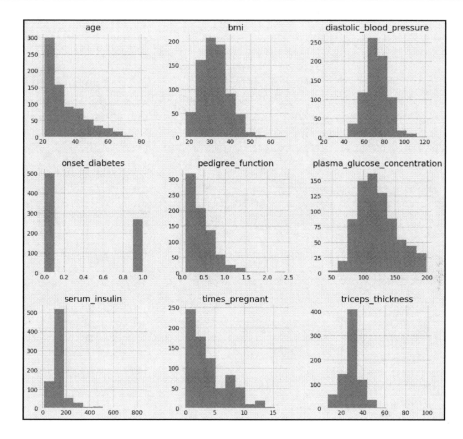

Nice, but notice anything off? Every single column has a vastly different mean, min, max, and standard deviation. This is also obvious through the describe method, using the following code:

```
pima_imputed_mean.describe()
```

The output is as follows:

	times _pregnant	plasma _glucose _concentration	diastolic_ blood_pressure	triceps _thickness	serum _insulin	bmi	pedigree _function	age	onset _diabetes
count	768.000000	768.000000	768.000000	768.000000	768.000000	768.000000	768.000000	768.000000	768.000000
mean	3.845052	121.686763	72.405184	29.153420	155.548223	32.457464	0.471876	33.240885	0.348958
std	3.369578	30.435949	12.096346	8.790942	85.021108	6.875151	0.331329	11.760232	0.476951
min	0.000000	44.000000	24.000000	7.000000	14.000000	18.200000	0.078000	21.000000	0.000000
25%	1.000000	99.750000	64.000000	25.000000	121.500000	27.500000	0.243750	24.000000	0.000000
50%	3.000000	117.000000	72.202592	29.153420	155.548223	32.400000	0.372500	29.000000	0.000000

75%	6.000000	140.250000	80.000000	32.000000	155.548223	36.600000	0.626250	41.000000	1.000000
max	17.000000	199.000000	122.000000	99.000000	846.000000	67.100000	2.420000	81.000000	1.000000

But why does this matter? Well, some machine learning models rely on learning methods that are affected greatly by the *scale* of the data, meaning that if we have a column such as `diastolic_blood_pressure` that lives between 24 and 122, and an age column between 21 and 81, then our learning algorithms will not learn optimally. To really see the differences in scales, let's invoke two optional parameters in the histogram method, `sharex` and `sharey`, so that we can see each graph on the same scale as every other graph, using the following code:

```
pima_imputed_mean.hist(figsize=(15, 15), sharex=True)
# with the same x axis (the y axis is not as important here)
```

The preceding code produces the following output:

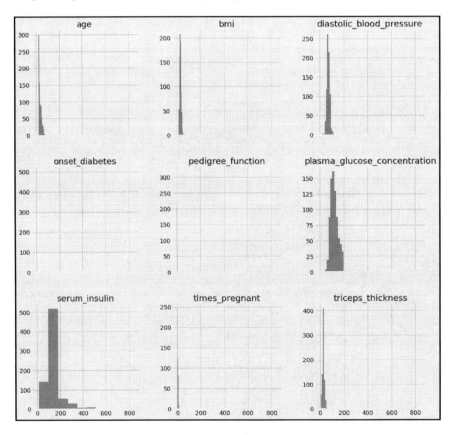

It is quite clear that our data all lives on vastly different scales. Data engineers have options on how to deal with this problem in our machine learning pipelines that are under a family of operations called **normalization**. Normalization operations are meant to align and transform both columns and rows to a consistent set of rules. For example, a common form of normalization is to transform all quantitative columns to be between a consistent and static range of values (for example all values must be between 0 and 1). We may also impose mathematical rules such as, *all columns must have the same mean and standard deviation* so that they appear nicely on the same histogram (unlike the pima histograms we computed recently). Normalization techniques are meant to *level the playing field* of data by ensuring that all rows and columns are treated equally under the eyes of machine learning.

We will focus on three methods of data normalization:

- Z-score standardization
- Min-max scaling
- Row normalization

The first two deal specifically with altering features in place, while the third option actually manipulates the rows of the data, but is still just as pertinent as the first two.

Z-score standardization

The most common of the normalization techniques, **z-score standardization**, utilizes a very simple statistical idea of a z-score. The output of a z-score normalization are features that are re-scaled to have a mean of zero and a standard deviation of one. By doing this, by re-scaling our features to have a uniform mean and variance (square of standard deviation), then we allow models such as KNN to learn optimally and not skew towards larger scaled features. The formula is simple: for every column, we replace the cells with the following value:

$$z = (x - \mu) / \sigma$$

Where:

- z is our new value (z-score)
- x is the previous value of the cell
- μ is the mean of the column
- σ is the standard deviation of the columns

Let's see an example by scaling the `plasma_glucose_concentration` column in our dataset:

```
print pima['plasma_glucose_concentration'].head()
```

```
0    148.0
1     85.0
2    183.0
3     89.0
4    137.0
Name: plasma_glucose_concentration, dtype: float64
```

And now let's manually compute z-scores for every value in our column, using the following code:

```
# get the mean of the column
mu = pima['plasma_glucose_concentration'].mean()

# get the standard deviation of the column
sigma = pima['plasma_glucose_concentration'].std()

# calculate z scores for every value in the column.
print ((pima['plasma_glucose_concentration'] - mu) / sigma).head()
```

```
0     0.864545
1    -1.205376
2     2.014501
3    -1.073952
4     0.503130
Name: plasma_glucose_concentration, dtype: float64
```

We see that every single value in the column will be replaced, and also notice how now some of them are negative. This is because the resulting values represent a *distance* from the mean. So, if a value originally was below the mean of the column, the resulting z-score will be negative. Of course, in scikit-learn, we have built-in objects to help us out, as shown in the following code:

```
# built in z-score normalizer
from sklearn.preprocessing import StandardScaler
```

Let's try it out, shown as follows:

```
# mean and std before z score standardizing
pima['plasma_glucose_concentration'].mean(),
pima['plasma_glucose_concentration'].std()

(121.68676277850591, 30.435948867207657)


ax = pima['plasma_glucose_concentration'].hist()
ax.set_title('Distribution of plasma_glucose_concentration')
```

The preceding code produces the following output:

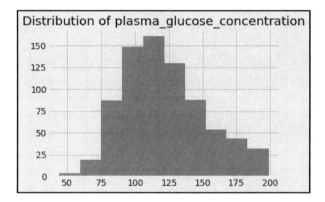

Here, we can see the distribution of the column before doing anything. Now, let's apply a z-score scaling, as shown in the following code:

```
scaler = StandardScaler()

glucose_z_score_standardized =
scaler.fit_transform(pima[['plasma_glucose_concentration']])
# note we use the double bracket notation [[ ]] because the transformer
requires a dataframe

# mean of 0 (floating point error) and standard deviation of 1
glucose_z_score_standardized.mean(), glucose_z_score_standardized.std()

(-3.5619655373390441e-16, 1.0)
```

We can see that after we apply our scaler to the column, or mean drops to zero and our standard deviation is one. Furthermore, if we take a look at the distribution of values across our recently scaled data:

```
ax = pd.Series(glucose_z_score_standardized.reshape(-1,)).hist()
ax.set_title('Distribution of plasma_glucose_concentration after Z Score
Scaling')
```

The output is as follows:

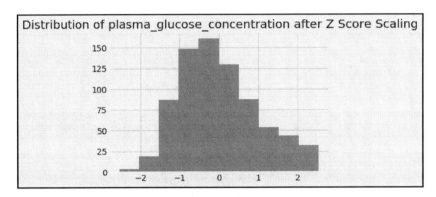

We will notice that our *x* axis is now much more constrained, while our *y* axis is unchanged. Also note that the shape of the data is unchanged entirely. Let's take a look at the histograms of our DataFrame after we apply a z-score transformation on every single column. When we do this, the `StandardScaler` will compute a mean and standard deviation for every column separately:

```
scale = StandardScaler() # instantiate a z-scaler object

pima_imputed_mean_scaled =
pd.DataFrame(scale.fit_transform(pima_imputed_mean),
columns=pima_column_names)
pima_imputed_mean_scaled.hist(figsize=(15, 15), sharex=True)
# now all share the same "space"
```

The preceding code produces the following output:

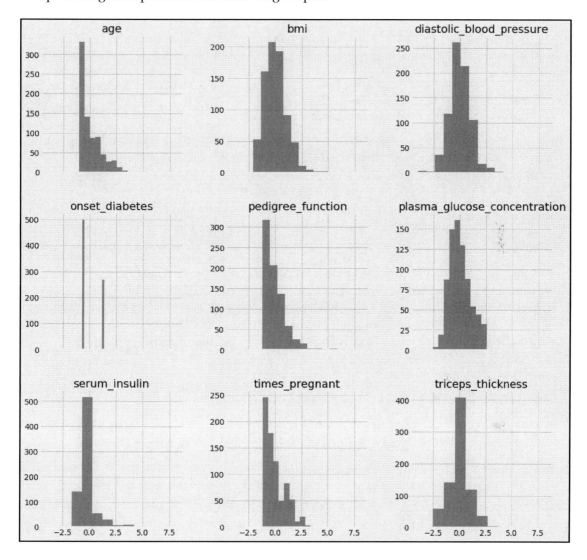

Notice that our *x* axes are all now much more constrained across the entire dataset. Let's now plug a `StandardScaler` into our machine learning pipeline from before:

```
knn_params = {'imputer__strategy':['mean', 'median'],
'classify__n_neighbors':[1, 2, 3, 4, 5, 6, 7]}

mean_impute_standardize = Pipeline([('imputer', Imputer()), ('standardize',
StandardScaler()), ('classify', knn)])
X = pima.drop('onset_diabetes', axis=1)
y = pima['onset_diabetes']

grid = GridSearchCV(mean_impute_standardize, knn_params)
grid.fit(X, y)

print grid.best_score_, grid.best_params_
```

```
0.7421875 {'imputer__strategy': 'median', 'classify__n_neighbors': 7}
```

Note a few things here. We included a new set of parameters to grid search, namely the strategy of imputing missing values. Now, I am looking for the best combination of strategy and number of neighbors in our KNN attached to a z-score scaling and our result is .742, which so far is the closest score we have gotten to our goal of beating .745, and this pipeline is learning from all 768 rows. Let's now look at another method of column normalization.

The min-max scaling method

Min-max scaling is similar to z-score normalization in that it will replace every value in a column with a new value using a formula. In this case, that formula is:

$$m = (x - x_{min}) / (x_{max} - x_{min})$$

Where:

- *m* is our new value
- *x* is the original cell value
- x_{min} is the minimum value of the column
- x_{max} is the maximum value of the column

Using this formula, we will see that the values of each column will now be between zero and one. Let's take a look at an example using a built-in scikit-learn module:

```
# import the sklearn module
from sklearn.preprocessing import MinMaxScaler

#instantiate the class
min_max = MinMaxScaler()

# apply the Min Max Scaling
pima_min_maxed = pd.DataFrame(min_max.fit_transform(pima_imputed),
columns=pima_column_names)

# spit out some descriptive statistics
pima_min_maxed.describe()
```

Here is the output of our `describe` method:

	times _pregnant	plasma _glucose _concentration	diastolic _blood _pressure	triceps _thickness	serum _insulin	bmi	pedigree _function	age	onset _diabetes
count	768.000000	768.000000	768.000000	768.000000	768.000000	768.000000	768.000000	768.000000	768.000000
mean	0.226180	0.501205	0.493930	0.240798	0.170130	0.291564	0.168179	0.204015	0.348958
std	0.198210	0.196361	0.123432	0.095554	0.102189	0.140596	0.141473	0.196004	0.476951
min	0.000000	0.000000	0.000000	0.000000	0.000000	0.000000	0.000000	0.000000	0.000000
25%	0.058824	0.359677	0.408163	0.195652	0.129207	0.190184	0.070773	0.050000	0.000000
50%	0.176471	0.470968	0.491863	0.240798	0.170130	0.290389	0.125747	0.133333	0.000000
75%	0.352941	0.620968	0.571429	0.271739	0.170130	0.376278	0.234095	0.333333	1.000000
max	1.000000	1.000000	1.000000	1.000000	1.000000	1.000000	1.000000	1.000000	1.000000

Notice how the `min` are all zeros and the `max` values are all ones. Note further that the standard deviations are now all very very small, a side effect of this type of scaling. This can hurt some models as it takes away weight from outliers. Let's plug our new normalization technique into our pipeline:

```
knn_params = {'imputer__strategy': ['mean', 'median'],
'classify__n_neighbors':[1, 2, 3, 4, 5, 6, 7]}

mean_impute_standardize = Pipeline([('imputer', Imputer()), ('standardize',
MinMaxScaler()), ('classify', knn)])
X = pima.drop('onset_diabetes', axis=1)
y = pima['onset_diabetes']

grid = GridSearchCV(mean_impute_standardize, knn_params)
```

```
grid.fit(X, y)

print grid.best_score_, grid.best_params_

0.74609375 {'imputer__strategy': 'mean', 'classify__n_neighbors': 4}
```

Woah, this is the best accuracy we've gotten so far working with the missing data and using all of the 768 original rows in the dataset. It seems as though the min-max scaling is helping our KNN a great deal! Wonderful; let's try a third type of normalization, and this time let's move away from normalizing columns and onto normalizing rows instead.

The row normalization method

Our final normalization method works row-wise instead of column-wise. Instead of calculating statistics on each column, mean, min, max, and so on, the row normalization technique will ensure that each row of data has a *unit norm*, meaning that each row will be the same vector length. Imagine if each row of data belonged to an n-dimensional space; each one would have a vector norm, or length. Another way to put it is if we consider every row to be a vector in space:

$$x = (x_1, x_2, ..., x_n)$$

Where 1, 2, ..., n in the case of Pima would be 8, 1 for each feature (not including the response), the norm would be calculated as:

$$||x|| = \sqrt{(x_1^{2+} x_2^{2+} ... + x_n^2)}$$

This is called the **L-2 Norm**. Other types of norms exist, but we will not get into that in this text. Instead, we are concerned with making sure that every single row has the same norm. This comes in handy, especially when working with text data or clustering algorithms.

Before doing anything, let's see the average norm of our mean-imputed matrix, using the following code:

```
np.sqrt((pima_imputed**2).sum(axis=1)).mean()
# average vector length of imputed matrix

223.36222025823744
```

Now, let's bring in our row-normalizer, as shown in the following code:

```
from sklearn.preprocessing import Normalizer # our row normalizer

normalize = Normalizer()

pima_normalized = pd.DataFrame(normalize.fit_transform(pima_imputed),
columns=pima_column_names)

np.sqrt((pima_normalized**2).sum(axis=1)).mean()
# average vector length of row normalized imputed matrix

1.0
```

After normalizing, we see that every single row has a norm of one now. Let's see how this method fares in our pipeline:

```
knn_params = {'imputer__strategy': ['mean', 'median'],
'classify__n_neighbors':[1, 2, 3, 4, 5, 6, 7]}

mean_impute_normalize = Pipeline([('imputer', Imputer()), ('normalize',
Normalizer()), ('classify', knn)])
X = pima.drop('onset_diabetes', axis=1)
y = pima['onset_diabetes']

grid = GridSearchCV(mean_impute_normalize, knn_params)
grid.fit(X, y)

print grid.best_score_, grid.best_params_

0.682291666667 {'imputer__strategy': 'mean', 'classify__n_neighbors': 6}
```

Ouch, not great, but worth a try. Now that we have seen three different methods of data normalization, let's put it all together and see how we did on this dataset.

There are many learning algorithms that are affected by the scale of data. Here is a list of some popular learning algorithms that are affected by the scale of data:

- KNN-due to its reliance on the Euclidean Distance
- K-Means Clustering - same reasoning as KNN
- Logistic regression, SVM, neural networks—if you are using gradient descent to learn weights
- Principal component analysis—eigen vectors will be skewed towards larger columns

Putting it all together

After dealing with a variety of problems with our dataset, from identifying missing values hidden as zeros, imputing missing values, and normalizing data at different scales, it's time to put all of our scores together into a single table and see what combination of feature engineering did the best:

Pipeline description	# rows model learned from	Cross-validated accuracy
Drop missing-valued rows	392	.7449
Impute values with 0	768	.7304
Impute values with mean of column	768	.7318
Impute values with median of column	768	.7357
Z-score normalization with median imputing	768	.7422
Min-max normalization with mean imputing	**768**	**.7461**
Row-normalization with mean imputing	768	.6823

It seems as though we were finally able to get a better accuracy by applying mean imputing and min-max normalization to our dataset and still use all 768 available rows. Great!

Summary

Feature improvement is about recognizing areas of issue and improvement in our data and figuring out which cleaning methods will be the most effective. Our main takeaway should be to look at data with the eyes of a data scientist. Instead of immediately dropping rows/columns with problems, we should think about the best ways of fixing these problems. More often than not, our machine learning performance will thank us in the end.

This chapter contains several ways of dealing with issues with our quantitative columns. The next chapter will deal with the imputing of categorical columns, as well as how to introduce brand new features into the mix from existing features. We will be working with scikit-learn pipelines with a mix of numerical and categorical columns to really expand the types of data we can work with.

4
Feature Construction

In the previous chapter, we worked with the `Pima Indian Diabetes Prediction` dataset to get a better understanding of which given features in our dataset are most valuable. Working with the features that were available to us, we identified missing values within our columns and employed techniques of dropping missing values, imputing, and normalizing/standardizing our data to improve the accuracy of our machine learning model.

It is important to note that, up to this point, we have only worked with features that are quantitative. We will now shift into dealing with categorical data, in addition to the quantitative data that has missing values. Our main focus will be to work with our given features to construct entirely new features for our models to learn from.

There are various methods we can utilize to construct our features, with the most basic starting with the pandas library in Python to scale an existing feature by a multiples. We will be diving into some more mathematically intensive methods, and will employ various packages available to us through the scikit-learn library; we will also create our own custom classes. We will go over these classes in detail as we get into the code.

We will be covering the following topics in our discussions:

- Examining our dataset
- Imputing categorical features
- Encoding categorical variables
- Extending numerical features
- Text-specific feature construction

Examining our dataset

For demonstrative purposes, in this chapter, we will utilize a dataset that we have created, so that we can showcase a variety of data levels and types. Let's set up our DataFrame and dive into our data.

We will use pandas to create the DataFrame we will work with, as this is the primary data structure in pandas. The advantage of a pandas DataFrame is that there are several attributes and methods available for us to perform on our data. This allows us to logically manipulate the data to develop a thorough understanding of what we are working with, and how best to structure our machine learning models:

1. First, let's import `pandas`:

    ```
    # import pandas as pd
    ```

2. Now, we can set up our `DataFrame X`. To do this, we will utilize the `DataFrame` method in pandas, which creates a tabular data structure (table with rows and columns). This method can take in a few types of data (NumPy arrays or dictionaries, to name a couple). Here, we will be passing-in a dictionary with keys as column headers and values as lists, with each list representing a column:

    ```
    X = pd.DataFrame({'city':['tokyo', None, 'london', 'seattle', 'san
    francisco', 'tokyo'],
                      'boolean':['yes', 'no', None, 'no', 'no', 'yes'],
                      'ordinal_column':['somewhat like', 'like',
    'somewhat like', 'like', 'somewhat like', 'dislike'],
                      'quantitative_column':[1, 11, -.5, 10, None,
    20]})
    ```

3. This will give us a DataFrame with four columns and six rows. Let's print our DataFrame X and take a look at the data:

    ```
    print X
    ```

We get the output as follows:

	boolean	city	ordinal_column	quantitative_column
0	yes	tokyo	somewhat like	1.0
1	no	None	like	11.0
2	None	london	somewhat like	-0.5
3	no	seattle	like	10.0

4	no	san francisco	somewhat like	NaN
5	yes	tokyo	dislike	20.0

Let's take a look at our columns and identify our data levels and types:

- `boolean`: This column is represented by binary categorical data (yes/no), and is at the nominal level
- `city`: This column is represented by categorical data, also at the nominal level
- `ordinal_column`: As you may have guessed by the column name, this column is represented by ordinal data, at the ordinal level
- `quantitative_column`: This column is represented by integers at the ratio level

Imputing categorical features

Now that we have an understanding of the data we are working with, let's take a look at our missing values:

- To do this, we can use the `isnull` method available to us in pandas for DataFrames. This method returns a `boolean` same-sized object indicating if the values are null.
- We will then `sum` these to see which columns have missing data:

```
X.isnull().sum()
>>>>
boolean                 1
city                    1
ordinal_column          0
quantitative_column     1
dtype: int64
```

Here, we can see that three of our columns are missing values. Our course of action will be to impute these missing values.

If you recall, we implemented scikit-learn's `Imputer` class in a previous chapter to fill in numerical data. `Imputer` does have a categorical option, `most_frequent`, however it only works on categorical data that has been encoded as integers.

We may not always want to transform our categorical data this way, as it can change how we interpret the categorical information, so we will build our own transformer. By transformer, we mean a method by which a column will impute missing values.

In fact, we will build several custom transformers in this chapter, as they are quite useful for making transformations to our data, and give us options that are not readily available in pandas or scikit-learn.

Let's start with our categorical column, `city`. Just as we have the strategy of imputing the mean value to fill missing rows for numerical data, we have a similar method for categorical data. To impute values for categorical data, fill missing rows with the most common category.

To do so, we will need to find out what the most common category is in our `city` column:

 Note that we need to specify the column we are working with to employ a method called `value_counts`. This will return an object that will be in descending order so that the first element is the most frequently-occurring element.

We will grab only the first element in the object:

```
# Let's find out what our most common category is in our city column
X['city'].value_counts().index[0]

>>>>
'tokyo'
```

We can see that `tokyo` appears to be the most common city. Now that we know which value to use to impute our missing rows, let's fill these slots. There is a `fillna` function that allows us to specify exactly how we want to fill missing values:

```
# fill empty slots with most common category
X['city'].fillna(X['city'].value_counts().index[0])
```

The `city` column now looks like this:

```
0              tokyo
1              tokyo
2             london
3            seattle
4      san francisco
5              tokyo
Name: city, dtype: object
```

Great, now our `city` column no longer has missing values. However, our other categorical column, `boolean`, still does. Rather than going through the same method, let's build a custom imputer that will be able to handle imputing all categorical data.

Custom imputers

Before we jump into the code, let's have a quick refresher of pipelines:

- Pipelines allow us to sequentially apply a list of transforms and a final estimator
- Intermediate steps of the pipeline must be **transforms**, meaning they must implement `fit` and `transform` methods
- The final estimator only needs to implement `fit`

The purpose of the pipeline is to assemble several steps that can be cross-validated together while setting different parameters. Once we have built our custom transformers for each column that needs imputing, we will pass them all through a pipeline so that our data can be transformed in one go. Let's build our custom category imputer to start.

Custom category imputer

First, we will utilize the scikit-learn `TransformerMixin` base class to create our own custom categorical imputer. This transformer (and all other custom transformers in this chapter) will work as an element in a pipeline with a fit and `transform` method.

The following code block will become very familiar throughout this chapter, so we will go over each line in detail:

```
from sklearn.base import TransformerMixin

class CustomCategoryImputer(TransformerMixin):
    def __init__(self, cols=None):
        self.cols = cols
    def transform(self, df):
        X = df.copy()
        for col in self.cols:
            X[col].fillna(X[col].value_counts().index[0], inplace=True)
        return X
    def fit(self, *_):
        return self
```

There is a lot happening in this code block, so let's break it down by line:

1. First, we have a new `import` statement:

   ```
   from sklearn.base import TransformerMixin
   ```

2. We will inherit the `TransformerMixin` class from scikit-learn, which includes a `.fit_transform` method that calls upon the `.fit` and `.transform` methods we will create. This allows us to maintain a similar structure in our transformer to that of scikit-learn. Let's initialize our custom class:

```
class CustomCategoryImputer(TransformerMixin):
    def __init__(self, cols=None):
        self.cols = cols
```

3. We have now instantiated our custom class and have our __init__ method that initializes our attributes. In our case, we only need to initialize one instance attribute, `self.cols` (which will be the columns that we specify as a parameter). Now, we can build our `fit` and `transform` methods:

```
def transform(self, df):
        X = df.copy()
        for col in self.cols:
            X[col].fillna(X[col].value_counts().index[0],
inplace=True)
        return X
```

4. Here, we have our `transform` method. It takes in a DataFrame, and the first step is to copy and rename the DataFrame to X. Then, we will iterate over the columns we have specified in our `cols` parameter to fill in the missing slots. The `fillna` portion may feel familiar, as it is the function we employed in our first example. We are using the same function and setting it up so that our custom categorical imputer can work across several columns at once. After the missing values have been filled, we return our filled DataFrame. Next comes our `fit` method:

```
def fit(self, *_):
        return self
```

We have set up our `fit` method to simply `return self`, as is the standard of `.fit` methods in scikit-learn.

5. Now we have a custom method that allows us to impute our categorical data! Let's see it in action with our two categorical columns, `city` and `boolean`:

```
# Implement our custom categorical imputer on our categorical
columns.

cci = CustomCategoryImputer(cols=['city', 'boolean'])
```

6. We have initialized our custom categorical imputer, and we now need to fit_transform this imputer to our dataset:

```
cci.fit_transform(X)
```

Our dataset now looks like this:

	boolean	city	ordinal_column	quantitative_column
0	yes	tokyo	somewhat like	1.0
1	no	tokyo	like	11.0
2	no	london	somewhat like	-0.5
3	no	seattle	like	10.0
4	no	san francisco	somewhat like	NaN
5	yes	tokyo	dislike	20.0

Great! Our city and boolean columns are no longer missing values. However, our quantitative column still has null values. Since the default imputer cannot select columns, let's make another custom one.

Custom quantitative imputer

We will use the same structure as our custom category imputer. The main difference here is that we will utilize scikit-learn's Imputer class to actually make the transformation on our columns:

```
# Lets make an imputer that can apply a strategy to select columns by name

from sklearn.preprocessing import Imputer
class CustomQuantitativeImputer(TransformerMixin):
    def __init__(self, cols=None, strategy='mean'):
        self.cols = cols
        self.strategy = strategy
    def transform(self, df):
        X = df.copy()
        impute = Imputer(strategy=self.strategy)
        for col in self.cols:
            X[col] = impute.fit_transform(X[[col]])
        return X
    def fit(self, *_):
        return self
```

For our `CustomQuantitativeImputer`, we have added a `strategy` parameter that will allow us to specify exactly how we want to impute missing values for our quantitative data. Here, we have selected the `mean` to replace missing values and still employ the `transform` and `fit` methods.

Once again, in order to impute our data, we will call the `fit_transform` method, this time specifying both the column and the `strategy` to use to impute:

```
cqi = CustomQuantitativeImputer(cols=['quantitative_column'],
strategy='mean')

cqi.fit_transform(X)
```

Alternatively, rather than calling and `fit_transforming` our `CustomCategoryImputer` and our `CustomQuantitativeImputer` separately, we can also set them up in a pipeline so that we can transform our dataset in one go. Let's see how:

1. Start with our `import` statement:

```
# import Pipeline from sklearn
from sklearn.pipeline import Pipeline
```

2. Now, we can pass through our custom imputers:

```
imputer = Pipeline([('quant', cqi), ('category', cci)])
imputer.fit_transform(X)
```

Let's see what our dataset looks like after our pipeline transformations:

	boolean	city	ordinal_column	quantitative_column
0	yes	tokyo	somewhat like	1.0
1	no	tokyo	like	11.0
2	no	london	somewhat like	-0.5
3	no	seattle	like	10.0
4	no	san francisco	somewhat like	8.3
5	yes	tokyo	dislike	20.0

Now we have a dataset with no missing values to work with!

Encoding categorical variables

To recap, thus far we have successfully imputed our dataset—both our categorical and quantitative columns. At this point, you may be wondering, *how do we utilize the categorical data with a machine learning algorithm?*

Simply put, we need to transform this categorical data into numerical data. So far, we have ensured that the most common category was used to fill the missing values. Now that this is done, we need to take it a step further.

Any machine learning algorithm, whether it is a linear-regression or a KNN-utilizing Euclidean distance, requires numerical input features to learn from. There are several methods we can rely on to transform our categorical data into numerical data.

Encoding at the nominal level

Let's begin with data at the nominal level. The main method we have is to transform our categorical data into dummy variables. We have two options to do this:

- Utilize pandas to automatically find the categorical variables and dummy code them
- Create our own custom transformer using dummy variables to work in a pipeline

Before we delve into these options, let's go over exactly what dummy variables are.

Dummy variables take the value zero or one to indicate the absence or presence of a category. They are proxy variables, or numerical stand-ins, for qualitative data.

Consider a simple regression analysis for wage determination. Say we are given gender, which is qualitative, and years of education, which is quantitative. In order to see if gender has an effect on wages, we would dummy code when the person is a female to female = 1, and female = 0 when the person is male.

When working with dummy variables, it is important to be aware of and avoid the dummy variable trap. The dummy variable trap is when you have independent variables that are multicollinear, or highly correlated. Simply put, these variables can be predicted from each other. So, in our gender example, the dummy variable trap would be if we include both female as (0|1) and male as (0|1), essentially creating a duplicate category. It can be inferred that a 0 female value indicates a male.

To avoid the dummy variable trap, simply leave out the constant term or one of the dummy categories. The left out dummy can become the base category to which the rest are compared to.

Let's come back to our dataset and employ some methods to encode our categorical data into dummy variables. pandas has a handy `get_dummies` method that actually finds all of the categorical variables and dummy codes them for us:

```
pd.get_dummies(X,
                columns = ['city', 'boolean'],  # which columns to dummify
                prefix_sep='__')  # the separator between the prefix (column
name) and cell value
```

We have to be sure to specify which columns we want to apply this to because it will also dummy code the ordinal columns, and this wouldn't make much sense. We will take a more in-depth look into why dummy coding ordinal data doesn't makes sense shortly.

Our data, with our dummy coded columns, now looks like this:

	ordinal_column	quantitative_column	city__london	city_san francisco	city_seattle	city_tokyo	boolean_no	boolean_yes
0	somewhat like	1.0	0	0	0	1	0	1
1	like	11.0	0	0	0	0	1	0
2	somewhat like	-0.5	1	0	0	0	0	0
3	like	10.0	0	0	1	0	1	0
4	somewhat like	NaN	0	1	0	0	1	0
5	dislike	20.0	0	0	0	1	0	1

Our other option for dummy coding our data is to create our own custom dummifier. Creating this allows us to set up a pipeline to transform our whole dataset in one go.

Once again, we will use the same structure as our previous two custom imputers. Here, our `transform` method will use the handy pandas `get_dummies` method to create dummy variables for specified columns. The only parameter we have in this custom dummifier is `cols`:

```
# create our custom dummifier
class CustomDummifier(TransformerMixin):
    def __init__(self, cols=None):
        self.cols = cols
    def transform(self, X):
        return pd.get_dummies(X, columns=self.cols)
    def fit(self, *_):
        return self
```

Our custom dummifier mimics scikit-learn's `OneHotEncoding`, but with the added advantage of working on our entire DataFrame.

Encoding at the ordinal level

Now, let's take a look at our ordinal columns. There is still useful information here, however, we need to transform the strings into numerical data. At the ordinal level, since there is meaning in the data having a specific order, it does not make sense to use dummy variables. To maintain the order, we will use a label encoder.

By a label encoder, we mean that each label in our ordinal data will have a numerical value associated to it. In our example, this means that the ordinal column values (`dislike`, `somewhat like`, and `like`) will be represented as 0, 1, and 2.

In the simplest form, the code is as follows:

```
# set up a list with our ordinal data corresponding the list index
ordering = ['dislike', 'somewhat like', 'like']  # 0 for dislike, 1 for
somewhat like, and 2 for like
# before we map our ordering to our ordinal column, let's take a look at
the column

print X['ordinal_column']
>>>>
0 somewhat like
1 like
2 somewhat like
3 like
4 somewhat like
5 dislike
Name: ordinal_column, dtype: object
```

Here, we have set up a list for ordering our labels. This is key, as we will be utilizing the index of our list to transform the labels to numerical data.

Here, we will implement a function called `map` on our column, that allows us to specify the function we want to implement on the column. We specify this function using a construct called `lambda`, which essentially allows us to create an anonymous function, or one that is not bound to a name:

```
lambda x: ordering.index(x)
```

This specific code is creating a function that will apply the index of our list called `ordering` to each element. Now, we map this to our ordinal column:

```
# now map our ordering to our ordinal column:
print X['ordinal_column'].map(lambda x: ordering.index(x))
>>>>
0    1
1    2
2    1
3    2
4    1
5    0
Name: ordinal_column, dtype: int64
```

Our ordinal column is now represented as labeled data.

Note that scikit-learn has a `LabelEncoder`, but we are not using this method because it does not include the ability to order categories (0 for dislike, 1 for somewhat like, 2 for like) as we have done previously. Rather, the default is a sorting method, which is not what we want to use here.

Once again, let us make a custom label encoder that will fit into our pipeline:

```
class CustomEncoder(TransformerMixin):
    def __init__(self, col, ordering=None):
        self.ordering = ordering
        self.col = col
    def transform(self, df):
        X = df.copy()
        X[self.col] = X[self.col].map(lambda x: self.ordering.index(x))
        return X
    def fit(self, *_):
        return self
```

We have maintained the structure of the other custom transformers in this chapter. Here, we have utilized the `map` and `lambda` functions detailed previously to transform the specified columns. Note the key parameter, `ordering`, which will determine which numerical values the labels will be encoding into.

Let's call our custom encoder:

```
ce = CustomEncoder(col='ordinal_column', ordering = ['dislike', 'somewhat
like', 'like'])

ce.fit_transform(X)
```

Our dataset after these transformations looks like the following:

	boolean	city	ordinal_column	quantitative_column
0	yes	tokyo	1	1.0
1	no	None	2	11.0
2	None	london	1	-0.5
3	no	seattle	2	10.0
4	no	san francisco	1	NaN
5	yes	tokyo	0	20.0

Our ordinal column is now labeled.

Up to this point, we have transformed the following columns accordingly:

- `boolean`, `city`: dummy encoding
- `ordinal_column`: label encoding

Bucketing continuous features into categories

Sometimes, when you have continuous numerical data, it may make sense to transform a continuous variable into a categorical variable. For example, say you have ages, but it would be more useful to work with age ranges.

pandas has a useful function called `cut` that will bin your data for you. By binning, we mean it will create the ranges for your data.

Let's see how this function could work on our `quantitative_column`:

```
# name of category is the bin by default
pd.cut(X['quantitative_column'], bins=3)
```

The output of the `cut` function for our quantitative column looks like this:

```
0        (-0.52, 6.333]
1        (6.333, 13.167]
2        (-0.52, 6.333]
3        (6.333, 13.167]
4                   NaN
5        (13.167, 20.0]
```

```
Name: quantitative_column, dtype: category
Categories (3, interval[float64]): [(-0.52, 6.333] < (6.333, 13.167] <
(13.167, 20.0]]
```

When we specify bins to be an integer (bins = 3), it defines the number of equal–width bins in the range of X. However, in this case, the range of X is extended by .1% on each side to include the min or max values of X.

We can also set labels to False, which will return only integer indicators of the bins:

```
# using no labels
pd.cut(X['quantitative_column'], bins=3, labels=False)
```

Here is what the integer indicators look like for our quantitative_column:

```
0      0.0
1      1.0
2      0.0
3      1.0
4      NaN
5      2.0
Name: quantitative_column, dtype: float64
```

Seeing our options with the cut function, we can also build our own CustomCutter for our pipeline. Once again, we will mimic the structure of our transformers. Our transform method will use the cut function, and so we will need to set bins and labels as parameters:

```
class CustomCutter(TransformerMixin):
    def __init__(self, col, bins, labels=False):
        self.labels = labels
        self.bins = bins
        self.col = col
    def transform(self, df):
        X = df.copy()
        X[self.col] = pd.cut(X[self.col], bins=self.bins,
labels=self.labels)
        return X
    def fit(self, *_):
        return self
```

Note that we have set the default labels parameter to False. Initialize our CustomCutter, specifying the column to transform and the number of bins to use:

```
cc = CustomCutter(col='quantitative_column', bins=3)

cc.fit_transform(X)
```

With our `CustomCutter` transforming our `quantitative_column`, our data now looks like this:

	boolean	city	ordinal_column	quantitative_column
0	yes	tokyo	somewhat like	1.0
1	no	None	like	11.0
2	None	london	somewhat like	-0.5
3	no	seattle	like	10.0
4	no	san francisco	somewhat like	NaN
5	yes	tokyo	dislike	20.0

Note that our `quantitative_column` is now ordinal, and so there is no need to dummify the data.

Creating our pipeline

To review, we have transformed the columns in our dataset in the following ways thus far:

- `boolean, city`: dummy encoding
- `ordinal_column`: label encoding
- `quantitative_column`: ordinal level data

Since we now have transformations for all of our columns, let's put everything together in a pipeline.

Start with importing our `Pipeline` class from scikit-learn:

```
from sklearn.pipeline import Pipeline
```

We will bring together each of the custom transformers that we have created. Here is the order we will follow in our pipeline:

1. First, we will utilize the `imputer` to fill in missing values
2. Next, we will dummify our categorical columns
3. Then, we will encode the `ordinal_column`
4. Finally, we will bucket the `quantitative_column`

Let's set up our pipeline as follows:

```
pipe = Pipeline([("imputer", imputer), ('dummify', cd), ('encode', ce),
('cut', cc)])
# will use our initial imputer
# will dummify variables first
# then encode the ordinal column
# then bucket (bin) the quantitative column
```

In order to see the full transformation of our data using our pipeline, let's take a look at our data with zero transformations:

```
# take a look at our data before fitting our pipeline
print X
```

This is what our data looked like in the beginning before any transformations were made:

	boolean	city	ordinal_column	quantitative_column
0	yes	tokyo	somewhat like	1.0
1	no	None	like	11.0
2	None	london	somewhat like	-0.5
3	no	seattle	like	10.0
4	no	san francisco	somewhat like	NaN
5	yes	tokyo	dislike	20.0

We can now `fit` our pipeline:

```
# now fit our pipeline
pipe.fit(X)

>>>>
Pipeline(memory=None,
     steps=[('imputer', Pipeline(memory=None,
     steps=[('quant', <__main__.CustomQuantitativeImputer object at
0x128bf00d0>), ('category', <__main__.CustomCategoryImputer object at
0x13666bf50>)])), ('dummify', <__main__.CustomDummifier object at
0x128bf0ed0>), ('encode', <__main__.CustomEncoder object at 0x127e145d0>),
('cut', <__main__.CustomCutter object at 0x13666bc90>)])
```

We have created our pipeline object, let's transform our DataFrame:

```
pipe.transform(X)
```

Here is what our final dataset looks like after undergoing all of the appropriate transformations by column:

	ordinal_column	quantitative_column	boolean_no	boolean_yes	city_london	city_san francisco	city_seattle	city_tokyo
0	1	0	0	1	0	0	0	1
1	2	1	1	0	0	0	0	1
2	1	0	1	0	1	0	0	0
3	2	1	1	0	0	0	1	0
4	1	1	1	0	0	1	0	0
5	0	2	0	1	0	0	0	1

Extending numerical features

Numerical features can undergo various methods to create extended features from them. Previously, we saw how we can transform continuous numerical data into ordinal data. Now, we will dive into extending our numerical features further.

Before we go any deeper into these methods, we will introduce a new dataset to work with.

Activity recognition from the Single Chest-Mounted Accelerometer dataset

This dataset collects data from a wearable accelerometer, mounted on the chest, collected from fifteen participants performing seven activities. The sampling frequency of the accelerometer is 52 Hz and the accelerometer data is uncalibrated.

The dataset is separated by participant and contains the following:

- Sequential number
- x acceleration
- y acceleration
- z acceleration
- Label

Labels are codified by numbers and represent an activity, as follows:

- Working at a computer
- Standing up, walking, and going up/down stairs
- Standing
- Walking
- Going up/down stairs
- Walking and talking with someone
- Talking while standing

Further information on this dataset is available on the UCI *Machine Learning Repository* at:

```
https://archive.ics.uci.edu/ml/datasets/Activity+Recognition+from+Single+Chest-
Mounted+Accelerometer
```

Let's take a look at our data. First, we need to load in our CSV file and set our column headers:

```
df = pd.read_csv('../data/activity_recognizer/1.csv', header=None)
df.columns = ['index', 'x', 'y', 'z', 'activity']
```

Now, let's examine the first few rows with the `.head` method, which will default to the first five rows, unless we specify how many rows to show:

```
df.head()
```

This shows us:

	index	x	y	z	activity
0	0.0	1502	2215	2153	1
1	1.0	1667	2072	2047	1
2	2.0	1611	1957	1906	1
3	3.0	1601	1939	1831	1
4	4.0	1643	1965	1879	1

This dataset is meant to train models to recognize a user's current physical activity given an accelerometer's x, y, and z position on a device such as a smartphone. According to the website, the options for the `activity` column are:

- **1**: Working at a computer

- **2**: Standing Up and Going updown stairs

- **3**: Standing

- **4**: Walking

- **5**: Going UpDown Stairs

- **6**: Walking and Talking with Someone

- **7**: Talking while Standing

The `activity` column will be the target variable we will be trying to predict, using the other columns. Let's determine the null accuracy to beat in our machine learning model. To do this, we will invoke the `value_counts` method with the `normalize` option set to `True` to give us the most commonly occurring activity as a percentage:

```
df['activity'].value_counts(normalize=True)

7    0.515369
1    0.207242
4    0.165291
3    0.068793
5    0.019637
6    0.017951
2    0.005711
0    0.000006
Name: activity, dtype: float64
```

The null accuracy to beat is 51.53%, meaning that if we guessed seven (talking while standing), then we would be right over half of the time. Now, let's do some machine learning! Let's step through, line by line, setting up our model.

First, we have our `import` statements:

```
from sklearn.neighbors import KNeighborsClassifier
from sklearn.model_selection import GridSearchCV
```

You may be familiar with these import statements from last chapter. Once again, we will be utilizing scikit-learn's **K-Nearest Neighbors** (**KNN**) classification model. We will also use the grid search module that automatically finds the best combination of parameters for the KNN model that best fits our data with respect to cross-validated accuracy. Next, we create a feature matrix (X) and a response variable (y) for our predictive model:

```
X = df[['x', 'y', 'z']]
# create our feature matrix by removing the response variable
y = df['activity']
```

Once our X and y are set up, we can introduce the variables and instances we need to successfully run a grid search:

```
# our grid search variables and instances

# KNN parameters to try
knn_params = {'n_neighbors':[3, 4, 5, 6]}
```

Next, we will instantiate a KNN model and a grid search module and fit it to our feature matrix and response variable:

```
knn = KNeighborsClassifier()
grid = GridSearchCV(knn, knn_params)
grid.fit(X, y)
```

Now, we can `print` the best accuracy and parameters that were used to learn from:

```
print grid.best_score_, grid.best_params_

0.720752487677 {'n_neighbors': 5}
```

Using five neighbors as its parameter, our KNN model was able to achieve a 72.07% accuracy, much better than our null accuracy of around 51.53%! Perhaps we can utilize another method to get our accuracy up even more.

Polynomial features

A key method of working with numerical data and creating more features is through scikit-learn's `PolynomialFeatures` class. In its simplest form, this constructor will create new columns that are products of existing columns to capture feature interactions.

More specifically, this class will generate a new feature matrix with all of the polynomial combinations of the features with a degree less than or equal to the specified degree. Meaning that, if your input sample is two-dimensional, like so: [a, b], then the degree-2 polynomial features are as follows: [1, a, b, a^2, ab, b^2].

Parameters

When instantiating polynomial features, there are three parameters to keep in mind:

- degree
- interaction_only
- include_bias

Degree corresponds to the degree of the polynomial features, with the default set to two.

interaction_only is a boolean that, when true, only interaction features are produced, meaning features that are products of degree distinct features. The default for interaction_only is false.

include_bias is also a boolean that, when true (default), includes a bias column, the feature in which all polynomial powers are zero, adding a column of all ones.

Let's set up a polynomial feature instance by first importing the class and instantiating with our parameters. At first, let's take a look at what features we get when setting interaction_only to False:

```
from sklearn.preprocessing import PolynomialFeatures

poly = PolynomialFeatures(degree=2, include_bias=False,
interaction_only=False)
```

Now, we can fit_transform these polynomial features to our dataset and look at the shape of our extended dataset:

```
X_poly = poly.fit_transform(X)
X_poly.shape

(162501, 9)
```

Our dataset has now expanded to 162501 rows and 9 columns.

Let's place our data into a DataFrame, setting the column headers to the feature_names, and taking a look at the first few rows:

```
pd.DataFrame(X_poly, columns=poly.get_feature_names()).head()
```

This shows us:

	x0	x1	x2	x0^2	x0 x1	x0 x2	x1^2	x1 x2	x2^2
0	1502.0	2215.0	2153.0	2256004.0	3326930.0	3233806.0	4906225.0	4768895.0	4635409.0
1	1667.0	2072.0	2047.0	2778889.0	3454024.0	3412349.0	4293184.0	4241384.0	4190209.0
2	1611.0	1957.0	1906.0	2595321.0	3152727.0	3070566.0	3829849.0	3730042.0	3632836.0
3	1601.0	1939.0	1831.0	2563201.0	3104339.0	2931431.0	3759721.0	3550309.0	3352561.0
4	1643.0	1965.0	1879.0	2699449.0	3228495.0	3087197.0	3861225.0	3692235.0	3530641.0

Exploratory data analysis

Now we can conduct some exploratory data analysis. Since the purpose of polynomial features is to get a better sense of feature interaction in the original data, the best way to visualize this is through a correlation heatmap.

We need to import a data visualization tool that will allow us to create a heatmap:

```
%matplotlib inline
import seaborn as sns
```

Matplotlib and Seaborn are popular data visualization tools. We can now visualize our correlation heatmap as follows:

```
sns.heatmap(pd.DataFrame(X_poly, columns=poly.get_feature_names()).corr())
```

.corr is a function we can call on our DataFrame that gives us a correlation matrix of our features. Let's take a look at our feature interactions:

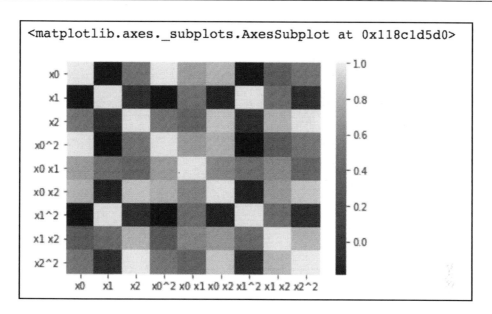

The colors on the `heatmap` are based on pure values; the darker the color, the greater the correlation of the features.

So far, we have looked at our polynomial features with our `interaction_only` parameter set to `False`. Let's set this to `True` and see what our features look like without repeat variables.

We will set up this polynomial feature instance the same as we did previously. Note the only difference is that `interaction_only` is now `True`:

```
poly = PolynomialFeatures(degree=2, include_bias=False,
interaction_only=True) X_poly = poly.fit_transform(X) print X_poly.shape
  (162501, 6)
```

We now have `162501` rows by `6` columns. Let's take a look:

```
pd.DataFrame(X_poly, columns=poly.get_feature_names()).head()
```

The DataFrame now looks as follows:

	x0	x1	x2	x0 x1	x0 x2	x1 x2
0	1502.0	2215.0	2153.0	3326930.0	3233806.0	4768895.0
1	1667.0	2072.0	2047.0	3454024.0	3412349.0	4241384.0
2	1611.0	1957.0	1906.0	3152727.0	3070566.0	3730042.0
3	1601.0	1939.0	1831.0	3104339.0	2931431.0	3550309.0
4	1643.0	1965.0	1879.0	3228495.0	3087197.0	3692235.0

Since `interaction_only` has been set to `True` this time, `x0^2`, `x1^2`, and `x2^2` have disappeared since they were repeat variables. Let's see what our correlation matrix looks like now:

```
sns.heatmap(pd.DataFrame(X_poly,
columns=poly.get_feature_names()).corr())
```

We get the following result:

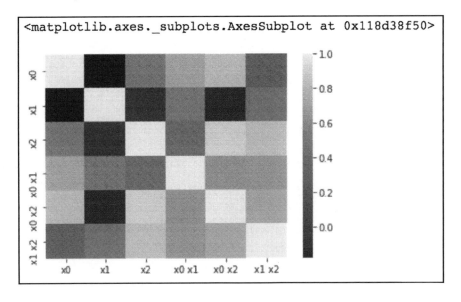

We are able to see how the features interact with each other. We can also perform a grid search of our KNN model with the new polynomial features, which can also be grid searched in a pipeline:

1. Let's set up our pipeline parameters first:

```
pipe_params = {'poly_features__degree':[1, 2, 3],
'poly_features__interaction_only':[True, False],
'classify__n_neighbors':[3, 4, 5, 6]}
```

2. Now, instantiate our `Pipeline`:

```
pipe = Pipeline([('poly_features', poly), ('classify', knn)])
```

3. From here, we can set up our grid search and print the best score and parameters to learn from:

```
grid = GridSearchCV(pipe, pipe_params)
grid.fit(X, y)

print grid.best_score_, grid.best_params_

0.721189408065 {'poly_features__degree': 2,
'poly_features__interaction_only': True, 'classify__n_neighbors':
5}
```

Our accuracy is now 72.12%, which is an improvement from our accuracy without expanding our features using polynomial features!

Text-specific feature construction

Until this point, we have been working with categorical and numerical data. While our categorical data has come in the form of a string, the text has been part of a single category. We will now dive deeper into longer—form text data. This form of text data is much more complex than single—category text, because we now have a series of categories, or tokens.

Before we get any further into working with text data, let's make sure we have a good understanding of what we mean when we refer to text data. Consider a service like Yelp, where users write up reviews of restaurants and businesses to share their thoughts on their experience. These reviews, all written in text format, contain a wealth of information that would be useful for machine learning purposes, for example, in predicting the best restaurant to visit.

In general, a large part of how we communicate in today's world is through written text, whether in messaging services, social media, or email. As a result, so much can be garnered from this information through modeling. For example, we can conduct a sentiment analysis from Twitter data.

This type of work can be referred to as **natural language processing (NLP)**. This is a field primarily concerned with interactions between computers and humans, specifically where computers can be programmed to process natural language.

Now, as we've mentioned before, it's important to note that all machine learning models require numerical inputs, so we have to be creative and think strategically when we work with text and convert such data into numerical features. There are several options for doing so, so let's get started.

Bag of words representation

The scikit-learn has a handy module called `feature_extraction` that allows us to, as the name suggests, extract features for data such as text in a format supported by machine learning algorithms. This module has methods for us to utilize when working with text.

Going forward, we may refer to our text data as a corpus, specifically meaning an aggregate of text content or documents.

The most common method to transform a corpus into a numerical representation, a process known as vectorization, is through a method called **bag-of-words**. The basic idea behind the bag of words approach is that documents are described by word occurrences while completely ignoring the positioning of words in the document. In its simplest form, text is represented as a **bag**, without regard for grammar or word order, and is maintained as a set, with importance given to multiplicity. A bag of words representation is achieved in the following three steps:

- Tokenizing
- Counting
- Normalizing

Let's start with tokenizing. This process uses white spaces and punctuation to separate words from each other, turning them into tokens. Each possible token is given an integer ID.

Next comes counting. This step simply counts the occurrences of tokens within a document.

Last comes normalizing, meaning that tokens are weighted with diminishing importance when they occur in the majority of documents.

Let's consider a couple more methods for vectorizing.

CountVectorizer

`CountVectorizer` is the most commonly used method to convert text data into their vector representations. It is similar to dummy variables, in the sense that `CountVectorizer` converts text columns into matrices where columns are tokens and cell values are counts of occurrences of each token in each document. The resulting matrix is referred to as a **document-term matrix** because each row will represent a **document** (in this case, a tweet) and each column represents a **term** (a word).

Let's take a look at a new dataset, and see how `CountVectorizer` works. The Twitter Sentiment Analysis dataset contains 1,578,627 classified tweets, and each row is marked as one for positive sentiment and zero for negative sentiment.

Further information on this dataset can be found at `http://thinknook.com/twitter-sentiment-analysis-training-corpus-dataset-2012-09-22/`.

Let's load in our data using pandas' `read_csv` method. Note that we are specifying an `encoding` as an optional parameter to ensure that we handle all special characters in the tweets properly:

```
tweets = pd.read_csv('../data/twitter_sentiment.csv', encoding='latin1')
```

This allows us to load in our data in a specific format and map text characters appropriately.

Take a look at the first few rows of data:

```
tweets.head()
```

We get the following data:

	ItemID	Sentiment	SentimentText
0	1	0	is so sad for my APL frie...
1	2	0	I missed the New Moon trail...
2	3	1	omg its already 7:30 :O
3	4	0	.. Omgaga. Im sooo im gunna CRy. I'...
4	5	0	i think mi bf is cheating on me!!! ...

We are only concerned with the `Sentiment` and `SentimentText` columns, so we will delete the `ItemID` column for now:

```
del tweets['ItemID']
```

Our data looks as follows:

	Sentiment	SentimentText
0	0	is so sad for my APL frie...
1	0	I missed the New Moon trail...
2	1	omg its already 7:30 :O
3	0	.. Omgaga. Im sooo im gunna CRy. I'...
4	0	i think mi bf is cheating on me!!! ...

Now, we can import `CountVectorizer` and get a better understanding of the text we are working with:

```
from sklearn.feature_extraction.text import CountVectorizer
```

Let's set up our X and y:

```
X = tweets['SentimentText']
y = tweets['Sentiment']
```

The `CountVectorizer` class works very similarly to the custom transformers we have been working with so far, and has a `fit_transform` function to manipulate the data:

```
vect = CountVectorizer()
_ = vect.fit_transform(X)
```

```
print _.shape
```

```
(99989, 105849)
```

After our `CountVectorizer` has transformed our data, we have 99,989 rows and 105,849 columns.

`CountVectorizer` has many different parameters that can change the number of features that are constructed. Let's go over a few of these parameters to get a better sense of how these features are created.

CountVectorizer parameters

A few parameters that we will go over include:

- `stop_words`
- `min_df`
- `max_df`
- `ngram_range`
- `analyzer`

`stop_words` is a frequently used parameter in `CountVectorizer`. You can pass in the string `english` to this parameter, and a built-in stop word list for English is used. You can also specify a list of words yourself. These words will then be removed from the tokens and will not appear as features in your data.

Here is an example:

```
vect = CountVectorizer(stop_words='english')  # removes a set of english
stop words (if, a, the, etc)
_ = vect.fit_transform(X)
print _.shape
```

```
(99989, 105545)
```

You can see that the feature columns have gone down from 105,849 when stop words were not used, to 105,545 when English stop words have been set. The idea behind using stop words is to remove noise within your features and take out words that occur so often that there won't be much meaning to garner from them in your models.

Another parameter is called `min_df`. This parameter is used to skim the number of features, by ignoring terms that have a document frequency lower than the given threshold or cut-off.

Here is an implementation of our `CountVectorizer` with `min_df`:

```
vect = CountVectorizer(min_df=.05)   # only includes words that occur in at
least 5% of the corpus documents
# used to skim the number of features
_ = vect.fit_transform(X)
print _.shape

(99989, 31)
```

This is a method that is utilized to significantly reduce the number of features created.

There is also a parameter called `max_df`:

```
vect = CountVectorizer(max_df=.8)   # only includes words that occur at most
80% of the documents
# used to "Deduce" stop words
_ = vect.fit_transform(X)
print _.shape

(99989, 105849)
```

This is similar to trying to understand what stop words exist in the document.

Next, let's look at the `ngram_range` parameter. This parameter takes in a tuple where the lower and upper boundary of the range of n-values indicates the number of different n-grams to be extracted. N-grams represent phrases, so a value of one would represent one token, however a value of two would represent two tokens together. As you can imagine, this will expand our feature set quite significantly:

```
vect = CountVectorizer(ngram_range=(1, 5))   # also includes phrases up to 5
words
_ = vect.fit_transform(X)
print _.shape   # explodes the number of features

(99989, 3219557)
```

See, we now have 3,219,557 features. Since sets of words (phrases) can sometimes have more meaning, using n-gram ranges can be useful for modeling.

You can also set an analyzer as a parameter in `CountVectorizer`. The analyzer determines whether the feature should be made of word or character n-grams. Word is the default:

```
vect = CountVectorizer(analyzer='word')  # default analyzer, decides to
split into words
_ = vect.fit_transform(X)
print _.shape

(99989, 105849)
```

Given that word is the default, our feature column number doesn't change much from the original.

We can even create our own custom analyzer. Conceptually, words are built from root words, or stems, and we can construct a custom analyzer that accounts for this.

Stemming is a common natural language processing method that allows us to stem our vocabulary, or make it smaller by converting words to their roots. There is a natural language toolkit, known as NLTK, that has several packages that allow us to perform operations on text data. One such package is a `stemmer`.

Let's see how it works:

1. First, import our `stemmer` and then initialize it:

```
from nltk.stem.snowball import SnowballStemmer
stemmer = SnowballStemmer('english')
```

2. Now, let's see how some words are stemmed:

```
stemmer.stem('interesting')
u'interest'
```

3. So, the word `interesting` can be reduced to the root stem. We can now use this to create a function that will allow us to tokenize words into their stems:

```
# define a function that accepts text and returns a list of lemmas
def word_tokenize(text, how='lemma'):
    words = text.split(' ')  # tokenize into words
    return [stemmer.stem(word) for word in words]
```

4. Let's see what our function outputs:

```
word_tokenize("hello you are very interesting")

[u'hello', u'you', u'are', u'veri', u'interest']
```

5. We can now place this tokenizer function into our analyzer parameter:

```
vect = CountVectorizer(analyzer=word_tokenize)
_ = vect.fit_transform(X)
print _.shape  # fewer features as stemming makes words smaller

(99989, 154397)
```

This yields us fewer features, which intuitively makes sense since our vocabulary has reduced with stemming.

`CountVectorizer` is a very useful tool to help us expand our features and convert text to numerical features. There is another common vectorizer that we will look into.

The Tf-idf vectorizer

A `Tf-idfVectorizer` can be broken down into two components. First, the *tf* part, which represents **term frequency**, and the *idf* part, meaning **inverse document frequency**. It is a term—weighting method that has applications in information—retrieval and clustering.

A weight is given to evaluate how important a word is to a document in a corpus. Let's look into each part a little more:

- **tf: term frequency**: Measures how frequently a term occurs in a document. Since documents can be different in length, it is possible that a term would appear many more times in longer documents than shorter ones. Thus, the term frequency is often divided by the document length, or the total number of terms in the document, as a way of normalization.
- **idf: inverse document frequency**: Measures how important a term is. While computing term frequency, all terms are considered equally important. However, certain terms, such as *is*, *of*, and *that*, may appear a lot of times but have little importance. So, we need to weight the frequent terms less, while we scale up the rare ones.

To re-emphasize, a `TfidfVectorizer` is the same as `CountVectorizer`, in that it constructs features from tokens, but it takes a step further and normalizes counts to frequency of occurrences across a corpus. Let's see an example of this in action.

First, our import:

```
from sklearn.feature_extraction.text import TfidfVectorizer
```

To bring up some code from before, a plain vanilla `CountVectorizer` will output a document-term matrix:

```
vect = CountVectorizer()
_ = vect.fit_transform(X)
print _.shape, _[0,:].mean()

(99989, 105849) 6.61319426731e-05
```

Our `TfidfVectorizer` can be set up as follows:

```
vect = TfidfVectorizer()
_ = vect.fit_transform(X)
print _.shape, _[0,:].mean() # same number of rows and columns, different
cell values

(99989, 105849) 2.18630609758e-05
```

We can see that both vectorizers output the same number of rows and columns, but produce different values in each cell. This is because `TfidfVectorizer` and `CountVectorizer` are both used to transform text data into quantitative data, but the way in which they fill in cell values differ.

Using text in machine learning pipelines

Of course, the ultimate goal of our vectorizers is to use them to make text data ingestible for our machine learning pipelines. Because `CountVectorizer` and `TfidfVectorizer` act like any other transformer we have been working with in this book, we will have to utilize a scikit-learn pipeline to ensure accuracy and honesty in our machine learning pipeline. In our example, we are going to be working with a large number of columns (in the hundreds of thousands), so I will use a classifier that is known to be more efficient in this case, a Naive Bayes model:

```
from sklearn.naive_bayes import MultinomialNB # for faster predictions with
large number of features...
```

Before we start building our pipelines, let's get our null accuracy of the response column, which is either zero (negative) or one (positive):

```
# get the null accuracy
y.value_counts(normalize=True)

1 0.564632 0 0.435368 Name: Sentiment, dtype: float64
```

Making the accuracy beat 56.5%. Now, let's create a pipeline with two steps:

- `CountVectorizer` to featurize the tweets
- `MultiNomialNB` Naive Bayes model to classify between positive and negative sentiment

First let's start with setting up our pipeline parameters as follows, and then instantiate our grid search as follows:

```
# set our pipeline parameters
pipe_params = {'vect__ngram_range':[(1, 1), (1, 2)],
'vect__max_features':[1000, 10000], 'vect__stop_words':[None, 'english']}

# instantiate our pipeline
pipe = Pipeline([('vect', CountVectorizer()), ('classify',
MultinomialNB())])

# instantiate our gridsearch object
grid = GridSearchCV(pipe, pipe_params)
# fit the gridsearch object
grid.fit(X, y)

# get our results
print grid.best_score_, grid.best_params_


0.755753132845 {'vect__ngram_range': (1, 2), 'vect__stop_words': None,
'vect__max_features': 10000}
```

And we got 75.6%, which is great! Now, let's kick things into high-gear and incorporate the `TfidfVectorizer`. Instead of rebuilding the pipeline using tf-idf instead of `CountVectorizer`, let's try using something a bit different. The scikit-learn has a `FeatureUnion` module that facilitates horizontal stacking of features (side-by-side). This allows us to use multiple types of text featurizers in the same pipeline.

For example, we can build a `featurizer` that runs both a `TfidfVectorizer` and a `CountVectorizer` on our tweets and concatenates them horizontally (keeping the same number of rows but increasing the number of columns):

```
from sklearn.pipeline import FeatureUnion
# build a separate featurizer object
featurizer = FeatureUnion([('tfidf_vect', TfidfVectorizer()),
('count_vect', CountVectorizer())])
```

Once we build the `featurizer`, we can use it to see how it affects the shape of our data:

```
_ = featurizer.fit_transform(X)
 print _.shape # same number of rows , but twice as many columns as either
CV or TFIDF

 (99989, 211698)
```

We can see that unioning the two featurizers results in a dataset with the same number of rows, but doubles the number of either the `CountVectorizer` or the `TfidfVectorizer`. This is because the resulting dataset is literally both datasets side-by-side. This way, our machine learning models may learn from both sets of data simultaneously. Let's change the `params` of our `featurizer` object slightly and see what difference it makes:

```
featurizer.set_params(tfidf_vect__max_features=100,
count_vect__ngram_range=(1, 2),
 count_vect__max_features=300)
 # the TfidfVectorizer will only keep 100 words while the CountVectorizer
will keep 300 of 1 and 2 word phrases
 _ = featurizer.fit_transform(X)
 print _.shape # same number of rows , but twice as many columns as either
CV or TFIDF
 (99989, 400)
```

Let's build a much more comprehensive pipeline that incorporates the feature union of both of our vectorizers:

```
pipe_params = {'featurizer__count_vect__ngram_range':[(1, 1), (1, 2)],
'featurizer__count_vect__max_features':[1000, 10000],
'featurizer__count_vect__stop_words':[None, 'english'],
 'featurizer__tfidf_vect__ngram_range':[(1, 1), (1, 2)],
'featurizer__tfidf_vect__max_features':[1000, 10000],
'featurizer__tfidf_vect__stop_words':[None, 'english']}
 pipe = Pipeline([('featurizer', featurizer), ('classify',
MultinomialNB())])
 grid = GridSearchCV(pipe, pipe_params)
 grid.fit(X, y)
 print grid.best_score_, grid.best_params_
```

```
0.758433427677 {'featurizer__tfidf_vect__max_features': 10000,
'featurizer__tfidf_vect__stop_words': 'english',
'featurizer__count_vect__stop_words': None,
'featurizer__count_vect__ngram_range': (1, 2),
'featurizer__count_vect__max_features': 10000,
'featurizer__tfidf_vect__ngram_range': (1, 1)}
```

Nice, even better than just `CountVectorizer` alone! It is also interesting to note that the best `ngram_range` for the `CountVectorizer` was (1, 2), while it was (1, 1) for the `TfidfVectorizer`, implying that word occurrences alone were not as important as two-word phrase occurrences.

By this point, it should be obvious that we could have made our pipeline much more complicated by:

- Grid searching across dozens of parameters for each vectorizer

- Adding in more steps to our pipeline such as polynomial feature construction

But this would have been very cumbersome for this text and would take hours to run on most commercial laptops. Feel free to expand on this pipeline and beat our score!

Phew, that was a lot. Text can be difficult to work with. Between sarcasm, misspellings, and vocabulary size, data scientists and machine learning engineers have their hands full. This introduction to working with text will allow you, the reader, to experiment with your own large text datasets and obtain your own results!

Summary

Thus far, we have gone over several methods of imputing missing values in our categorical and numerical data, encoding our categorical variables, and creating custom transformers to fit into a pipeline. We also dove into several feature construction methods for both numerical data and text-based data.

In the next chapter, we will take a look at the features we have constructed, and consider appropriate methods of selecting the right features to use for our machine learning models.

5
Feature Selection

We're halfway through our text and we have gotten our hands dirty with about a dozen datasets and have seen a great deal of feature selection methods that we, as data scientists and machine learning engineers, may utilize in our work and lives to ensure that we are getting the most out of our predictive modeling. So far, in dealing with data, we have worked with methods including:

- Feature understanding through the identification of levels of data
- Feature improvements and imputing missing values
- Feature standardization and normalization

Each of the preceding methods has a place in our data pipeline and, more often than not, two or more methods are used in tandem with one another.

The remainder of this text will focus on other methods of feature engineering that are, by nature, a bit more mathematical and complex than in the first half of this book. As the preceding workflow grows, we will do our best to spare the reader the inner workings of each and every statistical test we invoke and instead convey a broader picture of what the tests are trying to achieve. As authors and instructors, we are always open to your questions about any of the inner mechanisms of this work.

We have come across one problem quite frequently in our discussion of features, and that problem is **noise**. Often, we are left working with features that may not be highly predictive of the response and, sometimes, can even hinder our models' performance in the prediction of the response. We used tools such as standardization and normalization to try to mitigate such damage, but at the end of the day, noise must be dealt with.

In this chapter, we will address a subset of feature engineering called **feature selection**, which is the process of selecting which features, from the original batch of features, are the *best* when it comes to the model prediction pipeline. More formally, given n features, we search for a subset of k, where $k < n$ features that improve our machine learning pipeline. This generally comes down to the statement:

Feature Selection attempts to weed out the noise in our data and remove it.

The definition of feature selection touches on two major points that must be addressed:

- The methods in which we may find the subset of k features
- The definition of *better* in the context of machine learning

The majority of this chapter is dedicated to the methods in which we may find such subsets of features and the basis on which such methods work. This chapter will break up the methods of feature selection into two broad subsections: **statistical-based** and **model-based** feature selection. This separation may not 100% capture the complexity of the science and art of feature selection, but will work to drive real and actionable results in our machine learning pipeline.

Before we dive into the deep end of many of these methods, let's first discuss how we may better understand and define the idea of *better*, as it will frame the remainder of this chapter, as well as framing the remainder of this text.

We will cover the following topics in this chapter:

- Achieving better performance in feature engineering
- Creating a baseline machine learning pipeline
- The types of feature selection
- Choosing the right feature selection method

Achieving better performance in feature engineering

Throughout this book, we have relied on a base definition of *better* when it came to the various feature engineering methods we put into place. Our implicit goal was to achieve better predictive performance measured purely on simple metrics such as accuracy for classification tasks and RMSE for regression tasks (mostly accuracy). There are other metrics we may measure and track to gauge predictive performance. For example, we will use the following metrics for classification:

- True and false positive rate
- Sensitivity (AKA true positive rate) and specificity
- False negative and false positive rate

and for regression, the metrics that will be applied are:

- Mean absolute error
- R^2

These lists go on, and while we will not be abandoning the idea of quantifying performance through metrics such as the ones precedingly listed, we may also measure other *meta metrics*, or metrics that do not directly correlate to the performance of the prediction of the model, rather, so-called **meta metrics** attempt to measure the performance *around* the prediction and include such ideas as:

- Time in which the model needs to fit/train to the data
- Time it takes for a fitted model to predict new instances of data
- The size of the data in case data must be persisted (stored for later)

These ideas will add to our definition of *better* machine learning as they help to encompass a much larger picture of our machine learning pipeline outside of model predictive performance. In order to help us track these metrics, let's create a function that is generic enough to evaluate several models but specific enough to give us metrics for each one. We will call our function `get_best_model_and_accuracy` and it will do many jobs, such as:

- It will search across all given parameters in order to optimize the machine learning pipeline
- It will spit out some metrics that will help us assess the quality of the pipeline entered

Let's go ahead and define such a function with the help of the following code:

```
# import out grid search module
from sklearn.model_selection import GridSearchCV


def get_best_model_and_accuracy(model, params, X, y):
    grid = GridSearchCV(model, # the model to grid search
                        params, # the parameter set to try
                        error_score=0.) # if a parameter set raises an
error, continue and set the performance as a big, fat 0
    grid.fit(X, y) # fit the model and parameters
    # our classical metric for performance
    print "Best Accuracy: {}".format(grid.best_score_)
    # the best parameters that caused the best accuracy
    print "Best Parameters: {}".format(grid.best_params_)
    # the average time it took a model to fit to the data (in seconds)
    print "Average Time to Fit (s):
{}".format(round(grid.cv_results_['mean_fit_time'].mean(), 3))
    # the average time it took a model to predict out of sample data (in
seconds)
    # this metric gives us insight into how this model will perform in
real-time analysis
    print "Average Time to Score (s):
{}".format(round(grid.cv_results_['mean_score_time'].mean(), 3))
```

The overall goal of this function is to act as a ground truth in that we will use it to evaluate every feature selection method in this chapter to give us a sense of standardization of evaluation. This is not really any different to what we have been doing already, but we are now formalizing our work as a function, and also using metrics other than accuracy to grade our feature selection modules and machine learning pipelines.

A case study – a credit card defaulting dataset

By intelligently extracting the most important signals from our data and ignoring noise, feature selection algorithms achieve two major outcomes:

- **Improved model performance**: By removing redundant data, we are less likely to make decisions based on noisy and irrelevant data, and it also allows our models to hone in on the important features, thereby improving model pipeline predictive performance
- **Reduced training and predicting time**: By fitting pipelines to less data, this generally results in improved model fitting and predicting times, making our pipelines faster overall

In order to gain a realistic understanding of how and why noisy data gets in the way, let's introduce our newest dataset, a credit card defaulting dataset. We will work with 23 features and one response variable. That response variable will be a Boolean, meaning it will either be True or False. The reason we are working with 23 features is that we want to see if we can find which of the 23 features will help us in our machine learning pipelines and which ones will hurt us. We can import the datasets using the following code:

```
import pandas as pd
import numpy as np

# we will set a random seed to ensure that whenever we use random numbers
# which is a good amount, we will achieve the same random numbers
np.random.seed(123)
```

To start, let's bring in two common modules, `numpy` and `pandas`, and also set a random seed so that you and we will achieve the same results for consistency. Now, let's bring in our latest dataset, using the following code:

```
# archive.ics.uci.edu/ml/datasets/default+of+credit+card+clients
# import the newest csv
credit_card_default = pd.read_csv('../data/credit_card_default.csv')
```

Let's go ahead and do some mandatory EDA. Let's begin by checking how big a dataset we are working with, using the following code:

```
# 30,000 rows and 24 columns
credit_card_default.shape
```

So, we have `30,000 rows` (observations) and `24 columns` (1 response and 23 features). We will not go in depth to describe the columns meanings at this time, but we do encourage the reader to check out the source of the data (`http://archive.ics.uci.edu/ml/datasets/default+of+credit+card+clients#`). For now, we will rely on good old-fashioned statistics to tell us more:

```
# Some descriptive statistics
# We invoke the .T to transpose the matrix for better viewing
credit_card_default.describe().T
```

The output is as follows:

	count	mean	std	min	25%	50%	75%	max
LIMIT_BAL	30000.0	167484.322667	129747.661567	10000.0	50000.00	140000.0	240000.00	1000000.0
SEX	30000.0	1.603733	0.489129	1.0	1.00	2.0	2.00	2.0
EDUCATION	30000.0	1.853133	0.790349	0.0	1.00	2.0	2.00	6.0

MARRIAGE	30000.0	1.551867	0.521970	0.0	1.00	2.0	2.00	3.0
AGE	30000.0	35.485500	9.217904	21.0	28.00	34.0	41.00	79.0
PAY_0	30000.0	-0.016700	1.123802	-2.0	-1.00	0.0	0.00	8.0
PAY_2	30000.0	-0.133767	1.197186	-2.0	-1.00	0.0	0.00	8.0
PAY_3	30000.0	-0.166200	1.196868	-2.0	-1.00	0.0	0.00	8.0
PAY_4	30000.0	-0.220667	1.169139	-2.0	-1.00	0.0	0.00	8.0
PAY_5	30000.0	-0.266200	1.133187	-2.0	-1.00	0.0	0.00	8.0
PAY_6	30000.0	-0.291100	1.149988	-2.0	-1.00	0.0	0.00	8.0
BILL_AMT1	30000.0	51223.330900	73635.860576	-165580.0	3558.75	22381.5	67091.00	964511.0
BILL_AMT2	30000.0	49179.075167	71173.768783	-69777.0	2984.75	21200.0	64006.25	983931.0
BILL_AMT3	30000.0	47013.154800	69349.387427	-157264.0	2666.25	20088.5	60164.75	1664089.0
BILL_AMT4	30000.0	43262.948967	64332.856134	-170000.0	2326.75	19052.0	54506.00	891586.0
BILL_AMT5	30000.0	40311.400967	60797.155770	-81334.0	1763.00	18104.5	50190.50	927171.0
BILL_AMT6	30000.0	38871.760400	59554.107537	-339603.0	1256.00	17071.0	49198.25	961664.0
PAY_AMT1	30000.0	5663.580500	16563.280354	0.0	1000.00	2100.0	5006.00	873552.0
PAY_AMT2	30000.0	5921.163500	23040.870402	0.0	833.00	2009.0	5000.00	1684259.0
PAY_AMT3	30000.0	5225.681500	17606.961470	0.0	390.00	1800.0	4505.00	891586.0
PAY_AMT4	30000.0	4826.076867	15666.159744	0.0	296.00	1500.0	4013.25	621000.0
PAY_AMT5	30000.0	4799.387633	15278.305679	0.0	252.50	1500.0	4031.50	426529.0
PAY_AMT6	30000.0	5215.502567	17777.465775	0.0	117.75	1500.0	4000.00	528666.0
default payment next month	30000.0	0.221200	0.415062	0.0	0.00	0.0	0.00	1.0

The **default payment next month** is our response column and everything else is a feature/potential predictor of default. It is wildly clear that our features exist on wildly different scales, so that will be a factor in how we handle the data and which models we will pick. In previous chapters, we dealt heavily with data and features on different scales using solutions such as `StandardScalar` and normalization to alleviate some of these issues; however, in this chapter, we will largely choose to ignore such problems in order to focus on more relevant issues.

In the final chapter of this book, we will focus on several case studies that will marry almost all of the techniques in this book on a longer-term analysis of a dataset.

As we have seen in previous chapters, we know that null values are a big issue when dealing with machine learning, so let's do a quick check to make sure that we don't have any to deal with:

```
# check for missing values, none in this dataset
credit_card_default.isnull().sum()
LIMIT_BAL                        0
SEX                              0
EDUCATION                        0
MARRIAGE                         0
AGE                              0
PAY_0                            0
PAY_2                            0
PAY_3                            0
PAY_4                            0
PAY_5                            0
PAY_6                            0
BILL_AMT1                        0
BILL_AMT2                        0
BILL_AMT3                        0
BILL_AMT4                        0
BILL_AMT5                        0
BILL_AMT6                        0
PAY_AMT1                         0
PAY_AMT2                         0
PAY_AMT3                         0
PAY_AMT4                         0
PAY_AMT5                         0
PAY_AMT6                         0
default payment next month       0
dtype: int64
```

Phew! No missing values here. Again, we will deal with missing values again in future case studies, but for now, we have bigger fish to fry. Let's go ahead and set up some variables for our machine learning pipelines, using the following code:

```
# Create our feature matrix
X = credit_card_default.drop('default payment next month', axis=1)

# create our response variable
y = credit_card_default['default payment next month']
```

As usual, we created our X and y variables. Our X matrix will have 30,000 rows and 23 columns and our y is, as always, a 30,000 long pandas Series. Because we will be performing classification, we will, as usual, need to ascertain a null accuracy to ensure that our machine learning models are performing better than a baseline. We can get the null accuracy rate using the following code:

```
# get our null accuracy rate
y.value_counts(normalize=True)


0    0.7788
1    0.2212
```

So, the accuracy to beat, in this case, is **77.88%**, which is the percentage of people who did not default (0 meaning false to default).

Creating a baseline machine learning pipeline

In previous chapters, we offered to you, the reader, a single machine learning model to use throughout the chapter. In this chapter, we will do some work to find the best machine learning model for our needs and then work to enhance that model with feature selection. We will begin by importing four different machine learning models:

- Logistic Regression
- K-Nearest Neighbors
- Decision Tree
- Random Forest

The code for importing the learning models is given as follows:

```
# Import four machine learning models
from sklearn.linear_model import LogisticRegression
from sklearn.neighbors import KNeighborsClassifier
from sklearn.tree import DecisionTreeClassifier
from sklearn.ensemble import RandomForestClassifier
```

Once we are finished importing these modules, we will run them through our `get_best_model_and_accuracy` functions to get a baseline on how each one handles the raw data. We will have to first establish some variables to do so. We will use the following code to do this:

```
# Set up some parameters for our grid search
# We will start with four different machine learning model parameters

# Logistic Regression
lr_params = {'C':[1e-1, 1e0, 1e1, 1e2], 'penalty':['l1', 'l2']}

# KNN
knn_params = {'n_neighbors': [1, 3, 5, 7]}

# Decision Tree
tree_params = {'max_depth':[None, 1, 3, 5, 7]}

# Random Forest
forest_params = {'n_estimators': [10, 50, 100], 'max_depth': [None, 1, 3,
5, 7]}
```

 If you feel uncomfortable with any of the models listed above, we recommend reading up on documentation, or referring to the Packt book, *The Principles of Data Science*, `https://www.packtpub.com/big-data-and-business-intelligence/principles-data-science`, for a more detailed explanation of the algorithms.

Because we will be sending each model through our function, which invokes a grid search module, we need only create blank state models with no customized parameters set, as shown in the following code:

```
# instantiate the four machine learning models
lr = LogisticRegression()
knn = KNeighborsClassifier()
d_tree = DecisionTreeClassifier()
forest = RandomForestClassifier()
```

We are now going to run each of the four machine learning models through our evaluation function to see how well (or not) they do against our dataset. Recall that our number to beat at the moment is .7788, the baseline null accuracy. We will use the following code to run the models:

```
get_best_model_and_accuracy(lr, lr_params, X, y)

Best Accuracy: 0.809566666667
Best Parameters: {'penalty': 'l1', 'C': 0.1}
```

```
Average Time to Fit (s): 0.602
Average Time to Score (s): 0.002
```

We can see that the logistic regression has already beaten the null accuracy using the raw data and, on average, took 6/10 of a second to fit to a training set and only 20 milliseconds to score. This makes sense if we know that to fit, a logistic regression in **scikit-learn** must create a large matrix in memory, but to predict, it need only multiply and add scalars to one another.

Now, let's do the same with the KNN model, using the following code:

```
get_best_model_and_accuracy(knn, knn_params, X, y)

Best Accuracy: 0.760233333333
Best Parameters: {'n_neighbors': 7}
Average Time to Fit (s): 0.035
Average Time to Score (s): 0.88
```

Our KNN model, as expected, does much better on the fitting time. This is because, to fit to the data, the KNN only has to store the data in such a way that it is easily retrieved at prediction time, where it takes a hit on time. It's also worth mentioning the painfully obvious fact that the accuracy is not even better than the null accuracy! You might be wondering why, and if you're saying *hey wait a minute, doesn't KNN utilize the Euclidean Distance in order to make predictions, which can be thrown off by non-standardized data, a flaw that none of the other three machine learning models suffer?*, then you're 100% correct.

KNN is a distance-based model, in that it uses a metric of closeness in space that assumes that all features are on the same scale, which we already know that our data is not on. So, for KNN, we will have to construct a more complicated pipeline to more accurately assess its baseline performance, using the following code:

```
# bring in some familiar modules for dealing with this sort of thing
from sklearn.pipeline import Pipeline
from sklearn.preprocessing import StandardScaler

# construct pipeline parameters based on the parameters
# for KNN on its own
knn_pipe_params = {'classifier__{}'.format(k): v for k, v in
knn_params.iteritems()}

# KNN requires a standard scalar due to using Euclidean distance # as the
main equation for predicting observations
knn_pipe = Pipeline([('scale', StandardScaler()), ('classifier', knn)])

# quick to fit, very slow to predict
get_best_model_and_accuracy(knn_pipe, knn_pipe_params, X, y)
```

```
print knn_pipe_params  # {'classifier__n_neighbors': [1, 3, 5, 7]}

Best Accuracy: 0.8008
Best Parameters: {'classifier__n_neighbors': 7}
Average Time to Fit (s): 0.035
Average Time to Score (s): 6.723
```

The first thing to notice is that our modified code pipeline, which now includes a `StandardScalar` (which z-score normalizes our features) now beats the null accuracy at the very least, but also seriously hurts our predicting time, as we have added a step of preprocessing. So far, the logistic regression is in the lead with the best accuracy and the better overall timing of the pipeline. Let's move on to our two tree-based models and start with the simpler of the two, the decision tree, with the help of the following code:

```
get_best_model_and_accuracy(d_tree, tree_params, X, y)

Best Accuracy: 0.820266666667
Best Parameters: {'max_depth': 3}
Average Time to Fit (s): 0.158
Average Time to Score (s): 0.002
```

Amazing! Already, we have a new lead in accuracy and, also, the decision tree is quick to both fit and predict. In fact, it beats logistic regression in its time to fit and beats the KNN in its time to predict. Let's finish off our test by evaluating a random forest, using the following code:

```
get_best_model_and_accuracy(forest, forest_params, X, y)

Best Accuracy: 0.819566666667
Best Parameters: {'n_estimators': 50, 'max_depth': 7}
Average Time to Fit (s): 1.107
Average Time to Score (s): 0.044
```

Much better than either the Logistic Regression or the KNN, but not better than the decision tree. Let's aggregate these results to see which model we should move forward with in optimizing using feature selection:

Model Name	Accuracy (%)	Fit Time (s)	Predict Time (s)
Logistic Regression	.8096	.602	**.002**
KNN (with scaling)	.8008	**.035**	6.72
Decision Tree	**.8203**	.158	**.002**
Random Forest	.8196	1.107	.044

The decision tree comes in first for accuracy and tied for first for predict time with logistic regression, while KNN with scaling takes the trophy for being the fastest to fit to our data. Overall, the decision tree appears to be the best model to move forward with, as it came in first for, arguably, our two most important metrics:

- We definitely want the best accuracy to ensure that out of sample predictions are accurate
- Having a prediction time is useful considering that the models are being utilized for real-time production usage

The approach we are taking is one that selects a model before selecting any features. It is not required to work in this fashion, but we find that it generally saves the most time when working under pressure of time. For your purposes, we recommend that you experiment with many models concurrently and don't limit yourself to a single model.

Knowing that we will be using the decision tree for the remainder of this chapter, we know two more things:

- The new baseline accuracy to beat is .8203, the accuracy the tree obtained when fitting to the entire dataset
- We no longer have to use our `StandardScaler`, as decision trees are unaffected by it when it comes to model performance

The types of feature selection

Recall that our goal with feature selection is to improve our machine learning capabilities by increasing predictive power and reducing the time cost. To do this, we introduce two broad categories of feature selection: statistical-based and model-based. Statistical-based feature selection will rely heavily on statistical tests that are separate from our machine learning models in order to select features during the training phase of our pipeline. Model-based selection relies on a preprocessing step that involves training a secondary machine learning model and using that model's predictive power to select features.

Both of these types of feature selection attempt to reduce the size of our data by subsetting from our original features only the best ones with the highest predictive power. We may intelligently choose which feature selection method might work best for us, but in reality, a very valid way of working in this domain is to work through examples of each method and measure the performance of the resulting pipeline.

To begin, let's take a look at the subclass of feature selection modules that are reliant on statistical tests to select viable features from a dataset.

Statistical-based feature selection

Statistics provides us with relatively quick and easy methods of interpreting both quantitative and qualitative data. We have used some statistical measures in previous chapters to obtain new knowledge and perspective around our data, specifically in that we recognized mean and standard deviation as metrics that enabled us to calculate z-scores and scale our data. In this chapter, we will rely on two new concepts to help us with our feature selection:

- Pearson correlations
- hypothesis testing

Both of these methods are known as **univariate** methods of feature selection, meaning that they are quick and handy when the problem is to select out *single* features at a time in order to create a better dataset for our machine learning pipeline.

Using Pearson correlation to select features

We have actually looked at correlations in this book already, but not in the context of feature selection. We already know that we can invoke a correlation calculation in pandas by calling the following method:

```
credit_card_default.corr()
```

The output of the preceding code produces is the following:

	LIMIT_BAL	SEX	EDUCATION	MARRIAGE	AGE	PAY_0	PAY_2	PAY_3	PAY_4	PAY_5
LIMIT_BAL	1.000000	0.024755	-0.219161	-0.108139	0.144713	-0.271214	-0.296382	-0.286123	-0.267460	-0.249411
SEX	0.024755	1.000000	0.014232	-0.031389	-0.090874	-0.057643	-0.070771	-0.066096	-0.060173	-0.055064
EDUCATION	-0.219161	0.014232	1.000000	-0.143464	0.175061	0.105364	0.121566	0.114025	0.108793	0.097520
MARRIAGE	-0.108139	-0.031389	-0.143464	1.000000	-0.414170	0.019917	0.024199	0.032688	0.033122	0.035629
AGE	0.144713	-0.090874	0.175061	-0.414170	1.000000	-0.039447	-0.050148	-0.053048	-0.049722	-0.053826
PAY_0	-0.271214	-0.057643	0.105364	0.019917	-0.039447	1.000000	0.672164	0.574245	0.538841	0.509426
PAY_2	-0.296382	-0.070771	0.121566	0.024199	-0.050148	0.672164	1.000000	0.766552	0.662067	0.622780
PAY_3	-0.286123	-0.066096	0.114025	0.032688	-0.053048	0.574245	0.766552	1.000000	0.777359	0.686775
PAY_4	-0.267460	-0.060173	0.108793	0.033122	-0.049722	0.538841	0.662067	0.777359	1.000000	0.819835
PAY_5	-0.249411	-0.055064	0.097520	0.035629	-0.053826	0.509426	0.622780	0.686775	0.819835	1.000000
PAY_6	-0.235195	-0.044008	0.082316	0.034345	-0.048773	0.474553	0.575501	0.632684	0.716449	0.816900
BILL_AMT1	0.285430	-0.033642	0.023581	-0.023472	0.056239	0.187068	0.234887	0.208473	0.202812	0.206684
BILL_AMT2	0.278314	-0.031183	0.018749	-0.021602	0.054283	0.189859	0.235257	0.237295	0.225816	0.226913
BILL_AMT3	0.283236	-0.024563	0.013002	-0.024909	0.053710	0.179785	0.224146	0.227494	0.244983	0.243335
BILL_AMT4	0.293988	-0.021880	-0.000451	-0.023344	0.051353	0.179125	0.222237	0.227202	0.245917	0.271915
BILL_AMT5	0.295562	-0.017005	-0.007567	-0.025393	0.049345	0.180635	0.221348	0.225145	0.242902	0.269783
BILL_AMT6	0.290389	-0.016733	-0.009099	-0.021207	0.047613	0.176980	0.219403	0.222327	0.239154	0.262509
PAY_AMT1	0.195236	-0.000242	-0.037456	-0.005979	0.026147	-0.079269	-0.080701	0.001295	-0.009362	-0.006089
PAY_AMT2	0.178408	-0.001391	-0.030038	-0.008093	0.021785	-0.070101	-0.058990	-0.066793	-0.001944	-0.003191
PAY_AMT3	0.210167	-0.008597	-0.039943	-0.003541	0.029247	-0.070561	-0.055901	-0.053311	-0.069235	0.009062
PAY_AMT4	0.203242	-0.002229	-0.038218	-0.012659	0.021379	-0.064005	-0.046858	-0.046067	-0.043461	-0.058299
PAY_AMT5	0.217202	-0.001667	-0.040358	-0.001205	0.022850	-0.058190	-0.037093	-0.035863	-0.033590	-0.033337
PAY_AMT6	0.219595	-0.002766	-0.037200	-0.006641	0.019478	-0.058673	-0.036500	-0.035861	-0.026565	-0.023027
default payment next month	-0.153520	-0.039961	0.028006	-0.024339	0.013890	0.324794	0.263551	0.235253	0.216614	0.204149

As a continuation of the preceding table we have:

	BILL_AMT4	BILL_AMT5	BILL_AMT6	PAY_AMT1	PAY_AMT2	PAY_AMT3	PAY_AMT4	PAY_AMT5	PAY_AMT6	default payment next month
LIMIT_BAL	0.293988	0.295562	0.290389	0.195236	0.178408	0.210167	0.203242	0.217202	0.219595	-0.153520
SEX	-0.021880	-0.017005	-0.016733	-0.000242	-0.001391	-0.008597	-0.002229	-0.001667	-0.002766	-0.039961
EDUCATION	-0.000451	-0.007567	-0.009099	-0.037456	-0.030038	-0.039943	-0.038218	-0.040358	-0.037200	0.028006
MARRIAGE	-0.023344	-0.025393	-0.021207	-0.005979	-0.008093	-0.003541	-0.012659	-0.001205	-0.006641	-0.024339
AGE	0.051353	0.049345	0.047613	0.026147	0.021785	0.029247	0.021379	0.022850	0.019478	0.013890
PAY_0	0.179125	0.180635	0.176980	-0.079269	-0.070101	-0.070561	-0.064005	-0.058190	-0.058673	0.324794
PAY_2	0.222237	0.221348	0.219403	-0.080701	-0.058990	-0.055901	-0.046858	-0.037093	-0.036500	0.263551
PAY_3	0.227202	0.225145	0.222327	0.001295	-0.066793	-0.053311	-0.046067	-0.035863	-0.035861	0.235253
PAY_4	0.245917	0.242902	0.239154	-0.009362	-0.001944	-0.069235	-0.043461	-0.033590	-0.026565	0.216614
PAY_5	0.271915	0.269783	0.262509	-0.006089	-0.003191	0.009062	-0.058299	-0.033337	-0.023027	0.204149
PAY_6	0.266356	0.290894	0.285091	-0.001496	-0.005223	0.005834	0.019018	-0.046434	-0.025299	0.186866
BILL_AMT1	0.860272	0.829779	0.802650	0.140277	0.099355	0.156887	0.158303	0.167026	0.179341	-0.019644
BILL_AMT2	0.892482	0.859778	0.831594	0.280365	0.100851	0.150718	0.147398	0.157957	0.174256	-0.014193
BILL_AMT3	0.923969	0.883910	0.853320	0.244335	0.316936	0.130011	0.143405	0.179712	0.182326	-0.014076
BILL_AMT4	1.000000	0.940134	0.900941	0.233012	0.207564	0.300023	0.130191	0.160433	0.177637	-0.010156
BILL_AMT5	0.940134	1.000000	0.946197	0.217031	0.181246	0.252305	0.293118	0.141574	0.164184	-0.006760
BILL_AMT6	0.900941	0.946197	1.000000	0.199965	0.172663	0.233770	0.250237	0.307729	0.115494	-0.005372
PAY_AMT1	0.233012	0.217031	0.199965	1.000000	0.285576	0.252191	0.199558	0.148459	0.185735	-0.072929
PAY_AMT2	0.207564	0.181246	0.172663	0.285576	1.000000	0.244770	0.180107	0.180908	0.157634	-0.058579
PAY_AMT3	0.300023	0.252305	0.233770	0.252191	0.244770	1.000000	0.216325	0.159214	0.162740	-0.056250
PAY_AMT4	0.130191	0.293118	0.250237	0.199558	0.180107	0.216325	1.000000	0.151830	0.157834	-0.056827
PAY_AMT5	0.160433	0.141574	0.307729	0.148459	0.180908	0.159214	0.151830	1.000000	0.154896	-0.055124
PAY_AMT6	0.177637	0.164184	0.115494	0.185735	0.157634	0.162740	0.157834	0.154896	1.000000	-0.053183
default payment next month	-0.010156	-0.006760	-0.005372	-0.072929	-0.058579	-0.056250	-0.056827	-0.055124	-0.053183	1.000000

The Pearson correlation coefficient (which is the default for pandas) measures the *linear* relationship between columns. The value of the coefficient varies between -1 and +1, where 0 implies no correlation between them. Correlations closer to -1 or +1 imply an extremely strong linear relationship.

It is worth noting that Pearson's correlation generally requires that each column be normally distributed (which we are not assuming). We can also largely ignore this requirement because our dataset is large (over 500 is the threshold).

The pandas `.corr()` method calculates a Pearson correlation coefficient for every column versus every other column. This 24 column by 24 row matrix is very unruly, and in the past, we used `heatmaps` to try and make the information more digestible:

```
# using seaborn to generate heatmaps
import seaborn as sns
import matplotlib.style as style
# Use a clean stylizatino for our charts and graphs
style.use('fivethirtyeight')

sns.heatmap(credit_card_default.corr())
```

The `heatmap` generated will be as follows:

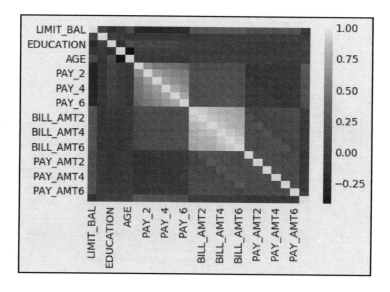

Note that the `heatmap` function automatically chose the most correlated features to show us. That being said, we are, for the moment, concerned with the features correlations to the response variable. We will assume that the more correlated a feature is to the response, the more useful it will be. Any feature that is not as strongly correlated will not be as useful to us.

Correlation coefficients are also used to determine feature interactions and redundancies. A key method of reducing overfitting in machine learning is spotting and removing these redundancies. We will be tackling this problem in our model-based selection methods.

Let's isolate the correlations between the features and the response variable, using the following code:

```
# just correlations between every feature and the response
credit_card_default.corr()['default payment next month']
```

```
LIMIT_BAL                       -0.153520
SEX                             -0.039961
EDUCATION                        0.028006
MARRIAGE                        -0.024339
AGE                              0.013890
PAY_0                            0.324794
PAY_2                            0.263551
PAY_3                            0.235253
PAY_4                            0.216614
PAY_5                            0.204149
PAY_6                            0.186866
BILL_AMT1                       -0.019644
BILL_AMT2                       -0.014193
BILL_AMT3                       -0.014076
BILL_AMT4                       -0.010156
BILL_AMT5                       -0.006760
BILL_AMT6                       -0.005372
PAY_AMT1                        -0.072929
PAY_AMT2                        -0.058579
PAY_AMT3                        -0.056250
PAY_AMT4                        -0.056827
PAY_AMT5                        -0.055124
PAY_AMT6                        -0.053183
default payment next month       1.000000
```

We can ignore the final row, as is it is the response variable correlated perfectly to itself. We are looking for features that have correlation coefficient values close to -1 or +1. These are the features that we might assume are going to be useful. Let's use pandas filtering to isolate features that have at least .2 correlation (positive or negative).

Let's do this by first defining a pandas *mask*, which will act as our filter, using the following code:

```
# filter only correlations stronger than .2 in either direction (positive
or negative)

credit_card_default.corr()['default payment next month'].abs() > .2
```

```
LIMIT_BAL                       False
SEX                             False
EDUCATION                       False
```

MARRIAGE	False
AGE	False
PAY_0	True
PAY_2	True
PAY_3	True
PAY_4	True
PAY_5	True
PAY_6	False
BILL_AMT1	False
BILL_AMT2	False
BILL_AMT3	False
BILL_AMT4	False
BILL_AMT5	False
BILL_AMT6	False
PAY_AMT1	False
PAY_AMT2	False
PAY_AMT3	False
PAY_AMT4	False
PAY_AMT5	False
PAY_AMT6	False
default payment next month	True

Every `False` in the preceding pandas Series represents a feature that has a correlation value between -.2 and .2 inclusive, while `True` values correspond to features with preceding correlation values .2 or less than -0.2. Let's plug this mask into our pandas filtering, using the following code:

```
# store the features
highly_correlated_features =
credit_card_default.columns[credit_card_default.corr()['default payment
next month'].abs() > .2]

highly_correlated_features

Index([u'PAY_0', u'PAY_2', u'PAY_3', u'PAY_4', u'PAY_5',
       u'default payment next month'],
     dtype='object')
```

The variable `highly_correlated_features` is supposed to hold the features of the dataframe that are highly correlated to the response; however, we do have to get rid of the name of the response column, as including that in our machine learning pipeline would be cheating:

```
# drop the response variable
highly_correlated_features = highly_correlated_features.drop('default
payment next month')
```

```
highly_correlated_features

Index([u'PAY_0', u'PAY_2', u'PAY_3', u'PAY_4', u'PAY_5'], dtype='object')
```

So, now we have five features from our original dataset that are meant to be predictive of the response variable, so let's try it out with the help of the following code:

```
# only include the five highly correlated features
X_subsetted = X[highly_correlated_features]

get_best_model_and_accuracy(d_tree, tree_params, X_subsetted, y)

# barely worse, but about 20x faster to fit the model
Best Accuracy: 0.819666666667
Best Parameters: {'max_depth': 3}
Average Time to Fit (s): 0.01
Average Time to Score (s): 0.002
```

Our accuracy is definitely worse than the accuracy to beat, .8203, but also note that the fitting time saw about a 20-fold increase. Our model is able to learn almost as well as with the entire dataset with only five features. Moreover, it is able to learn as much in a much shorter timeframe.

Let's bring back our scikit-learn pipelines and include our correlation choosing methodology as a part of our preprocessing phase. To do this, we will have to create a custom transformer that invokes the logic we just went through, as a pipeline-ready class.

We will call our class the CustomCorrelationChooser and it will have to implement both a fit and a transform logic, which are:

- The fit logic will select columns from the features matrix that are higher than a specified threshold
- The transform logic will subset any future datasets to only include those columns that were deemed important

```
from sklearn.base import TransformerMixin, BaseEstimator

class CustomCorrelationChooser(TransformerMixin, BaseEstimator):
    def __init__(self, response, cols_to_keep=[], threshold=None):
        # store the response series
        self.response = response
        # store the threshold that we wish to keep
        self.threshold = threshold
        # initialize a variable that will eventually
        # hold the names of the features that we wish to keep
        self.cols_to_keep = cols_to_keep
```

```
def transform(self, X):
    # the transform method simply selects the appropiate
    # columns from the original dataset
    return X[self.cols_to_keep]
def fit(self, X, *_):
    # create a new dataframe that holds both features and response
    df = pd.concat([X, self.response], axis=1)
    # store names of columns that meet correlation threshold
    self.cols_to_keep = df.columns[df.corr()[df.columns[-1]].abs() >
self.threshold]
    # only keep columns in X, for example, will remove response
variable
    self.cols_to_keep = [c for c in self.cols_to_keep if c in
X.columns]
    return self
```

Let's take our new correlation feature selector for a spin, with the help of the following code:

```
# instantiate our new feature selector
ccc = CustomCorrelationChooser(threshold=.2, response=y)
ccc.fit(X)

ccc.cols_to_keep

['PAY_0', 'PAY_2', 'PAY_3', 'PAY_4', 'PAY_5']
```

Our class has selected the same five columns as we found earlier. Let's test out the transform functionality by calling it on our X matrix, using the following code:

```
ccc.transform(X).head()
```

The preceding code produces the following table as the output:

	PAY_0	PAY_2	PAY_3	PAY_4	PAY_5
0	2	2	-1	-1	-2
1	-1	2	0	0	0
2	0	0	0	0	0
3	0	0	0	0	0
4	-1	0	-1	0	0

We see that the `transform` method has eliminated the other columns and kept only the features that met our `.2` correlation threshold. Now, let's put it all together in our pipeline, with the help of the following code:

```
# instantiate our feature selector with the response variable set
ccc = CustomCorrelationChooser(response=y)

# make our new pipeline, including the selector
ccc_pipe = Pipeline([('correlation_select', ccc),
  ('classifier', d_tree)])

# make a copy of the decisino tree pipeline parameters
ccc_pipe_params = deepcopy(tree_pipe_params)

# update that dictionary with feature selector specific parameters
ccc_pipe_params.update({
  'correlation_select__threshold':[0, .1, .2, .3]})

print ccc_pipe_params  #{'correlation_select__threshold': [0, 0.1, 0.2,
0.3], 'classifier__max_depth': [None, 1, 3, 5, 7, 9, 11, 13, 15, 17, 19,
21]}

# better than original (by a little, and a bit faster on
# average overall
get_best_model_and_accuracy(ccc_pipe, ccc_pipe_params, X, y)

Best Accuracy: 0.8206
Best Parameters: {'correlation_select__threshold': 0.1,
'classifier__max_depth': 5}
Average Time to Fit (s): 0.105
Average Time to Score (s): 0.003
```

Wow! Our first attempt at feature selection and we have already beaten our goal (albeit by a little bit). Our pipeline is showing us that if we threshold at `0.1`, we have eliminated noise enough to improve accuracy and also cut down on the fitting time (from .158 seconds without the selector). Let's take a look at which columns our selector decided to keep:

```
# check the threshold of .1
ccc = CustomCorrelationChooser(threshold=0.1, response=y)
ccc.fit(X)

# check which columns were kept
ccc.cols_to_keep
['LIMIT_BAL', 'PAY_0', 'PAY_2', 'PAY_3', 'PAY_4', 'PAY_5', 'PAY_6']
```

It appears that our selector has decided to keep the five columns that we found, as well as two more, the `LIMIT_BAL` and the `PAY_6` columns. Great! This is the beauty of automated pipeline gridsearching in scikit-learn. It allows our models to do what they do best and intuit things that we could not have on our own.

Feature selection using hypothesis testing

Hypothesis testing is a methodology in statistics that allows for a bit more complex statistical testing for individual features. Feature selection via hypothesis testing will attempt to select only the best features from a dataset, just as we were doing with our custom correlation chooser, but these tests rely more on formalized statistical methods and are interpreted through what are known as **p-values**.

A hypothesis test is a statistical test that is used to figure out whether we can apply a certain condition for an entire population, given a data sample. The result of a hypothesis test tells us whether we should believe the hypothesis or reject it for an alternative one. Based on sample data from a population, a hypothesis test determines whether or not to reject the null hypothesis. We usually use a **p-value** (a non-negative decimal with an upper bound of 1, which is based on our significance level) to make this conclusion.

In the case of feature selection, the hypothesis we wish to test is along the lines of: *True or False: This feature has no relevance to the response variable.* We want to test this hypothesis for every feature and decide whether the features hold some significance in the prediction of the response. In a way, this is how we dealt with the correlation logic. We basically said that, if a column's correlation with the response is too weak, then we say that the hypothesis that the feature has no relevance is true. If the correlation coefficient was strong enough, then we can reject the hypothesis that the feature has no relevance in favor of an alternative hypothesis, that the feature does have some relevance.

To begin to use this for our data, we will have to bring in two new modules: `SelectKBest` and `f_classif`, using the following code:

```
# SelectKBest selects features according to the k highest scores of a given
scoring function
from sklearn.feature_selection import SelectKBest

# This models a statistical test known as ANOVA
from sklearn.feature_selection import f_classif

# f_classif allows for negative values, not all do
```

```
# chi2 is a very common classification criteria but only allows for
positive values
# regression has its own statistical tests
```

`SelectKBest` is basically just a wrapper that keeps a set amount of features that are the highest ranked according to some criterion. In this case, we will use the p-values of completed hypothesis testings as a ranking.

Interpreting the p-value

The p-values are a decimals between 0 and 1 that represent the probability that the data given to us occurred by chance under the hypothesis test. Simply put, the lower the p-value, the better the chance that we can reject the null hypothesis. For our purposes, the smaller the p-value, the better the chances that the feature has some relevance to our response variable and we should keep it.

> For a more in-depth handling of statistical testing, check out *Principles of Data Science*, `https://www.packtpub.com/big-data-and-business-intelligence/principles-data-science`, by Packt Publishing.

The big take away from this is that the `f_classif` function will perform an ANOVA test (a type of hypothesis test) on each feature on its own (hence the name univariate testing) and assign that feature a p-value. The `SelectKBest` will rank the features by that p-value (the lower the better) and keep only the best k (a human input) features. Let's try this out in Python.

Ranking the p-value

Let's begin by instantiating a `SelectKBest` module. We will manually enter a k value, 5, meaning we wish to keep only the five best features according to the resulting p-values:

```
# keep only the best five features according to p-values of ANOVA test
k_best = SelectKBest(f_classif, k=5)
```

We can then fit and transform our X matrix to select the features we want, as we did before with our custom selector:

```
# matrix after selecting the top 5 features
k_best.fit_transform(X, y)

# 30,000 rows x 5 columns
array([[ 2,   2,  -1,  -1,  -2],
       [-1,   2,   0,   0,   0],
```

```
    [ 0,   0,   0,   0,   0],
    ...,
    [ 4,   3,   2,  -1,   0],
    [ 1,  -1,   0,   0,   0],
    [ 0,   0,   0,   0,   0]])
```

If we want to inspect the `p-values` directly and see which columns were chosen, we can dive deeper into the select `k_best` variables:

```
# get the p values of columns
k_best.pvalues_

# make a dataframe of features and p-values
# sort that dataframe by p-value
p_values = pd.DataFrame({'column': X.columns, 'p_value':
k_best.pvalues_}).sort_values('p_value')

# show the top 5 features
p_values.head()
```

The preceding code produces the following table as the output:

	column	p_value
5	PAY_0	0.000000e+00
6	PAY_2	0.000000e+00
7	PAY_3	0.000000e+00
8	PAY_4	1.899297e-315
9	PAY_5	1.126608e-279

We can see that, once again, our selector is choosing the `PAY_X` columns as the most important. If we take a look at our `p-value` column, we will notice that our values are extremely small and close to zero. A common threshold for p-values is 0.05, meaning that anything less than 0.05 may be considered significant, and these columns are extremely significant according to our tests. We can also directly see which columns meet a threshold of 0.05 using the pandas filtering methodology:

```
# features with a low p value
p_values[p_values['p_value'] < .05]
```

The preceding code produces the following table as the output:

	column	p_value
5	PAY_0	0.000000e+00
6	PAY_2	0.000000e+00
7	PAY_3	0.000000e+00
8	PAY_4	1.899297e-315
9	PAY_5	1.126608e-279
10	PAY_6	7.296740e-234
0	LIMIT_BAL	1.302244e-157
17	PAY_AMT1	1.146488e-36
18	PAY_AMT2	3.166657e-24
20	PAY_AMT4	6.830942e-23
19	PAY_AMT3	1.841770e-22
21	PAY_AMT5	1.241345e-21
22	PAY_AMT6	3.033589e-20
1	SEX	4.395249e-12
2	EDUCATION	1.225038e-06
3	MARRIAGE	2.485364e-05
11	BILL_AMT1	6.673295e-04
12	BILL_AMT2	1.395736e-02
13	BILL_AMT3	1.476998e-02
4	AGE	1.613685e-02

The majority of the columns have a low `p-value`, but not all. Let's see the columns with a higher `p_value`, using the following code:

```
# features with a high p value
p_values[p_values['p_value'] >= .05]
```

The preceding code produces the following table as the output:

	column	p_value
14	BILL_AMT4	0.078556
15	BILL_AMT5	0.241634
16	BILL_AMT6	0.352123

These three columns have quite a high `p-value`. Let's use our `SelectKBest` in a pipeline to see if we can grid search our way into a better machine learning pipeline, using the following code:

```
k_best = SelectKBest(f_classif)

# Make a new pipeline with SelectKBest
select_k_pipe = Pipeline([('k_best', k_best),
  ('classifier', d_tree)])

select_k_best_pipe_params = deepcopy(tree_pipe_params)
# the 'all' literally does nothing to subset
select_k_best_pipe_params.update({'k_best__k':range(1,23) + ['all']})

print select_k_best_pipe_params # {'k_best__k': [1, 2, 3, 4, 5, 6, 7, 8, 9,
10, 11, 12, 13, 14, 15, 16, 17, 18, 19, 20, 21, 22, 'all'],
'classifier__max_depth': [None, 1, 3, 5, 7, 9, 11, 13, 15, 17, 19, 21]}

# comparable to our results with correlationchooser
get_best_model_and_accuracy(select_k_pipe, select_k_best_pipe_params, X, y)


Best Accuracy: 0.8206
Best Parameters: {'k_best__k': 7, 'classifier__max_depth': 5}
Average Time to Fit (s): 0.102
Average Time to Score (s): 0.002
```

It seems that our `SelectKBest` module is getting about the same accuracy as our custom transformer, but it's getting there a bit quicker! Let's see which columns our tests are selecting for us, with the help of the following code:

```
k_best = SelectKBest(f_classif, k=7)

# lowest 7 p values match what our custom correlationchooser chose before
# ['LIMIT_BAL', 'PAY_0', 'PAY_2', 'PAY_3', 'PAY_4', 'PAY_5', 'PAY_6']

p_values.head(7)
```

The preceding code produces the following table as the output:

	column	p_value
5	PAY_0	0.000000e+00
6	PAY_0	0.000000e+00
7	PAY_0	0.000000e+00
8	PAY_0	1.899297e-315
9	PAY_0	1.126608e-279
10	PAY_0	7.296740e-234
0	LIMIT_BAL	1.302244e-157

They appear to be the same columns that were chosen by our other statistical method. It's possible that our statistical method is limited to continually picking these seven columns for us.

There are other tests available besides ANOVA, such as Chi^2 and others, for regression tasks. They are all included in scikit-learn's documentation. For more info on feature selection through univariate testing, check out the scikit-learn documentation here: `http://scikit-learn.org/stable/modules/feature_selection.html#univariate-feature-selection`

Before we move on to model-based feature selection, it's helpful to do a quick sanity check to ensure that we are on the right track. So far, we have seen two statistical methods for feature selection that gave us the same seven columns for optimal accuracy. But what if we were to take every column **except** those seven? We should expect a much lower accuracy and worse pipeline overall, right? Let's make sure. The following code helps us to implement sanity checks:

```
# sanity check
# If we only the worst columns
the_worst_of_X = X[X.columns.drop(['LIMIT_BAL', 'PAY_0', 'PAY_2', 'PAY_3',
'PAY_4', 'PAY_5', 'PAY_6'])]

# goes to show, that selecting the wrong features will
# hurt us in predictive performance
get_best_model_and_accuracy(d_tree, tree_params, the_worst_of_X, y)

Best Accuracy: 0.783966666667
```

```
Best Parameters: {'max_depth': 5}
Average Time to Fit (s): 0.21
Average Time to Score (s): 0.002
```

OK, so by selecting the columns except those seven, we see not only worse accuracy (almost as bad as the null accuracy), but also slower fitting times on average. With this, I believe we may move on to our next subset of feature selection techniques, the model-based methods.

Model-based feature selection

Our last section dealt with using statistical methods and testing in order to select features from the original dataset to improve our machine learning pipeline, both in predictive performance, as well as in time-complexity. In doing so, we were able to see first-hand the effects of using feature selection.

A brief refresher on natural language processing

If talking about feature selection has sounded familiar from the very beginning of this chapter, almost as if we were doing it even before we began with correlation coefficients and statistical testing, well, you aren't wrong. In Chapter 4, *Feature Construction* when dealing with feature construction, we introduced the concept of the CountVectorizer, a module in scikit-learn designed to construct features from text columns and use them in machine learning pipelines.

The CountVectorizer had many parameters that we could alter in search of the best pipeline. Specifically, there were a few built-in feature selection parameters:

- max_features: This integer set a hard limit of the maximum number of features that the featurizer could remember. The features that were remembered were decided based on a ranking system where the rank of a token was the count of the token in the corpus.
- min_df: This float limited the number of features by imposing a rule stating that a token may only appear in the dataset if it appeared in the corpus as a rate strictly greater than the value for min_df.
- max_df: Similar to min_df, this float limits the number of features by only allowing tokens that appear in the corpus at a rate strictly lower than the value set for max_df.

- `stop_words`: Limits the type of tokens allowed by matching them against a static list of tokens. If a token is found that exists in the `stop_words` set, that word, no matter if it occurs at the right amount to be allowed by `min_df` and `max_df`, is ignored.

In the previous chapter, we briefly introduced a dataset aimed at predicting the sentiment of a tweet based purely on the words in that tweet. Let's take some time to refresh our memories on how to use these parameters. Let's begin by bringing in our `tweet` dataset, with the help of the following code:

```
# bring in the tweet dataset
tweets = pd.read_csv('../data/twitter_sentiment.csv',
 encoding='latin1')
```

To refresh our memory, let's look at the first five `tweets`, using the following code:

```
tweets.head()
```

The preceding code produces the following table as the output:

	ItemID	Sentiment	SentimentText
0	1	0	is so sad for my APL frie...
1	2	0	I missed the New Moon trail...
2	3	1	omg its already 7:30 :O
3	4	0	.. Omgaga. Im sooo im gunna CRy. I'...
4	5	0	i think mi bf is cheating on me!!! ...

Let's create a feature and a response variable. Recall that, because we are working with text, our feature variable will simply be the text column and not a two-dimensional matrix like it usually is:

```
tweets_X, tweets_y = tweets['SentimentText'], tweets['Sentiment']
```

Let's set up a pipeline and evaluate it using the same function that we've been using in this chapter, with the help of the following code:

```
from sklearn.feature_extraction.text import CountVectorizer
# import a naive bayes to help predict and fit a bit faster
from sklearn.naive_bayes import MultinomialNB

featurizer = CountVectorizer()
```

```
text_pipe = Pipeline([('featurizer', featurizer),
                ('classify', MultinomialNB())])

text_pipe_params = {'featurizer__ngram_range':[(1, 2)],
            'featurizer__max_features': [5000, 10000],
            'featurizer__min_df': [0., .1, .2, .3],
            'featurizer__max_df': [.7, .8, .9, 1.]}


get_best_model_and_accuracy(text_pipe, text_pipe_params,
                tweets_X, tweets_y)

Best Accuracy: 0.755753132845
Best Parameters: {'featurizer__min_df': 0.0, 'featurizer__ngram_range': (1,
2), 'featurizer__max_df': 0.7, 'featurizer__max_features': 10000}
Average Time to Fit (s): 5.808
Average Time to Score (s): 0.957
```

A decent score (recalling that the null accuracy was .564), but we were able to beat this in the last chapter by using a `FeatureUnion` module to combine features from `TfidfVectorizer` and `CountVectorizer`.

To try out the techniques we've seen in this chapter, let's go ahead and apply a `SelectKBest` in a pipeline with a `CountVectorizer`. Let's see if we can rely not on the built-in `CountVectorizer` feature selection parameters, but instead, on statistical testing:

```
# Let's try a more basic pipeline, but one that relies on SelectKBest as
well
featurizer = CountVectorizer(ngram_range=(1, 2))

select_k_text_pipe = Pipeline([('featurizer', featurizer),
                ('select_k', SelectKBest()),
                ('classify', MultinomialNB())])

select_k_text_pipe_params = {'select_k__k': [1000, 5000]}

get_best_model_and_accuracy(select_k_text_pipe,
                select_k_text_pipe_params,
                tweets_X, tweets_y)

Best Accuracy: 0.755703127344
Best Parameters: {'select_k__k': 10000}
Average Time to Fit (s): 6.927
Average Time to Score (s): 1.448
```

It seems that `SelectKBest` didn't do as well for text tokens, and without `FeatureUnion`, we were unable to compete with the previous chapter's accuracy scores. Either way, for both pipelines, it is worth noting that the time it takes to both fit and predict are extremely poor. This is because statistical univariate methods are not optimal for a very large number of features, such as the features obtained from text vectorization.

Using machine learning to select features

Using `CountVectorizer` built-in feature selection tools is great when you are dealing with text; however, we are usually dealing with data already built into a row/column structure. We've seen the power of using purely statistical methodology for feature selection, and now let's see how we can invoke the awesome power of machine learning to, hopefully, do even more. The two main machine learning models that we will use in this section for the purposes of feature selection are tree-based models and linear models. They both have a notion of feature ranking that are useful when subsetting feature sets.

Before we go further, we believe it is worth mentioning again that these methods, while different in their methodology of selection, are attempting to find the optimal subset of features to improve our machine learning pipelines. The first method we will dive into will involve the internal importance metrics that algorithms such as decision trees and random forest models generate whilst fitting to training data.

Tree-based model feature selection metrics

When fitting decision trees, the tree starts at the root node and greedily chooses the optimal split at every junction that optimizes a certain metric of **node purity**. By default, scikit-learn optimizes for the **gini** metric at every step. While each split is created, the model keeps track of how much each split helps the overall optimization goal. In doing so, tree-based models that choose splits based on such metrics have a notion of **feature importance**.

To illustrate this further, let's go ahead and fit a decision tree to our data and output the feature importance' with the help of the following code:

```
# create a brand new decision tree classifier
tree = DecisionTreeClassifier()

tree.fit(X, y)
```

Once our tree has fit to the data, we can call on the `feature_importances_` attribute to capture the importance of the feature, relative to the fitting of the tree:

```
# note that we have some other features in play besides what our last two
selectors decided for us

importances = pd.DataFrame({'importance': tree.feature_importances_,
'feature':X.columns}).sort_values('importance', ascending=False)

importances.head()
```

The preceding code produces the following table as the output:

	feature	importance
5	PAY_0	0.161829
4	AGE	0.074121
11	BILL_AMT1	0.064363
0	LIMIT_BAL	0.058788
19	PAY_AMT3	0.054911

What this table is telling us is that the most important feature while fitting was the column `PAY_0`, which matches up to what our statistical models were telling us earlier in this chapter. What is more notable are the second, third, and fifth most important features, as they didn't really show up before using our statistical tests. This is a good indicator that this method of feature selection might yield some new results for us.

Recall that, earlier, we relied on a built in scikit-learn wrapper called SelectKBest to capture the top *k* features based on a ranking function like ANOVA p-values. We will introduce another similar style of wrapper called `SelectFromModel` which, like `SelectKBest`, will capture the top k most importance features. However, it will do so by listening to a machine learning model's internal metric for feature importance rather than the p-values of a statistical test. We will use the following code to define the `SelectFromModel`:

```
# similar to SelectKBest, but not with statistical tests
from sklearn.feature_selection import SelectFromModel
```

The biggest difference in usage between `SelectFromModel` and `SelectKBest` is that `SelectFromModel` doesn't take in an integer k, which represents the number of features to keep, but rather `SelectFromModel` uses a threshold for selection which acts as a hard minimum of importance to be selected. In this way, the model-based selectors of this chapter are able to move away from a human-inputted number of features to keep and instead rely on relative importance to include only as many features as the pipeline needs. Let's instantiate our class as follows:

```
# instantiate a class that choses features based
# on feature importances according to the fitting phase
# of a separate decision tree classifier
select_from_model = SelectFromModel(DecisionTreeClassifier(),
 threshold=.05)
```

Let's fit this `SelectFromModel` class to our data and invoke the transform method to watch our data get subsetted, with the help of the following code:

```
selected_X = select_from_model.fit_transform(X, y)
selected_X.shape

(30000, 9)
```

Now that we know the basic mechanics of the module, let's use it to select features for us in a pipeline. Recall that the accuracy to beat is .8206, which we got both from our correlation chooser and our ANOVA test (because they both returned the same features):

```
# to speed things up a bit in the future
tree_pipe_params = {'classifier__max_depth': [1, 3, 5, 7]}

from sklearn.pipeline import Pipeline

# create a SelectFromModel that is tuned by a DecisionTreeClassifier
select = SelectFromModel(DecisionTreeClassifier())

select_from_pipe = Pipeline([('select', select),
                             ('classifier', d_tree)])

select_from_pipe_params = deepcopy(tree_pipe_params)

select_from_pipe_params.update({
 'select__threshold': [.01, .05, .1, .2, .25, .3, .4, .5, .6, "mean",
"median", "2.*mean"],
 'select__estimator__max_depth': [None, 1, 3, 5, 7]
 })

print select_from_pipe_params  # {'select__threshold': [0.01, 0.05, 0.1,
```

```
'mean', 'median', '2.*mean'], 'select__estimator__max_depth': [None, 1, 3,
5, 7], 'classifier__max_depth': [1, 3, 5, 7]}


get_best_model_and_accuracy(select_from_pipe,
 select_from_pipe_params,
 X, y)


# not better than original
Best Accuracy: 0.820266666667
Best Parameters: {'select__threshold': 0.01,
'select__estimator__max_depth': None, 'classifier__max_depth': 3}
Average Time to Fit (s): 0.192
Average Time to Score (s): 0.002
```

Note first that, as part of the threshold parameter, we are able to include some reserved words rather than a float that represents the minimum importance to use. For example, the threshold of mean only selects features with an importance that is higher than average. Similarly, a value of median as a threshold only selects features that are more important than the median value. We may also include multiples to these reserved words so that 2.*mean will only include features that are more important than twice the mean importance value.

Let's take a peak as to which features our decision tree-based selector is choosing for us. We can do this by invoking a method within SelectFromModel called get_support(). It will return an array of Booleans, one for each original feature column, and tell us which of the features it decided to keep, as follows:

```
# set the optimal params to the pipeline
select_from_pipe.set_params(**{'select__threshold': 0.01,
 'select__estimator__max_depth': None,
 'classifier__max_depth': 3})


# fit our pipeline to our data
select_from_pipe.steps[0][1].fit(X, y)


# list the columns that the SVC selected by calling the get_support()
method from SelectFromModel
X.columns[select_from_pipe.steps[0][1].get_support()]


[u'LIMIT_BAL', u'SEX', u'EDUCATION', u'MARRIAGE', u'AGE', u'PAY_0',
u'PAY_2', u'PAY_3', u'PAY_6', u'BILL_AMT1', u'BILL_AMT2', u'BILL_AMT3',
u'BILL_AMT4', u'BILL_AMT5', u'BILL_AMT6', u'PAY_AMT1', u'PAY_AMT2',
u'PAY_AMT3', u'PAY_AMT4', u'PAY_AMT5', u'PAY_AMT6']
```

Wow! So the tree decided to keep all but two features, and still only did just as good as the tree did without selecting anything:

 For more information on decision trees and how they are fit using gini or entropy, look into the scikit-learn documentation or other texts that handle this topic in more depth.

We could continue onward by trying several other tree-based models, such as RandomForest, ExtraTreesClassifier, and others, but perhaps we may be able to do better by utilizing a model other than a tree-based model.

Linear models and regularization

The `SelectFromModel` selector is able to handle any machine learning model that exposes a `feature_importances_` or `coef_` attribute post-fitting. Tree-based models expose the former, while linear models expose the latter. After fitting, linear models such as Linear Regression, Logistic Regression, Support Vector Machines, and others all place coefficients in front of features that represent the slope of that feature/how much it affects the response when that feature is changed. `SelectFromModel` can equate this to a feature importance and choose features based on the coefficients given to features while fitting.

Before we can use these models, however, we must introduce a concept called **regularization**, which will help us select truly only the most important features.

A brief introduction to regularization

In linear models, **regularization** is a method for imposing additional constraints to a learning model, where the goal is to prevent overfitting and improve the generalization of the data. This is done by adding extra terms to the *loss function* being optimized, meaning that, while fitting, regularized linear models may severely diminish, or even destroy features along the way. There are two widely used regularization methods, called L1 and L2 regularization. Both regularization techniques rely on the L-p Norm, which is defined for a vector as being:

$$L^{p}\left(x\right) = ||x||_{p} = \sqrt[1/p]{\sum_{k=1}^{n} |x_{k}|^{p}}$$

- **L1 regularization**, also known as **lasso** regularization, uses the L1 Norm, which, using the above formula, reduces to the sum of the absolute values of the entries of a vector to limit the coefficients in such a way that they may disappear entirely and become 0. If the coefficient of a feature drops to 0, then that feature will not have any say in the prediction of new data observations and definitely will not be chosen by a `SelectFromModel` selector.

- **L2 regularization**, also known as **ridge** regularization, imposes the L2 norm as a penalty (sum of the square of vector entries) so that coefficients cannot drop to 0, but they can become very, very tiny.

Regularization also helps with multicollinearity, the problem of having multiple features in a dataset that are linearly related to one another. A Lasso Penalty (L1) will force coefficients of dependent features to 0, ensuring that they aren't chosen by the selector module, helping combat overfitting.

Linear model coefficients as another feature importance metric

We can use L1 and L2 regularization to find optimal coefficients for our feature selection, just as we did with our tree-based models. Let's use a logistic regression model as our model-based selector and gridsearch across both the L1 and L2 norm:

```
# a new selector that uses the coefficients from a regularized logistic
regression as feature importances
logistic_selector = SelectFromModel(LogisticRegression())

# make a new pipeline that uses coefficients from LogistisRegression as a
feature ranker
regularization_pipe = Pipeline([('select', logistic_selector),
  ('classifier', tree)])

regularization_pipe_params = deepcopy(tree_pipe_params)

# try l1 regularization and l2 regularization
regularization_pipe_params.update({
  'select__threshold': [.01, .05, .1, "mean", "median", "2.*mean"],
  'select__estimator__penalty': ['l1', 'l2'],
  })

print regularization_pipe_params  # {'select__threshold': [0.01, 0.05, 0.1,
'mean', 'median', '2.*mean'], 'classifier__max_depth': [1, 3, 5, 7],
'select__estimator__penalty': ['l1', 'l2']}
```

```
get_best_model_and_accuracy(regularization_pipe,
 regularization_pipe_params,
 X, y)


# better than original, in fact the best so far, and much faster on the
scoring side
Best Accuracy: 0.821166666667 Best Parameters: {'select__threshold': 0.01,
'classifier__max_depth': 5, 'select__estimator__penalty': 'l1'}
Average Time to Fit (s): 0.51
Average Time to Score (s): 0.001
```

Finally! We got an accuracy better than our statistical testing selector. Let's see which features our model-based selector decided to keep by invoking the `get_support()` method of `SelectFromModel` again:

```
# set the optimal params to the pipeline
regularization_pipe.set_params(**{'select__threshold': 0.01,
 'classifier__max_depth': 5,
 'select__estimator__penalty': 'l1'})

# fit our pipeline to our data
regularization_pipe.steps[0][1].fit(X, y)

# list the columns that the Logisti Regression selected by calling the
get_support() method from SelectFromModel
X.columns[regularization_pipe.steps[0][1].get_support()]

[u'SEX', u'EDUCATION', u'MARRIAGE', u'PAY_0', u'PAY_2', u'PAY_3', u'PAY_4',
u'PAY_5']
```

Fascinating! Our logistic regression based selector kept most of the PAY_X columns but was also able to figure out that the sex, education, and marriage status of the person was going to play a hand in prediction. Let's continue our adventure by using one more model with our `SelectFromModel` selector module, a support vector machine classifier.

If you are unfamiliar with support vector machines, they are classification models that attempt to draw linear boundaries in space to separate binary labels. These linear boundaries are known as support vectors. For now, the most important difference between logistic regression and support vector classifiers are that SVCs are usually better equipped to optimize coefficients for maximizing accuracy for binary classification tasks, while logistic regression is better at modeling the probabilistic attributes of binary classification tasks. Let's implement a Linear SVC model from scikit-learn as we did for decision trees and logistic regression and see how it fares, using the following code:

```
# SVC is a linear model that uses linear supports to
# seperate classes in euclidean space
# This model can only work for binary classification tasks
from sklearn.svm import LinearSVC

# Using a support vector classifier to get coefficients
svc_selector = SelectFromModel(LinearSVC())

svc_pipe = Pipeline([('select', svc_selector),
  ('classifier', tree)])

svc_pipe_params = deepcopy(tree_pipe_params)

svc_pipe_params.update({
  'select__threshold': [.01, .05, .1, "mean", "median", "2.*mean"],
  'select__estimator__penalty': ['l1', 'l2'],
  'select__estimator__loss': ['squared_hinge', 'hinge'],
  'select__estimator__dual': [True, False]
  })

print svc_pipe_params  # 'select__estimator__loss': ['squared_hinge',
'hinge'], 'select__threshold': [0.01, 0.05, 0.1, 'mean', 'median',
'2.*mean'], 'select__estimator__penalty': ['l1', 'l2'],
'classifier__max_depth': [1, 3, 5, 7], 'select__estimator__dual': [True,
False]}

get_best_model_and_accuracy(svc_pipe,
  svc_pipe_params,
  X, y)


# better than original, in fact the best so far, and much faster on the
scoring side
Best Accuracy: 0.821233333333
Best Parameters: {'select__estimator__loss': 'squared_hinge',
'select__threshold': 0.01, 'select__estimator__penalty': 'l1',
'classifier__max_depth': 5, 'select__estimator__dual': False}
```

```
Average Time to Fit (s): 0.989
Average Time to Score (s): 0.001
```

Great! The best accuracy we've gotten so far. We can see that the fitting time took a hit but if we are OK with that, couple the best accuracy so far with an outstandingly quick predicting time and we've got a great machine learning pipeline on our hands; one that leverages the power of regularization in the context of support vector classification to feed significant features into a decision tree classifier. Let's see which features our selector chose to give us our best accuracy to date:

```
# set the optimal params to the pipeline
svc_pipe.set_params(**{'select__estimator__loss': 'squared_hinge',
 'select__threshold': 0.01,
 'select__estimator__penalty': 'l1',
 'classifier__max_depth': 5,
 'select__estimator__dual': False})

# fit our pipeline to our data
svc_pipe.steps[0][1].fit(X, y)

# list the columns that the SVC selected by calling the get_support()
method from SelectFromModel
X.columns[svc_pipe.steps[0][1].get_support()]

[u'SEX', u'EDUCATION', u'MARRIAGE', u'PAY_0', u'PAY_2', u'PAY_3', u'PAY_5']
```

The only difference between these features and what our logistic regression got was the PAY_4 column. But we can see that even removing a single column can affect our entire pipeline's performance.

Choosing the right feature selection method

At this point, you may be feeling a bit overwhelmed with the information in this chapter. We have presented several ways of performing feature selection, some based on pure statistics and others based on the output of secondary machine learning models. It is natural to wonder how to decide which feature selection method is right for your data. In theory, if you are able to try multiple options, as we did in this chapter, that would be ideal, but we understand that it might not be feasible to do so. The following are some rules of thumbs that you can follow when you are trying to prioritize which feature selection module is more likely to offer greater results:

- If your features are mostly categorical, you should start by trying to implement a SelectKBest with a Chi^2 ranker or a tree-based model selector.

- If your features are largely quantitative (like ours were), using linear models as model-based selectors and relying on correlations tends to yield greater results, as was shown in this chapter.
- If you are solving a binary classification problem, using a Support Vector Classification model along with a `SelectFromModel` selector will probably fit nicely, as the SVC tries to find coefficients to optimize for binary classification tasks.
- A little bit of EDA can go a long way in manual feature selection. The importance of having domain knowledge in the domain from which the data originated cannot be understated.

That being said, these are meant only to be used as guidelines. As a data scientist, ultimately you decide which features you wish to keep to optimize the metric of your choosing. The methods that we provide in this text are here to help you in your discovery of the latent power of features hidden by noise and multicollinearity.

Summary

In this chapter, we learned a great deal about methodologies for selecting subsets of features in order to increase the performance of our machine learning pipelines in both a predictive capacity as well in-time-complexity.

The dataset that we chose had a relatively low number of features. If selecting, however, from a very large set of features (over a hundred), then the methods in this chapter will likely start to become entirely too cumbersome. We saw that in this chapter, when attempting to optimize a `CountVectorizer` pipeline, the time it would take to run a univariate test on every feature is not only astronomical; we would run a greater risk of experiencing multicollinearity in our features by sheer coincidence.

In the next chapter, we will introduce purely mathematical transformations that we may apply to our data matrices in order to alleviate the trouble of working with vast quantities of features, or even a few highly uninterpretable features. We will begin to work with datasets that stray away from what we have seen before, such as image data, topic modeling data, and more.

6
Feature Transformations

So far, in this text, we have encountered feature engineering tools from what seems like all possible angles of data. From analyzing tabular data in order to ascertain levels of data to constructing and selecting columns using statistical measures in order to optimize our machine learning pipelines, we have been on a remarkable journey of dealing with features in our data.

It is worth mentioning once more that enhancements of machine learning come in many forms. We generally consider our two main metrics as accuracy and prediction/fit times. This means that if we can utilize feature engineering tools to make our pipeline have higher accuracy in a cross-validated setting, or be able to fit and/or predict data quicker, then we may consider that a success. Of course, our ultimate hope is to optimize for both accuracy and time, giving us a much better pipeline to work with.

The past five chapters have dealt with what is considered classical feature engineering. We have looked at five main categories/steps in feature engineering so far:

- **Exploratory data analysis**: In the beginning of our work with machine learning pipelines, before even touching machine learning algorithms or feature engineering tools, it is encouraged to perform some basic descriptive statistics on our datasets and create visualizations to better understand the nature of the data
- **Feature understanding**: Once we have a sense of the size and shape of the data, we should take a closer look at each of the columns in our dataset (if possible) and outline characteristics, including the level of data, as that will dictate how to clean specific columns if necessary
- **Feature improvement**: This phase is about altering data values and entire columns by imputing missing values depending on the level of the columns and performing dummy variable transformations and scaling operations if possible

- **Feature construction**: Once we have the best possible dataset at our disposal, we can think about constructing new columns to account for feature interaction
- **Feature selection**: In the selection phase of our pipeline, we take all original and constructed columns and perform (usually univariate) statistical tests in order to isolate the best performing columns for the purpose of removing noise and speeding up calculations

The following figure sums up this procedure and shows us how to think about each step in the process:

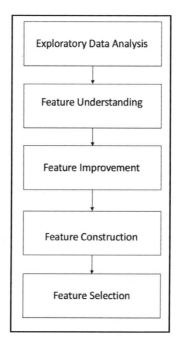

Machine learning pipeline

This is an example of a machine learning pipeline using methods from earlier in this text. It consists of five main steps: analysis, understanding, improvement, construction, and selection. In the upcoming chapters, we will be focusing on a new method of transforming data that partly breaks away from this classical notion.

At this stage of the book, the reader is more than ready to start tackling the datasets of the world with reasonable confidence and expectations of performance. The following two `Chapters 6`, *Feature Transformations*, and `Chapter 7`, *Feature Learning*, will focus on two subsets of feature engineering that are quite heavy in both programming and mathematics, specifically linear algebra. We will, as always, do our best to explain all lines of code used in this chapter and only describe mathematical procedures where necessary.

This chapter will deal with **feature transformations**, a suite of algorithms designed to alter the internal structure of data to produce mathematically superior *super-columns*, while the following chapter will focus on feature learning using non-parametric algorithms (those that do not depend on the shape of the data) to automatically learn new features. The final chapter of this text contains several worked out case studies to show the end-to-end process of feature engineering and its effects on machine learning pipelines.

For now, let us begin with our discussion of feature transformation. As we mentioned before, feature transformations are a set of matrix algorithms that will structurally alter our data and produce what is essentially a brand new matrix of data. The basic idea is that original features of a dataset are the descriptors/characteristics of data-points and we should be able to create a new set of features that explain the data-points just as well, perhaps even better, with fewer columns.

Imagine a simple, rectangular room. The room is empty except for a single mannequin standing in the center. The mannequin never moves and is always facing the same way. You have been charged with the task of monitoring that room 24/7. Of course, you come up with the idea of adding security cameras to the room to make sure that all activity is captured and recorded. You place a single camera in a top corner of the room, facing down to look at the face of the mannequin and, in the process, catch a large part of the room on camera. With one camera, you are able to see virtually all aspects of the room. The problem is that the camera has blind spots. For example, you won't be able to see directly below the camera (due to its physical inability to see there) and behind the mannequin (as the dummy itself is blocking the camera's view). Being brilliant, you add a second camera to the opposite top corner, behind the mannequin, to compensate for the blind spots of the first camera. Using two cameras, you can now see greater than 99% of the room from a security office.

In this example, the room represents the original feature space of data and the mannequin represents a data-point, standing at a certain section of the feature space. More formally, I'm asking you to consider a three-dimensional feature space with a single data-point:

$$[X, Y, Z]$$

To try and capture this data-point with a single camera is like squashing down our dataset to have only one new dimension, namely, the data seen by camera one:

$$[X, Y, Z] \approx [C1]$$

However, only using one dimension likely will not be enough, as we were able to conceive blind spots for that single camera so we added a second camera:

$$[X, Y, Z] \approx [C1, C2]$$

These two cameras (new dimensions produced by feature transformations) capture the data in a new way, but give us enough of the information we needed with only two columns instead of three. The toughest part of feature transformations is the suspension of our belief that the original feature space is the best. We must be open to the fact that there may be other mathematical axes and systems that describe our data just as well with fewer features, or possibly even better.

Dimension reduction – feature transformations versus feature selection versus feature construction

In the last section, I mentioned how we could squish datasets to have fewer columns to describe data in new ways. This sounds similar to the concept of feature selection: removing columns from our original dataset to create a different, potentially better, views of our dataset by cutting out the noise and enhancing signal columns. While both feature selection and feature transformation are methods of performing dimension reduction, it is worth mentioning that they could not be more different in their methodologies.

Feature selection processes are limited to only being able to select features from the original set of columns, while feature transformation algorithms use these original columns and combine them in useful ways to create new columns that are better at describing the data than any single column from the original dataset. Therefore, feature selection methods reduce dimensions by isolating signal columns and ignoring noise columns.

Feature transformation methods create new columns using hidden structures in the original datasets to produce an entirely new, structurally different dataset. These algorithms create brand new columns that are so powerful that we only need a few of them to explain our entire dataset accurately.

We also mentioned that feature transformation works by producing new columns that capture the essence (variance) of the data. This is similar to the crux of feature construction: creating new features for the purpose of capturing latent structures in data. Again, we should mention that these two different processes achieve similar results using vastly different methods.

Feature construction is again limited to constructing new columns using simple operations (addition, multiplication, and so on) between a few columns at a time. This implies that any constructed features using classical feature construction are constructed using only a few columns from the original dataset at a time. If our goal is to create enough features to capture all possible feature interactions, that might take an absurd number of additional columns. For example, if given a dataset had 1,000 features or more, we would need to create tens of thousands of columns to construct enough features to capture even a subset of all possible feature interactions.

Feature transformation methods are able to utilize small bits of information from all columns in every new super-column, so we do not need to create an inordinate amount of new columns to capture latent feature interactions. Due to the nature of feature transformation algorithms and its use of matrixes/linear algebra, feature transformation methods never create more columns than we start with, and are still able to extract the latent structure that features construction columns attempt to extract.

Feature transformation algorithms are able to *construct* new features by *selecting* the best of all columns and combining this latent structure with a few brand new columns. In this way, we may consider feature transformation as one of the most powerful sets of algorithms that we will discuss in this text. That being said, it is time to introduce our first algorithm and dataset in the book: **Principal Components Analysis (PCA)** and the `iris` dataset.

Principal Component Analysis

Principal Component Analysis is a technique that takes datasets that have several correlated features and projects them onto a coordinate (axis) system that has fewer correlated features. These new, uncorrelated features (which I referred to before as a super-columns) are called **principal components**. The principal components serve as an alternative coordinate system to the original feature space that requires fewer features and captures as much variance as possible. If we refer back to our example with the cameras, the principal components are exemplified by the cameras themselves.

Put another way, the goal of the PCA is to identify patterns and latent structures within datasets in order to create new columns and use these columns instead of the original features. Just as in feature selection, if we start with a data matrix of size $n \times d$ where n is the number of observations and d is the number of original features, we are projecting this matrix onto a matrix of size $n \times k$ (where $k < d$).

Our principal components give rise to new columns that maximize the variance in our data. This means that each column is trying to explain the shape of our data. Principal components are ordered by variance explained so that the first principal component does the most to explain the variance of the data, while the second component does the second most to explain the variance of the data. The goal is to utilize as many components as we need in order to optimize the machine learning task, whether it be supervised or unsupervised learning:

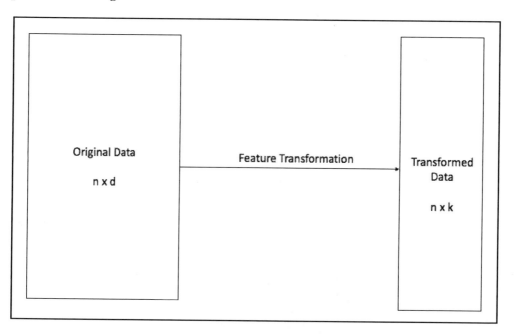

Feature transformation is about transforming datasets into matrices with the same number of rows with a reduced number of features. This is similar to the point of feature selection but in this case, we are concerned with the creation of brand new features.

PCA is itself an unsupervised task, meaning that it does not utilize a response column in order to make the projection/transformation. This matters because the second feature transformation algorithm that we will work with will be supervised and will utilize the response variable in order to create super-columns in a different way that optimizes predictive tasks.

How PCA works

A PCA works by invoking a process called the **eigenvalue decomposition** of the covariance of a matrix. The mathematics behind this was first published in the 1930s and involves a bit of multivariable calculus and linear algebra. For the purposes of this text, we will skip over that and get to the good part.

 PCA may also work on the correlation matrix. You may choose to use the correlation matrix if the features are on a similar scale while covariance matrices are more useful when using different scales. We generally recommend using the covariance matrix with scaled data.

This process happens in four steps:

1. Create the covariance matrix of the dataset
2. Calculate the eigenvalues of the covariance matrix
3. Keep the top k eigenvalues (sorted by the descending eigenvalues)
4. Use the kept eigenvectors to transform new data-points

Let's look at an example of this using a dataset called the `iris` dataset. In this fairly small dataset, we will take a look at a step by step performance of a PCA followed by the scikit-learn implementation.

PCA with the Iris dataset – manual example

The `iris` dataset consists of 150 rows and four columns. Each row/observation represents a single flower while the columns/features represent four different quantitative characteristics about the flower. The goal of the dataset is to fit a classifier that attempts to predict one of three types of `iris` given the four features. The flower may be considered either a setosa, a virginica, or a versicolor.

This dataset is so common in the field of machine learning instruction, scikit-learn has a built-in module for downloading the dataset:

1. Let's first import the module and then extract the dataset into a variable called `iris`:

```
# import the Iris dataset from scikit-learn
from sklearn.datasets import load_iris
# import our plotting module
import matplotlib.pyplot as plt
```

```
%matplotlib inline

# load the Iris dataset
iris = load_iris()
```

2. Now, let's store the extracted data matrix and response variables into two new variables, `iris_X` and `iris_y`, respectively:

```
# create X and y variables to hold features and response column
iris_X, iris_y = iris.data, iris.target
```

3. Let's take a look at the names of the flowers that we are trying to predict:

```
# the names of the flower we are trying to predict.
iris.target_names

array(['setosa', 'versicolor', 'virginica'], dtype='|S10')
```

4. Along with the names of the flowers, we can also look at the names of the features that we are utilizing to make these predictions:

```
# Names of the features
iris.feature_names

['sepal length (cm)',
 'sepal width (cm)',
 'petal length (cm)',
 'petal width (cm)']
```

5. To get a sense of what our data looks like, let's write some code that will display the data-points of two of the four features:

```
# for labelling
label_dict = {i: k for i, k in enumerate(iris.target_names)}
# {0: 'setosa', 1: 'versicolor', 2: 'virginica'}

def plot(X, y, title, x_label, y_label):
  ax = plt.subplot(111)
  for label,marker,color in zip(
  range(3),('^', 's', 'o'),('blue', 'red', 'green')):

    plt.scatter(x=X[:,0].real[y == label],
    y=X[:,1].real[y == label],
    color=color,
    alpha=0.5,
    label=label_dict[label]
    )
```

```
plt.xlabel(x_label)
plt.ylabel(y_label)

leg = plt.legend(loc='upper right', fancybox=True)
leg.get_frame().set_alpha(0.5)
plt.title(title)

plot(iris_X, iris_y, "Original Iris Data", "sepal length (cm)",
"sepal width (cm)")
```

The following is the output of the preceding code:

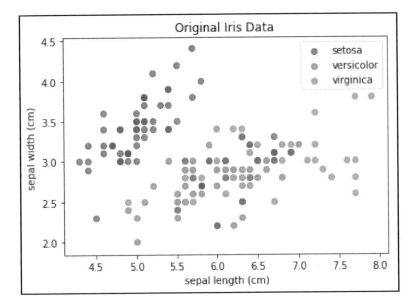

Let us now perform a PCA of the `iris` dataset in order to obtain our principal components. Recall that this happens in four steps.

Creating the covariance matrix of the dataset

To calculate the covariance matrix of `iris`, we will first calculate the feature-wise mean vector (for use in the future) and then calculate our covariance matrix using NumPy.

The covariance matrix is a *d x d* matrix (square matrix with the same number of features as the number of rows and columns) that represents feature interactions between each feature. It is quite similar to a correlation matrix:

```
# Calculate a PCA manually

# import numpy
import numpy as np

# calculate the mean vector
mean_vector = iris_X.mean(axis=0)
print mean_vector
[ 5.84333333  3.054        3.75866667  1.19866667]

# calculate the covariance matrix
cov_mat = np.cov((iris_X-mean_vector).T)
print cov_mat.shape
(4, 4)
```

The variable cov_mat stores our 4 x 4 covariance matrix.

Calculating the eigenvalues of the covariance matrix

NumPy is a handy function that computes eigenvectors and eigenvalues that we can use in order to get the principal components of our iris dataset:

```
# calculate the eigenvectors and eigenvalues of our covariance matrix of
the iris dataset
eig_val_cov, eig_vec_cov = np.linalg.eig(cov_mat)

# Print the eigen vectors and corresponding eigenvalues
# in order of descending eigenvalues
for i in range(len(eig_val_cov)):
 eigvec_cov = eig_vec_cov[:,i]
 print 'Eigenvector {}: \n{}'.format(i+1, eigvec_cov)
 print 'Eigenvalue {} from covariance matrix: {}'.format(i+1,
eig_val_cov[i])
 print 30 * '-'

Eigenvector 1:
[ 0.36158968 -0.08226889  0.85657211  0.35884393]
Eigenvalue 1 from covariance matrix: 4.22484076832
------------------------------
Eigenvector 2:
[-0.65653988 -0.72971237  0.1757674   0.07470647]
Eigenvalue 2 from covariance matrix: 0.242243571628
```

```
---------------------------
Eigenvector 3:
[-0.58099728  0.59641809  0.07252408  0.54906091]
Eigenvalue 3 from covariance matrix: 0.0785239080942
---------------------------
Eigenvector 4:
[ 0.31725455 -0.32409435 -0.47971899  0.75112056]
Eigenvalue 4 from covariance matrix: 0.023683027126
---------------------------
```

Keeping the top *k* eigenvalues (sorted by the descending eigenvalues)

Now that we have our four eigenvalues, we will choose the appropriate number of them to keep to consider them principal components. We can choose all four if we wish, but we generally wish to choose a number less than the original number of features. But what is the right number? We could grid search and find the answer using the brute-force method, however, we have another tool in our arsenal, called the **scree plot**.

A scree plot is a simple line graph that shows the percentage of total variance explained in the data by each principal component. To build this plot, we will sort the eigenvalues in order of descending value and plot the *cumulative* variance explained by each component and all components prior. In the case of `iris`, we will have four points on our scree plot, one for each principal component. Each component on its own explains a percentage of the total variance captured, and all components, when the percentages are added up, should account for 100% of the total variance in the dataset.

Let's calculate the percentage of variance explained by each eigenvector (principal component) by taking the eigenvalue associated with that eigenvector and dividing it by the sum of all eigenvalues:

```
# the percentages of the variance captured by each eigenvalue
# is equal to the eigenvalue of that components divided by
# the sum of all eigen values

explained_variance_ratio = eig_val_cov/eig_val_cov.sum()
explained_variance_ratio

array([ 0.92461621,  0.05301557,  0.01718514,  0.00518309])
```

What this is telling us is that our four principal components differ vastly in the amount of variance that they account for. The first principal component, as a single feature/column, is able to account for over 92% of the variance in the data. That is astonishing! This means that this single super-column theoretically can do nearly all of the work of the four original columns.

To visualize our scree plot, let's create a plot with the four principal components on the x axis and the cumulative variance explained on the y axis. For every data-point, the y position will represent the total percentage of variance explained using all principal components up until that one:

```
# Scree Plot

plt.plot(np.cumsum(explained_variance_ratio))
plt.title('Scree Plot')
plt.xlabel('Principal Component (k)')
plt.ylabel('% of Variance Explained <= k')
```

The following is the output of the preceding code:

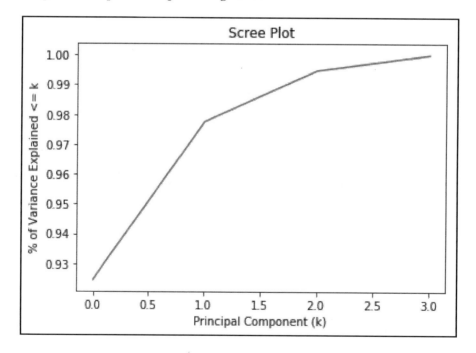

This is telling us that the first two components, by themselves, account for nearly 98% of the total variance of the original dataset, meaning that if we only used the first two eigenvectors and used them as our new principal components, then we would be in good shape. We would be able to shrink the size of our dataset by half (from four to two columns) while maintaining integrity in performance and speeding up performance. We will taking a closer look at examples of machine learning to validate these theoretical notions in the upcoming sections.

 An eigenvalue decomposition will always result in as many eigenvectors as we have features. It is up to us to choose how many principal components we wish to use once they are all calculated. This highlights the fact that PCA, like most other algorithms in this text, is semi-supervised and require some human input.

Using the kept eigenvectors to transform new data-points

Once we decide to keep two principal components (whether we use a grid search module or the analysis of a scree plot to find the optimal number doesn't matter), we have to be able to use these components to transform incoming, out of sample data-points. To do this, let's first isolate the top two eigenvectors and store them in a new variable called `top_2_eigenvectors`:

```
# store the top two eigenvectors in a variable
top_2_eigenvectors = eig_vec_cov[:,:2].T

# show the transpose so that each row is a principal component, we have two
rows == two components
top_2_eigenvectors

array([[ 0.36158968, -0.08226889,  0.85657211,  0.35884393],
       [-0.65653988, -0.72971237,  0.1757674 ,  0.07470647]])
```

This array represents the top two eigenvectors:

- [0.36158968, -0.08226889, 0.85657211, 0.35884393]
- [-0.65653988, -0.72971237, 0.1757674 , 0.07470647]]

With these vectors in place, we can use them to project our data into the new and improved super-dataset by multiplying the two matrices together: `iris_X` and `top_2_eigenvectors`. The following image shows us how we are going to make sure that the numbers work out:

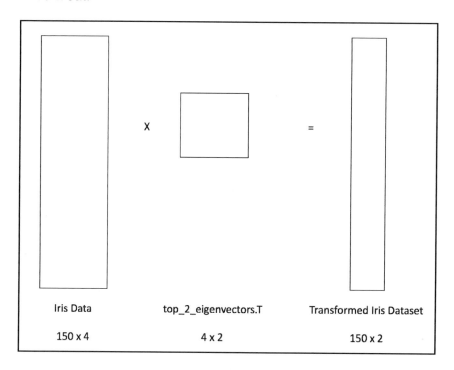

The preceding figure shows how to utilize principal components to transform datasets from their original feature spaces to the new coordinate systems. In the case of `iris`, we take our original 150 x 4 dataset and multiply it by the transpose of the top two eigenvectors. We utilize the transpose to ensure that the matrix sizes match up. The result is a matrix with the same number of rows but a reduced number of columns. Each row is multiplied by the two principal components.

By multiplying these matrices together, we are *projecting* our original dataset onto this new space of two dimensions:

```
# to transform our data from having shape (150, 4) to (150, 2)
# we will multiply the matrices of our data and our eigen vectors together

np.dot(iris_X, top_2_eigenvectors.T)[:5,]

array([[ 2.82713597, -5.64133105],
       [ 2.79595248, -5.14516688],
       [ 2.62152356, -5.17737812],
       [ 2.7649059 , -5.00359942],
       [ 2.78275012, -5.64864829]])
```

And that's it. We have transformed our four-dimensional iris data into a new matrix with only two columns. This new matrix may serve in place of the original dataset in our machine learning pipeline.

Scikit-learn's PCA

As usual, scikit-learn saves the day by implementing this procedure in an easy to use transformer so that we don't have to go through that manual process each time we wish to use this powerful process:

1. We can import it from scikit-learn's decomposition module:

```
# scikit-learn's version of PCA
from sklearn.decomposition import PCA
```

2. To mimic the process we performed with the `iris` dataset, let's instantiate a PCA object with only two components:

```
# Like any other sklearn module, we first instantiate the class
pca = PCA(n_components=2)
```

3. Now, we can fit our PCA to the data:

```
# fit the PCA to our data
pca.fit(iris_X)
```

4. Let's take a look at some of the attributes of the PCA object to see if they match up with what we achieved in our manual process. Let's take a look at the `components_` attribute of our object to see if this matches up without the `top_2_eigenvectors` variable:

```
pca.components_

array([[ 0.36158968, -0.08226889,  0.85657211,  0.35884393],
       [ 0.65653988,  0.72971237, -0.1757674 , -0.07470647]])

# note that the second column is the negative of the manual process
# this is because eignevectors can be positive or negative
# It should have little to no effect on our machine learning
pipelines
```

5. Our two components match, almost exactly, our previous variable, `top_2_eigenvectors`. We say almost because the second component is actually the negative of the eigenvector we calculated. This is fine because, mathematically, both eigenvectors are 100% valid and still achieve the primary goal of creating uncorrelated columns.

6. So far, this process is much less painful than what we were doing before. To complete the process, we need to use the transform method of the PCA object to project data onto our new two-dimensional plane:

```
pca.transform(iris_X)[:5,]

array([[-2.68420713,  0.32660731],
       [-2.71539062, -0.16955685],
       [-2.88981954, -0.13734561],
       [-2.7464372 , -0.31112432],
       [-2.72859298,  0.33392456]])

# sklearn PCA centers the data first while transforming, so these
numbers won't match our manual process.
```

 Notice that our projected data does not match up with the projected data we got before at all. This is because the scikit-learn version of PCA automatically centers data in the prediction phase, which changes the outcome.

7. We can mimic this by altering a single line in our version to match:

```
# manually centering our data to match scikit-learn's
implementation of PCA
np.dot(iris_X-mean_vector, top_2_eigenvectors.T)[:5,]

array([[-2.68420713, -0.32660731],
       [-2.71539062,  0.16955685],
       [-2.88981954,  0.13734561],
       [-2.7464372 ,  0.31112432],
       [-2.72859298, -0.33392456]])
```

8. Let's make a quick plot of the projected `iris` data and compare what the dataset looks like before and after projecting onto our new coordinate system:

```
# Plot the original and projected data
plot(iris_X, iris_y, "Original Iris Data", "sepal length (cm)",
"sepal width (cm)")
plt.show()
plot(pca.transform(iris_X), iris_y, "Iris: Data projected onto
first two PCA components", "PCA1", "PCA2")
```

The following is the output of the preceding code:

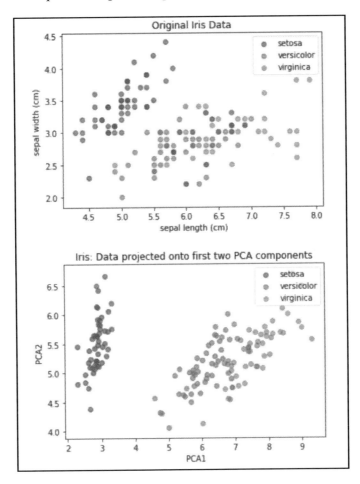

In our original dataset, we can see the irises in their original feature space along the first two columns. Notice that in our projected space, the flowers are much more separated from one another and also rotated on their axis a bit. It looks like the data clusters are *standing upright*. This phenomenon is because our principal components are working to capture variance in our data, and it shows in our plots.

We can extract the amount of variance explained by each component as we did in our manual example:

```
# percentage of variance in data explained by each component
# same as what we calculated earlier
pca.explained_variance_ratio_

array([ 0.92461621,  0.05301557])
```

Now, that we can perform all of the basic functions with scikit-learn's PCA, let's use this information to display one of the main benefits of PCA: de-correlating features.

By nature, in the eigenvalue decomposition procedure, the resulting principal components are perpendicular to each other, meaning that they are linearly independent of one another.

This is a major benefit because many machine learning models and preprocessing techniques make the assumption that inputted features are independent, and utilizing PCA ensures this for us.

To show this, let's create the correlation matrix of the original `iris` dataset and find the average linear correlation coefficient between each of the features. Then, we will do the same for a PCA projected dataset and compare the values. We expect that the average correlation of the projected dataset should be much closer to zero, implying that they are all linearly independent.

Let's begin by calculating the correlation matrix of the original `iris` dataset:

1. It will be a 4 x 4 matrix where the values represent the correlation coefficient of every feature versus each other:

    ```
    # show how pca attempts to eliminate dependence between columns

    # show the correlation matrix of the original dataset
    np.corrcoef(iris_X.T)


    array([[ 1.        ,  -0.10936925,  0.87175416,  0.81795363],
    ```

```
       [-0.10936925,  1.          ,  -0.4205161 ,  -0.35654409],
       [ 0.87175416, -0.4205161 ,  1.          ,   0.9627571 ],
       [ 0.81795363, -0.35654409,  0.9627571 ,   1.          ]])
```

2. We will then extract all values above the diagonal of 1s to use them to find the average correlation between all of the features:

```
# correlation coefficients above the diagonal
np.corrcoef(iris_X.T)[[0, 0, 0, 1, 1], [1, 2, 3, 2, 3]]
```

```
array([-0.10936925, 0.87175416, 0.81795363, -0.4205161 ,
-0.35654409])
```

3. Finally, we will take the mean of this array:

```
# average correlation of original iris dataset.
np.corrcoef(iris_X.T)[[0, 0, 0, 1, 1], [1, 2, 3, 2, 3]].mean()
```

```
0.16065567094168495
```

4. The average correlation coefficient of the original features is .16, which is pretty small, but definitely not zero. Now, let's create a full PCA that captures all four principal components:

```
# capture all four principal components
full_pca = PCA(n_components=4)

# fit our PCA to the iris dataset
full_pca.fit(iris_X)
```

5. Once we've done this, we will use the same method as before and calculate the average correlation coefficient between the new, supposedly linearly independent columns:

```
pca_iris = full_pca.transform(iris_X)
# average correlation of PCAed iris dataset.
np.corrcoef(pca_iris.T)[[0, 0, 0, 1, 1], [1, 2, 3, 2, 3]].mean()
# VERY close to 0 because columns are independent from one another
# This is an important consequence of performing an eigenvalue
decomposition
```

```
7.2640855025557061e-17 # very close to 0
```

This shows how data projected onto principal components end up having fewer correlated features, which is helpful in general in machine learning.

How centering and scaling data affects PCA

As with many of the transformations that we have worked with previously in this text, the scaling of features tends to matter a great deal to the transformations. PCA is no different. Previously, we mentioned that the scikit-learn version of PCA automatically centers data in the prediction phase, but why doesn't it do so at the fitting time? If the scikit-learn PCA module goes through the trouble of centering data in the predict method, why doesn't it do so while calculating the eigenvectors? The hypothesis here is that centering data doesn't affect the principal components. Let's test this:

1. Let's import out `StandardScaler` module from scikit-learn and center the `iris` dataset:

```
# import our scaling module
from sklearn.preprocessing import StandardScaler
# center our data, not a full scaling
X_centered = StandardScaler(with_std=False).fit_transform(iris_X)

X_centered[:5,]

array([[-0.74333333, 0.446 , -2.35866667, -0.99866667],
[-0.94333333, -0.054 , -2.35866667, -0.99866667], [-1.14333333,
0.146 , -2.45866667, -0.99866667], [-1.24333333, 0.046 ,
-2.25866667, -0.99866667], [-0.84333333, 0.546 , -2.35866667,
-0.99866667]])
```

2. Let's take a look at the now centered dataset:

```
# Plot our centered data
plot(X_centered, iris_y, "Iris: Data Centered", "sepal length
(cm)", "sepal width (cm)")
```

We get the following output for the code:

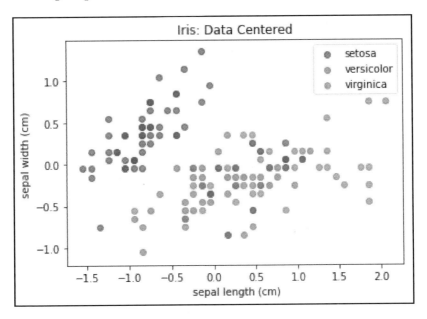

3. We can then fit the PCA class that we instanstiated before, with `n_components` set to 2, to our centered `iris` dataset:

```
# fit our PCA (with n_components still set to 2) on our centered
data
 pca.fit(X_centered)
```

4. Once this is done, we can call the `components_` attribute of the PCA module and compare the resulting principal components with the PCs that we got with the original `iris` dataset:

```
# same components as before
 pca.components_

 array([[ 0.36158968, -0.08226889, 0.85657211, 0.35884393], [
 0.65653988, 0.72971237, -0.1757674 , -0.07470647]])
```

5. It seems that the PCs that resulted from the centered data are exactly the same as the PCs that we saw earlier. To clarify this, let's transform the centered data using the PCA module and look at the first five rows and see if they match up with the previously obtained projection:

```
# same projection when data are centered because PCA does this
automatically
 pca.transform(X_centered)[:5,]

 array([[-2.68420713,  0.32660731],  [-2.71539062, -0.16955685],
 [-2.88981954, -0.13734561],  [-2.7464372 , -0.31112432],
 [-2.72859298,  0.33392456]])
```

6. The rows match up! If we look at the graph of the projected centered data and the explained variance ratios, we will that these also match up:

```
# Plot PCA projection of centered data, same as previous PCA
projected data
 plot(pca.transform(X_centered), iris_y, "Iris: Data projected onto
first two PCA components with centered data", "PCA1", "PCA2")
```

We get the following output:

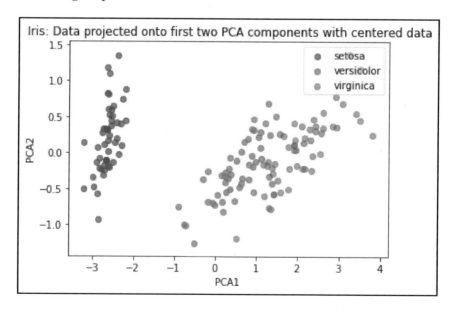

For percentage variance, we implement the following:

```
# percentage of variance in data explained by each component
pca.explained_variance_ratio_

array([ 0.92461621, 0.05301557])
```

The reason this is happening is because matrices have the same covariance matrix as their centered counterparts. If two matrices have the same covariance matrix, then they will have the same eigenvalue decomposition. This is why the scikit-learn version of PCA doesn't bother to center data while finding the eigenvalues and eigenvectors, because they would have found the same ones regardless of centering, so why add an extra, unnecessary step?

Now, let's take a look at what happens to our principal components when we scale data using standard z-score scaling:

```
# doing a normal z score scaling
X_scaled = StandardScaler().fit_transform(iris_X)

# Plot scaled data
plot(X_scaled, iris_y, "Iris: Data Scaled", "sepal length (cm)", "sepal
width (cm)")
```

We get the output, as follows:

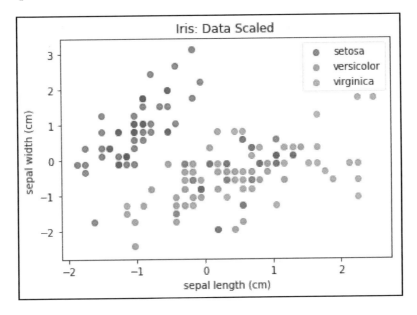

It is worth mentioning that at this point, we have plotted the iris data in its original format, centered, and now scaled completely. In each graph, the data-points are exactly the same, but the axes are different. This is expected. Centering and scaling data doesn't change the shape of the data, but it does effect feature interaction for our feature engineering and machine learning pipelines.

Let's fit our PCA module on our newly scaled data and see if our PCs are different:

```
# fit our 2-dimensional PCA on our scaled data
pca.fit(X_scaled)

# different components as cenetered data
pca.components_

array([[ 0.52237162, -0.26335492, 0.58125401, 0.56561105], [ 0.37231836,
0.92555649, 0.02109478, 0.06541577]])
```

These are different components, as before. PCA is scale-invariant, meaning that scale affects the components. Note that when we say scaling, we mean centering and dividing by the standard deviation. Let's project our dataset onto our new components and ensure that the newly projected data is indeed different:

```
# different projection when data are scaled
pca.transform(X_scaled)[:5,]

array([[-2.26454173, 0.5057039 ], [-2.0864255 , -0.65540473],
[-2.36795045, -0.31847731], [-2.30419716, -0.57536771], [-2.38877749,
0.6747674 ]])
```

Finally, let's take a look at our explained variance ratios:

```
# percentage of variance in data explained by each component
pca.explained_variance_ratio_

array([ 0.72770452, 0.23030523])
```

This is interesting. Scaling our data is usually a good idea when performing feature engineering/machine learning and usually we recommend it to our readers, but why does our first component have a much lower explained variance ratio than it did before?

It's because once we scaled our data, the columns' covariance with one another became more consistent and the variance explained by each principal component was spread out instead of being solidified in a single PC. In practice and production, we generally recommend scaling, but it is a good idea to test your pipeline's performance on both scaled and un-scaled data.

Let's top off this section with a look at the projected iris data on our scaled data:

```
# Plot PCA projection of scaled data
plot(pca.transform(X_scaled), iris_y, "Iris: Data projected onto first two
PCA components", "PCA1", "PCA2")
```

We get the following output:

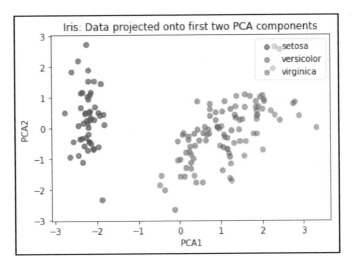

It is subtle, but if you look at this graph and compare it to the previous plots of projected data under the original and centered data, you will notice slight differences between them.

A deeper look into the principal components

Before we take a look at our second feature transformation algorithm, it is important to take a look at how principal components are interpreted:

1. Our `iris` dataset is a 150 x 4 matrix, and when we calculated our PCA components when `n_components` was set to 2, we obtained a components matrix of size 2 x 4:

    ```
    # how to interpret and use components
    pca.components_ # a 2 x 4 matrix

    array([[ 0.52237162, -0.26335492, 0.58125401, 0.56561105], [
    0.37231836, 0.92555649, 0.02109478, 0.06541577]])
    ```

2. Just like in our manual example of calculating eigenvectors, the `components_` attribute can be used to project data using matrix multiplication. We do so by multiplying our original dataset with the transpose of the `components_` matrix:

```
# Multiply original matrix (150 x 4) by components transposed (4 x
2) to get new columns (150 x 2)
np.dot(X_scaled, pca.components_.T)[:5,]
```

```
array([[-2.26454173, 0.5057039 ], [-2.0864255 , -0.65540473],
[-2.36795045, -0.31847731], [-2.30419716, -0.57536771],
[-2.38877749, 0.6747674 ]])
```

3. We invoke the transpose function here so that the matrix dimensions match up. What is happening at a low level is that for every row, we are calculating the dot product between the original row and each of the principal components. The results of the dot product become the elements of the new row:

```
# extract the first row of our scaled data
first_scaled_flower = X_scaled[0]

# extract the two PC's
first_Pc = pca.components_[0]
second_Pc = pca.components_[1]

first_scaled_flower.shape # (4,)
print first_scaled_flower # array([-0.90068117, 1.03205722,
-1.3412724 , -1.31297673])


# same result as the first row of our matrix multiplication
np.dot(first_scaled_flower, first_Pc), np.dot(first_scaled_flower,
second_Pc)

(-2.2645417283949003, 0.50570390277378274)
```

4. Luckily, we can rely on the built-in transform method to do this work for us:

```
# This is how the transform method works in pca
pca.transform(X_scaled)[:5,]

array([[-2.26454173, 0.5057039 ], [-2.0864255 , -0.65540473],
[-2.36795045, -0.31847731], [-2.30419716, -0.57536771],
[-2.38877749, 0.6747674 ]])
```

Put another way, we can interpret each component as being a combination of the original columns. In this case, our first principal component is:

```
[ 0.52237162, -0.26335492, 0.58125401, 0.56561105]
```

The first scaled flower is:

```
[-0.90068117, 1.03205722, -1.3412724 , -1.31297673]
```

To get the first element of the first row of our projected data, we can use the following formula:

$$(0.52237162 \times -0.90068117) + (-0.26335492 \times 1.03205722) + (0.58125401 \times -1.3412724) + (0.56561105 \times -1.31297673) = -2.264541736368$$

In fact, in general, for any flower with the coordinates (a, b, c, d), where a is the sepal length of the iris, b the sepal width, c the petal length, and d the petal width (this order was taken from `iris.feature_names` from before), the first value of the new coordinate system can be calculated by the following:

$$0.52237162a - 0.26335492b + 0.58125401c + 0.56561105d$$

Let's take this a step further and visualize the components in space alongside our data. We will truncate our original data to only keep two of its original features, sepal length and sepal width. The reason we are doing this is so that we can visualize the data easier without having to worry about four dimensions:

```python
# cut out last two columns of the original iris dataset
iris_2_dim = iris_X[:,2:4]

# center the data
iris_2_dim = iris_2_dim - iris_2_dim.mean(axis=0)

plot(iris_2_dim, iris_y, "Iris: Only 2 dimensions", "sepal length", "sepal width")
```

We get the output, as follows:

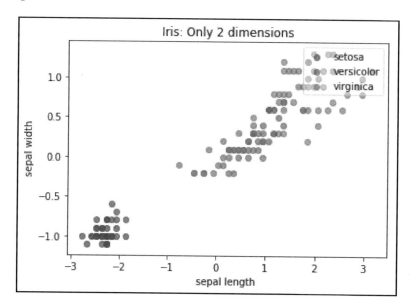

We can see a cluster of flowers (**setosas**) on the bottom left and a larger cluster of both **versicolor** and **virginicia** flowers on the top right. It appears obvious right away that the data, as a whole, is stretched along a diagonal line stemming from the bottom left to the top right. The hope is that our principal components also pick up on this and rearrange our data accordingly.

Let's instantiate a PCA class that keeps two principal components and then use that class to transform our truncated **iris data** into new columns:

```
# instantiate a PCA of 2 components
twodim_pca = PCA(n_components=2)

# fit and transform our truncated iris data
iris_2_dim_transformed = twodim_pca.fit_transform(iris_2_dim)

plot(iris_2_dim_transformed, iris_y, "Iris: PCA performed on only 2
dimensions", "PCA1", "PCA2")
```

We get the output, as follows:

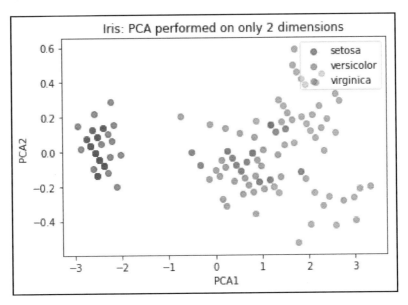

PCA 1, our first principal component, should be carrying the majority of the variance within it, which is why the projected data is spread out mostly across the new *x* axis. Notice how the scale of the *x* axis is between -3 and 3 while the *y* axis is only between -0.4 and 0.6. To further clarify this, the following code block will graph both the original and projected iris scatter plots, as well as an overlay the principal components of `twodim_pca` on top of them, in both the original coordinate system as well as the new coordinate system.

The goal is to interpret the components as being guiding vectors, showing the way in which the data is moving and showing how these guiding vectors become perpendicular coordinate systems:

```
# This code is graphing both the original iris data and the projected
version of it using PCA.
 # Moreover, on each graph, the principal components are graphed as vectors
on the data themselves
 # The longer of the arrows is meant to describe the first principal
component and
 # the shorter of the arrows describes the second principal component
def draw_vector(v0, v1, ax):
arrowprops=dict(arrowstyle='->',linewidth=2,
shrinkA=0, shrinkB=0)
ax.annotate('', v1, v0, arrowprops=arrowprops)
```

```
fig, ax = plt.subplots(2, 1, figsize=(10, 10))
fig.subplots_adjust(left=0.0625, right=0.95, wspace=0.1)

# plot data
ax[0].scatter(iris_2_dim[:, 0], iris_2_dim[:, 1], alpha=0.2)
for length, vector in zip(twodim_pca.explained_variance_,
twodim_pca.components_):
 v = vector * np.sqrt(length) # elongdate vector to match up to
explained_variance
 draw_vector(twodim_pca.mean_,
 twodim_pca.mean_ + v, ax=ax[0])
ax[0].set(xlabel='x', ylabel='y', title='Original Iris Dataset',
xlim=(-3, 3), ylim=(-2, 2))


ax[1].scatter(iris_2_dim_transformed[:, 0], iris_2_dim_transformed[:, 1],
alpha=0.2)
for length, vector in zip(twodim_pca.explained_variance_,
twodim_pca.components_):
 transformed_component = twodim_pca.transform([vector])[0] # transform
components to new coordinate system
 v = transformed_component * np.sqrt(length) # elongdate vector to match up
to explained_variance
 draw_vector(iris_2_dim_transformed.mean(axis=0),
 iris_2_dim_transformed.mean(axis=0) + v, ax=ax[1])
ax[1].set(xlabel='component 1', ylabel='component 2',
title='Projected Data',
xlim=(-3, 3), ylim=(-1, 1))
```

This is the **Original Iris Dataset** and **Projected Data** using PCA:

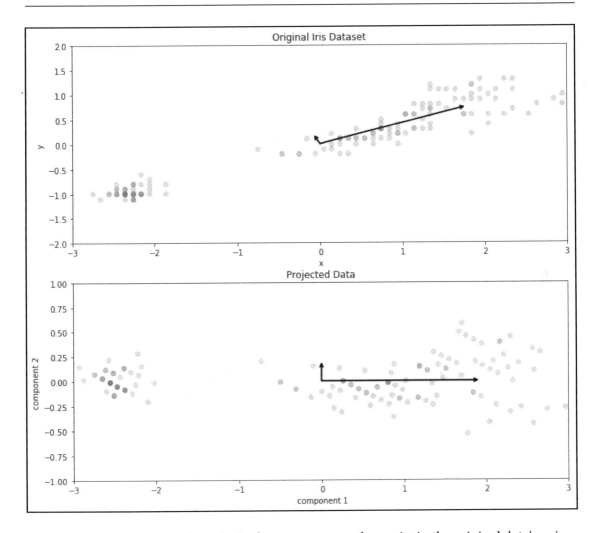

The top graph is showing the principal components as they exist in the original data's axis system. They are not perpendicular and they are pointing in the direction that the data naturally follows. We can see that the longer of the two vectors, the first principal component, is clearly following that diagonal direction that the iris data is following the most.

The secondary principal component is pointing in a direction of variance that explains a portion of the shape of the data, but not all of it. The bottom graph shows the projected iris data onto these new components accompanied by the same components, but acting as perpendicular coordinate systems. They have become the new x and y axes.

The PCA is a feature transformation tool that allows us to construct brand new super-features as linear combinations of previous features. We have seen that these components carry the maximum amount of variance within them, and act as new coordinate systems for our data. Our next feature transformation algorithm is similar in that it, too, will extract components from our data, but it does so in a machine learning-type manner.

Linear Discriminant Analysis

Linear Discriminant Analysis (LDA) is a feature transformation technique as well as a supervised classifier. It is commonly used as a preprocessing step for classification pipelines. The goal of LDA, like PCA, is to extract a new coordinate system and project datasets onto a lower-dimensional space. The main difference between LDA and PCA is that instead of focusing on the variance of the data as a whole like PCA, LDA optimizes the lower-dimensional space for the best class separability. This means that the new coordinate system is more useful in finding decision boundaries for classification models, which is perfect for us when building classification pipelines.

The reason that LDA is extremely useful is that separating based on class separability helps us avoid overfitting in our machine learning pipelines. This is also known as *preventing the curse of dimensionality*. LDA also reduces computational costs.

How LDA works

LDA works as a dimensionality reduction tool, just like PCA, however instead of calculating the eigenvalues of the covariance matrix of the data as a whole, LDA calculates eigenvalues and eigenvectors of within-class and between-class scatter matrices. Performing LDA can be broken down into five steps:

1. Calculate mean vectors of each class

2. Calculate within-class and between-class scatter matrices

3. Calculate eigenvalues and eigenvectors for $S_W^{-1} S_B$

4. Keep the top k eigenvectors by ordering them by descending eigenvalues

5. Use the top eigenvectors to project onto the new space

Let's look at an example.

Calculating the mean vectors of each class

First, we need to calculate a column-wise mean vector for each of our classes. One for setosa, one for versicolor, and another for virginica:

```
# calculate the mean for each class
# to do this we will separate the iris dataset into three dataframes
# one for each flower, then we will take one's mean columnwise
mean_vectors = []
for cl in [0, 1, 2]:
class_mean_vector = np.mean(iris_X[iris_y==cl], axis=0)
mean_vectors.append(class_mean_vector)
print label_dict[cl], class_mean_vector

setosa [ 5.006 3.418 1.464 0.244]
versicolor [ 5.936 2.77 4.26 1.326]
virginica [ 6.588 2.974 5.552 2.026]
```

Calculating within-class and between-class scatter matrices

We will now calculate a **within-class** scatter matrix, defined by the following:

$$S_W = \sum_{i=1}^{c} S_i$$

Where we define S_i as:

$$S_i = \sum_{x \in D_i}^{n} (x - m_i)(x - m_i)^T$$

Here, m_i represents the mean vector for the i class, and a **between-class scatter** matrix defined by the following:

$$S_B = \sum_{i=1}^{c} N_i (m_i - m)(m_i - m)^T$$

m is the overall mean of the dataset, m_i is the sample mean for each class, and N_i is the sample size for each class (number of observations per class):

```
# Calculate within-class scatter matrix
S_W = np.zeros((4,4))
# for each flower
for cl,mv in zip([0, 1, 2], mean_vectors):
# scatter matrix for every class, starts with all 0's
class_sc_mat = np.zeros((4,4))
# for each row that describes the specific flower
for row in iris_X[iris_y == cl]:
# make column vectors
row, mv = row.reshape(4,1), mv.reshape(4,1)
# this is a 4x4 matrix
class_sc_mat += (row-mv).dot((row-mv).T)
# sum class scatter matrices
S_W += class_sc_mat

S_W
```

```
array([[ 38.9562, 13.683 , 24.614 , 5.6556], [ 13.683 , 17.035 , 8.12 ,
4.9132], [ 24.614 , 8.12 , 27.22 , 6.2536], [ 5.6556, 4.9132, 6.2536,
6.1756]])
```

```
# calculate the between-class scatter matrix

# mean of entire dataset
overall_mean = np.mean(iris_X, axis=0).reshape(4,1)

# will eventually become between class scatter matrix
S_B = np.zeros((4,4))
for i,mean_vec in enumerate(mean_vectors):
# number of flowers in each species
n = iris_X[iris_y==i,:].shape[0]
# make column vector for each specied
mean_vec = mean_vec.reshape(4,1)
S_B += n * (mean_vec - overall_mean).dot((mean_vec - overall_mean).T)

S_B
```

```
array([[ 63.2121, -19.534 , 165.1647, 71.3631], [ -19.534 , 10.9776,
-56.0552, -22.4924], [ 165.1647, -56.0552, 436.6437, 186.9081], [ 71.3631,
-22.4924, 186.9081, 80.6041]])
```

Within-class and between-class scatter matrices are generalizations of a step in the ANOVA test (mentioned in the previous chapter). The idea here is to decompose our iris dataset into two distinct parts.

Once we have calculated these matrices, we can move onto the next step, which uses matrix algebra to extract linear discriminants.

Calculating eigenvalues and eigenvectors for $S_W^{-1}SB$

Just as we did in PCA, we rely on eigenvalue decompositions of a specific matrix. In the case of LDA, we will be decomposing the matrix $S_W^{-1} S_B$:

```
# calculate eigenvalues and eigenvectors of S-1W x SB
eig_vals, eig_vecs = np.linalg.eig(np.dot(np.linalg.inv(S_W), S_B))
eig_vecs = eig_vecs.real
eig_vals = eig_vals.real

for i in range(len(eig_vals)):
eigvec_sc = eig_vecs[:,i]
print 'Eigenvector {}: {}'.format(i+1, eigvec_sc)
print 'Eigenvalue {:}: {}'.format(i+1, eig_vals[i])
print

Eigenvector 1: [-0.2049 -0.3871 0.5465 0.7138]
Eigenvalue 1: 32.2719577997 Eigenvector 2: [ 0.009 0.589 -0.2543 0.767 ]
Eigenvalue 2: 0.27756686384 Eigenvector 3: [ 0.2771 -0.3863 -0.4388 0.6644]
Eigenvalue 3: -6.73276389619e-16 . # basically 0 Eigenvector 4: [ 0.2771
-0.3863 -0.4388 0.6644] Eigenvalue 4: -6.73276389619e-16 . # basically 0
```

Note that the third and fourth eigenvalues are basically zero. This is because the way LDA is trying to work is by drawing decision boundaries between our classes. Because we only have three classes in the iris, we may only draw up to two decision boundaries. In general, fitting LDA to a dataset with n classes will only produce up to n-1 components.

Keeping the top k eigenvectors by ordering them by descending eigenvalues

As in PCA, we only wish to keep the eigenvectors that are doing most of the work:

```
# keep the top two linear discriminants
linear_discriminants = eig_vecs.T[:2]

linear_discriminants

array([[-0.2049, -0.3871, 0.5465, 0.7138], [ 0.009 , 0.589 , -0.2543,
0.767 ]])
```

We can look at the ratio of explained variance in each component/linear discriminant by dividing each eigenvalue by the sum total of all eigenvalues:

```
#explained variance ratios
eig_vals / eig_vals.sum()

array([ .99147, .0085275, -2.0685e-17, -2.0685e-17])
```

It appears that the first component is doing a vast majority of the work and holding over 99% of the information on its own.

Using the top eigenvectors to project onto the new space

Now that we have our components, let's plot the projected iris data by first using the eigenvectors to project the original data onto the new space and then calling our plot function:

```
# LDA projected data
lda_iris_projection = np.dot(iris_X, linear_discriminants.T)
lda_iris_projection[:5,]

plot(lda_iris_projection, iris_y, "LDA Projection", "LDA1", "LDA2")
```

We get the following output:

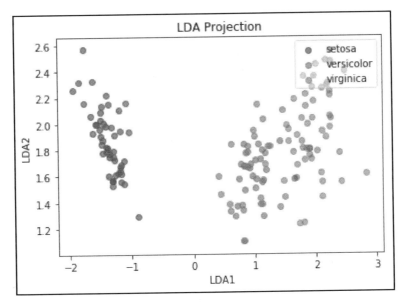

Notice that in this graph, the data is *standing* almost fully upright (even more than PCA projected data), as if the LDA components are trying to help machine learning models separate the flowers as much as possible by drawing these decision boundaries and providing eigenvectors/linear discriminants. This helps us project data into a space that separates classes as much as possible.

How to use LDA in scikit-learn

LDA has an implementation in scikit-learn to avoid this very laborious process. It is easily imported:

```
from sklearn.discriminant_analysis import LinearDiscriminantAnalysis
```

From there, let's use it to fit and transform our original iris data and plot the resulting projected dataset so that we may compare it to the projection using PCA. The biggest thing to notice in the following code block is that the fit function requires two inputs.

Recall how we mentioned that LDA is actually a classifier disguised as a feature transformation algorithm. Unlike PCA, which finds components in an unsupervised manner (without a response variable), LDA will attempt to find the best coordinate system *with respect to* a response variable that optimizes for class separability. This implies that LDA only works if we have a response variable. If we do, we input the response as a second input to our fit method and let LDA do its thing:

```
# instantiate the LDA module
lda = LinearDiscriminantAnalysis(n_components=2)

# fit and transform our original iris data
X_lda_iris = lda.fit_transform(iris_X, iris_y)

# plot the projected data
plot(X_lda_iris, iris_y, "LDA Projection", "LDA1", "LDA2")
```

We get the following output:

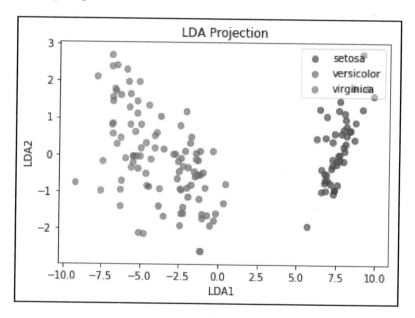

This graph is a mirror image of the manual LDA that we performed. This is OK. Recall in PCA that the manual version we had contained eigenvectors that had opposite signs (positive versus negative). This does not affect our machine learning pipelines. Within the LDA module, we have some differences to keep note of. Instead of a `.components_` attribute, we have a `.scalings_` attribute, which acts almost the same:

```
# essentially the same as pca.components_, but transposed (4x2 instead of
2x4)
 lda.scalings_


 array([[ 0.81926852, 0.03285975], [ 1.5478732 , 2.15471106], [-2.18494056,
-0.93024679], [-2.85385002, 2.8060046 ]])


 # same as manual calculations
 lda.explained_variance_ratio_
 array([ 0.9915, 0.0085])
```

The explained variance ratios for the two linear discriminants are exactly the same as the ones we calculated before and notice that they omit the third and fourth eigenvalues because they are virtually zero.

These components, however, at first glance, look nothing like the manual eigenvectors that we achieved before. The reason for this is that the way that scikit-learn calculates the eigenvectors produces the same eigenvectors, but scaled by a scalar, as follows:

```
# show that the sklearn components are just a scalar multiplication from
the manual components we calculateda
 for manual_component, sklearn_component in zip(eig_vecs.T[:2],
lda.scalings_.T):
 print sklearn_component / manual_component

 [-3.9982 -3.9982 -3.9982 -3.9982] [ 3.6583 3.6583 3.6583 3.6583]
```

The scikit-learn linear discriminants are a scalar multiplication of the manual eigenvectors, which means that they are both valid eigenvectors. The only difference is in the scaling of the projected data.

These components are organized as a 4 x 2 matrix, instead of the PCA components, which was given to us as a 2 x 4 matrix. This was a choice when developing the module and doesn't affect the math at all for us. LDA, like PCA, scales invariant, so scaling the data matters.

Let's fit the LDA module to scaled iris data and look at the components to see the difference:

```
# fit our LDA to scaled data
X_lda_iris = lda.fit_transform(X_scaled, iris_y)

lda.scalings_ # different scalings when data are scaled

array([[ 0.67614337, 0.0271192 ], [ 0.66890811, 0.93115101], [-3.84228173,
-1.63586613], [-2.17067434, 2.13428251]])
```

The scalings_ attribute (akin to PCA's components_ attribute) is showing us different arrays, which means that the projection will also be different. To finish our (briefer) description of LDA, let's apply the same code block that we did with PCA and interpret the scalings_ arrays as we did with the components_ attribute of PCA.

Let's first fit and transform LDA on our truncated iris dataset, where we have only kept the first two features:

```
# fit our LDA to our truncated iris dataset
iris_2_dim_transformed_lda = lda.fit_transform(iris_2_dim, iris_y)
```

Let's take a look at the first five rows of our projected dataset:

```
# project data
iris_2_dim_transformed_lda[:5,]

array([[-6.04248571, 0.07027756], [-6.04248571, 0.07027756], [-6.19690803,
0.28598813], [-5.88806338, -0.14543302], [-6.04248571, 0.07027756]])
```

Our scalings_ matrix is now a 2 x 2 matrix (2 rows and 2 columns) where the columns are the components (instead of the rows being components in PCA). To adjust for this, let's make a new variable called components that holds the transposed version of the scalings_ attribute:

```
# different notation
components = lda.scalings_.T # transposing gives same style as PCA. We
want rows to be components

print components
[[ 1.54422328 2.40338224] [-2.15710573 5.02431491]]


np.dot(iris_2_dim, components.T)[:5,] # same as transform method


array([[-6.04248571, 0.07027756], [-6.04248571, 0.07027756], [-6.19690803,
0.28598813], [-5.88806338, -0.14543302], [-6.04248571, 0.07027756]])
```

We can see that se uses the components variable in the same way that we did the PCA `components_` attribute. This implies that the projection is another linear combination of original columns, just as they were in PCA. It is also worth noting that LDA still de-correlates features, just as PCA did. To show this, let us calculate the correlation coefficient matrix of both the original truncated iris data and the correlation matrix of the projected data:

```
# original features are highly correlated
np.corrcoef(iris_2_dim.T)
 array([[ 1. , 0.9627571],
 [ 0.9627571, 1. ]])

 # new LDA features are highly uncorrelated, like in PCA
 np.corrcoef(iris_2_dim_transformed_lda.T)
 array([[ 1.00000000e+00, 1.03227536e-15], [ 1.03227536e-15,
1.00000000e+00]])
```

Note that in the top right value in each matrix, the original matrix is showing *highly* correlated features, while the projected data using LDA has highly independent features (given the close to zero correlation coefficient). To wrap up our interpretation of LDA before we move onto the real fun (using both PCA and LDA for machine learning), let's take a look at a visualization of the `scalings_` attribute of LDA, just as we did for PCA:

```
# This code is graphing both the original iris data and the projected
version of it using LDA.
 # Moreover, on each graph, the scalings of the LDA are graphed as vectors
on the data themselves
 # The longer of the arrows is meant to describe the first scaling vector
and
 # the shorter of the arrows describes the second scaling vector
def draw_vector(v0, v1, ax):
arrowprops=dict(arrowstyle='->',
linewidth=2,
shrinkA=0, shrinkB=0)
ax.annotate('', v1, v0, arrowprops=arrowprops)

fig, ax = plt.subplots(2, 1, figsize=(10, 10))
fig.subplots_adjust(left=0.0625, right=0.95, wspace=0.1)

# plot data
ax[0].scatter(iris_2_dim[:, 0], iris_2_dim[:, 1], alpha=0.2)
for length, vector in zip(lda.explained_variance_ratio_, components):
v = vector * .5
draw_vector(lda.xbar_, lda.xbar_ + v, ax=ax[0]) # lda.xbar_ is equivalent
to pca.mean_
ax[0].axis('equal')
```

```
ax[0].set(xlabel='x', ylabel='y', title='Original Iris Dataset',
xlim=(-3, 3), ylim=(-3, 3))

ax[1].scatter(iris_2_dim_transformed_lda[:, 0],
iris_2_dim_transformed_lda[:, 1], alpha=0.2)
for length, vector in zip(lda.explained_variance_ratio_, components):
transformed_component = lda.transform([vector])[0]
v = transformed_component * .1
draw_vector(iris_2_dim_transformed_lda.mean(axis=0),
iris_2_dim_transformed_lda.mean(axis=0) + v, ax=ax[1])
ax[1].axis('equal')
ax[1].set(xlabel='lda component 1', ylabel='lda component 2',
title='Linear Discriminant Analysis Projected Data',
xlim=(-10, 10), ylim=(-3, 3))
```

We get the following output:

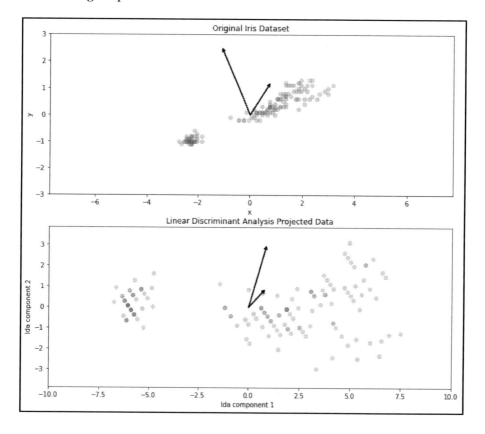

Notice how the component, instead of going with the variance of the data, goes almost perpendicular to it; it's following the separation of the classes instead. Also, note how it's almost parallel with the gap between the flowers on the left and right side. LDA is trying to capture the separation between classes

In the top graph, we can see the original iris dataset with the `scalings_` vectors overlaid on top of the data-points. The longer vector is pointing almost parallel to the large gap between the setosas on the bottom left and the rest of the flowers on the top right. This is indicative that the LDA is trying to point out the best directions to look in to separate the classes of flowers in the original coordinate system.

It is important to note here that the `scalings_ attribute` of LDA does not correlate 1:1 to the new coordinate system as it did in PCA. This is because the goal of `scalings_` is not to create a new coordinate system, but just to point in the direction of boundaries in the data that optimizes for class separability. We will not go into detail about the calculation of these new coordinate systems as we did with PCA. It is sufficient to understand that the main difference between PCA and LDA is that PCA is an unsupervised method that captures the variance of the data as a whole whereas LDA, a supervised method, uses the response variable to capture class separability.

 Limitations of supervised feature transformations like LDA mean that they cannot help with tasks such as clustering, whereas PCA can help. This is because clustering is an unsupervised task and does not have a response variable for LDA to use.

LDA versus PCA – iris dataset

Finally, we arrive at the moment where we can try using both PCA and LDA in our machine learning pipelines. Because we have been working with the `iris` dataset extensively in this chapter, we will continue to demonstrate the utility of both LDA and PCA as feature transformational pre-processing steps for supervised and unsupervised machine learning.

We will start with supervised machine learning and attempt to build a classifier to recognize the species of flower given the four quantitative flower traits:

1. We begin by importing three modules from scikit-learn:

```
from sklearn.neighbors import KNeighborsClassifier
from sklearn.pipeline import Pipeline
from sklearn.model_selection import cross_val_score
```

We will use KNN as our supervised model and the pipeline module to combine our KNN model with our feature transformation tools to create machine learning pipelines that can be cross-validated using the `cross_val_score` module. We will try a few different machine learning pipelines and record their performance:

2. Let's begin by creating three new variables, one to hold our LDA, one to hold our PCA, and another to hold a KNN model:

```
# Create a PCA module to keep a single component
single_pca = PCA(n_components=1)

# Create a LDA module to keep a single component
single_lda = LinearDiscriminantAnalysis(n_components=1)

# Instantiate a KNN model
knn = KNeighborsClassifier(n_neighbors=3)
```

3. Let's invoke the KNN model without any transformational techniques to get the baseline accuracy. We will use this to compare the two feature transformation algorithms:

```
# run a cross validation on the KNN without any feature
transformation
knn_average = cross_val_score(knn, iris_X, iris_y).mean()

# This is a baseline accuracy. If we did nothing, KNN on its own
achieves a 98% accuracy
knn_average

0.98039215686274517
```

4. The baseline accuracy to beat is 98.04%. Let's use our LDA, which keeps only the most powerful component:

```
lda_pipeline = Pipeline([('lda', single_lda), ('knn', knn)])
lda_average = cross_val_score(lda_pipeline, iris_X, iris_y).mean()
```

```
# better prediction accuracy than PCA by a good amount, but not as
good as original
lda_average
```

0.9673202614379085

5. It seems that only using a single linear discriminant isn't enough to beat our baseline accuracy. Let us now try the PCA. Our hypothesis here is that the PCA will not outperform the LDA for the sole reason that the PCA is not trying to optimize for class separation as LDA is:

```
# create a pipeline that performs PCA
pca_pipeline = Pipeline([('pca', single_pca), ('knn', knn)])

pca_average = cross_val_score(pca_pipeline, iris_X, iris_y).mean()

pca_average
```

0.8941993464052288

Definitely the worst so far.

It is worth exploring whether adding another LDA component will help us:

```
# try LDA with 2 components
lda_pipeline = Pipeline([('lda',
LinearDiscriminantAnalysis(n_components=2)),
('knn', knn)])

lda_average = cross_val_score(lda_pipeline, iris_X, iris_y).mean()

# Just as good as using original data
lda_average
```

0.98039215686274517

With two components, we are able to achieve the original accuracy! This is great, but we want to do better than our baseline. Let's see if a feature selection module from the last chapter can help us. Let's import and use the SelectKBest module and see if statistical feature selection would best our LDA module:

```
# compare our feature transformation tools to a feature selection tool
from sklearn.feature_selection import SelectKBest
# try all possible values for k, excluding keeping all columns
for k in [1, 2, 3]:
# make the pipeline
select_pipeline = Pipeline([('select', SelectKBest(k=k)), ('knn', knn)])
```

```
# cross validate the pipeline
select_average = cross_val_score(select_pipeline, iris_X, iris_y).mean()
print k, "best feature has accuracy:", select_average

# LDA is even better than the best selectkbest
1 best feature has accuracy: 0.953839869281 2 best feature has accuracy:
0.960784313725 3 best feature has accuracy: 0.97385620915
```

Our LDA with two components is so far winning. In production, it is quite common to use both unsupervised and supervised feature transformations. Let's set up a `GridSearch` module to find the best combination across:

- Scaling data (with or without mean/std)
- PCA components
- LDA components
- KNN neighbors

The following code block is going to set up a function called `get_best_model_and_accuracy` which will take in a model (scikit-learn pipeline or other), a parameter grid in the form of a dictionary, our X and y datasets, and output the result of the grid search module. The output will be the model's best performance (in terms of accuracy), the best parameters that led to the best performance, the average time it took to fit, and the average time it took to predict:

```
def get_best_model_and_accuracy(model, params, X, y):
    grid = GridSearchCV(model, # the model to grid search
                        params, # the parameter set to try
                        error_score=0.) # if a parameter set raises an
error, continue and set the performance as a big, fat 0

    grid.fit(X, y) # fit the model and parameters
    # our classical metric for performance
    print "Best Accuracy: {}".format(grid.best_score_)
    # the best parameters that caused the best accuracy
    print "Best Parameters: {}".format(grid.best_params_)
    # the average time it took a model to fit to the data (in seconds)
    avg_time_fit = round(grid.cv_results_['mean_fit_time'].mean(), 3)
    print "Average Time to Fit (s): {}".format(avg_time_fit)
    # the average time it took a model to predict out of sample data (in
seconds)
    # this metric gives us insight into how this model will perform in
real-time analysis
    print "Average Time to Score (s):
{}".format(round(grid.cv_results_['mean_score_time'].mean(), 3))
```

Once we have our function set up to take in models and parameters, let's use it to test our pipeline with our combinations of scaling, PCA, LDA, and KNN:

```
from sklearn.model_selection import GridSearchCV
iris_params = {
    'preprocessing__scale__with_std': [True, False],
    'preprocessing__scale__with_mean': [True, False],
    'preprocessing__pca__n_components':[1, 2, 3, 4], # according to
scikit-learn docs, max allowed n_components for LDA is number of classes -
1
    'preprocessing__lda__n_components':[1, 2],

    'clf__n_neighbors': range(1, 9)
}
# make a larger pipeline
preprocessing = Pipeline([('scale', StandardScaler()), ('pca', PCA()),
('lda', LinearDiscriminantAnalysis())])


iris_pipeline = Pipeline(steps=[('preprocessing', preprocessing),('clf',
KNeighborsClassifier())])


get_best_model_and_accuracy(iris_pipeline, iris_params, iris_X, iris_y)

Best Accuracy: 0.986666666667 Best Parameters:
{'preprocessing__scale__with_std': False,
'preprocessing__pca__n_components': 3, 'preprocessing__scale__with_mean':
True, 'preprocessing__lda__n_components': 2, 'clf__n_neighbors': 3} Average
Time to Fit (s): 0.002 Average Time to Score (s): 0.001
```

The best accuracy so far (near 99%) uses a combination of scaling, PCA, and LDA. It is common to correctly use all three of these algorithms in the same pipelines and perform hyper-parameter tuning to fine-tune the process. This shows us that more often than not, the best production-ready machine learning pipelines are in fact a combination of multiple feature engineering methods.

Summary

To summarize our findings, both PCA and LDA are feature transformation tools in our arsenal that are used to find optimal new features to use. LDA specifically optimizes for class separation while PCA works in an unsupervised way to capture variance in the data in fewer columns. Usually, the two are used in conjunction with supervised pipelines, as we showed in the iris pipeline. In the final chapter, we will go through two longer case studies that utilize both PCA and LDA for text clustering and facial recognition software.

PCA and LDA are extremely powerful tools, but have limitations. Both of them are linear transformations, which means that they can only create linear boundaries and capture linear qualities in our data. They are also static transformations. No matter what data we input into a PCA or LDA, the output is expected and mathematical. If the data we are using isn't a good fit for PCA or LDA (they exhibit non-linear qualities, for example, they are circular), then the two algorithms will not help us, no matter how much we grid search.

The next chapter will focus on feature learning algorithms. These are arguably the most powerful feature engineering algorithms. They are built to learn new features based on the input data without assuming qualities such as PCA and LDA. In this chapter, we will use complex structures including neural networks to achieve the highest level of feature engineering yet.

7
Feature Learning

In our final chapter, where we will be exploring feature engineering techniques, we will be taking a look at what is likely the most powerful feature engineering tool at our disposal. Feature learning algorithms are able to take in cleaned data (yes, you still need to do some work) and create brand-new features by exploiting latent structures within data. If all of this sounds familiar, that is because this is the description that we used in the previous chapter for feature transformations. The differences between these two families of algorithms are in the *parametric* assumptions that they make when attempting to create new features.

We will be covering the following topics:

- Parametric assumptions of data
- Restricted Boltzmann Machines
- The BernoulliRBM
- Extracting RBM components from MNIST
- Using RBMs in a machine learning pipeline
- Learning text features—word vectorization

Parametric assumptions of data

When we say **parametric assumptions**, we are referring to base assumptions that algorithms make about the *shape* of the data. In the previous chapter, while exploring **principal component analysis** (**PCA**), we discovered that the end result of the algorithm produced components that we could use to transform data through a single matrix multiplication. The assumption that we were making was that the original data took on a shape that could be decomposed and represented by a single linear transformation (the matrix operation). But what if that is not true? What if PCA is unable to extract *useful* features from the original dataset? Algorithms such as PCA and **linear discriminate analysis** (**LDA**) will always be able to find features, but they may not be useful at all. Moreover, these algorithms rely on a predetermined equation and will always output the same features each and every time they are run. This is why we consider both LDA and PCA as being *linear transformations*.

Feature learning algorithms attempt to solve this issue by removing that parametric assumption. They do not make any assumptions about the shape of the incoming data and rely on *stochastic learning*. This means that, instead of throwing the same equation at the matrix of data every time, they will attempt to figure out the best features to extract by looking at the data points over and over again (in epochs) and converge onto a solution (potentially different ones at runtime).

 For more information on how stochastic learning (and stochastic gradient descent) works, please refer to the *Principles of Data Science*, by Sinan Ozdemir at:
https://www.packtpub.com/big-data-and-business-intelligence/principles-data-science

This allows feature learning algorithms to bypass the parametric assumption made by algorithms such as PCA and LDA and opens us up to solve much more difficult questions than we could previously in this text. Such a complex idea (bypassing parametric assumptions) requires the use of complex algorithms. *Deep learning* algorithms are the choice of many data scientists and machine learning to learn new features from raw data.

We will assume that the reader has a basic familiarity with the neural network architecture in order to focus on applications of these architectures for feature learning. The following table summarizes the basic differences between feature learning and transformation:

	Parametric?	Simple to use?	Creates new feature set?	Deep learning?
Feature transformation algorithms	Yes	Yes	Yes	No
Feature learning algorithms	No	No (usually)	Yes	Yes (usually)

The fact that both feature learning and feature transformation algorithms create new feature sets means that we regard both of them as being under the umbrella of *feature extraction*. The following figure shows this relationship:

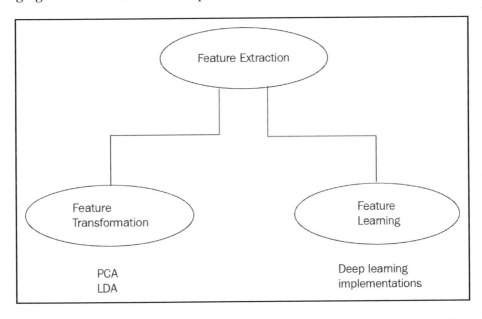

Feature extraction as a superset of feature learning and feature transformation. Both families of algorithms work to exploit latent structure in order to transform raw data into a new feature set

Both **feature learning** and **feature transformation** fall under the category of feature extraction as they are both trying to create a new feature set from the latent structure of raw data. The methods in which they are allowed to work, though, are the main differentiators.

Non-parametric fallacy

It is important to mention that a model being non-parametric doesn't mean that there are no assumptions at all made by the model during training.

While the algorithms that we will be introducing in this chapter forgo the assumption on the shape of the data, they still may make assumptions on other aspects of the data, for example, the values of the cells.

The algorithms of this chapter

In this chapter, we will focus on two feature learning areas:

- **Restricted Boltzmann Machines (RBM)**: A simple deep learning architecture that is set up to learn a set number of new dimensions based on a probabilistic model that data follows. These machines are in fact a family of algorithms with only one implemented in scikit-learn. The **BernoulliRBM** may be a non-parametric feature learner; however, as the name suggests, some expectations are set as to the values of the cells of the dataset.
- **Word embeddings**: Likely one of the biggest contributors to the recent deep learning-fueled advancements of natural language processing/understanding/generation is the ability to project strings (words and phrases) into an n-dimensional feature set in order to grasp context and minute detail in wording. We will use the `gensim` Python package to prepare our own word embeddings and then use pre-trained word embeddings to see some examples of how these word embeddings can be used to enhance the way we interact with text.

All of these examples have something in common. They all involve learning brand new features from raw data. They then use these new features to enhance the way that they interact with data. For the latter two examples, we will have to move away from scikit-learn as these more advanced techniques are not (yet) implemented in the latest versions. Instead, we will see examples of deep learning neural architectures implemented in TensorFlow and Keras.

For all of these techniques, we will be focusing less on the very low-level inner workings of the models, and more on how they work to interpret data. We will go in order and start with the only algorithm that has a scikit-learn implementation, the restricted Boltzmann machine family of algorithms.

Restricted Boltzmann Machines

RBMs are a family of unsupervised feature learning algorithms that use probabilistic models to learn new features. Like PCA and LDA, we can use RBMs to extract a new feature set from raw data and use them to enhance machine learning pipelines. The features that are extracted by RBMs tend to work best when followed by linear models such as linear regression, logistic regression, perceptron's, and so on.

The unsupervised nature of RBMs is important as they are more similar to PCA algorithms than they are to LDA. They do not require a ground-truth label for data points to extract new features. This makes them useful in a wider variety of machine learning problems.

Conceptually, RBMs are shallow (two-layer) neural networks. They are thought to be the building blocks of a class of algorithms called **Deep Belief Networks** (**DBN**). Keeping with standard terminology, there is a visible layer (the first layer), followed by a hidden layer (the second layer). These are the only two layers of the network:

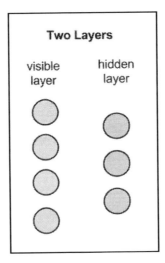

The setup for a restricted Boltzmann Machine. The circles represent nodes in the graph

Like any neural network, we have nodes in our two layers. The first visible layer of the network has as many layers as the input feature dimension. In our upcoming example, we will be working with 28 x 28 images necessitating 784 (28 x 28) nodes in our input layer. The number of nodes in the hidden layer is a human-chosen number and represents the number of features that we wish to learn.

Not necessarily dimension reduction

In PCA and LDA, we had severe limits to the number of components we were allowed to extract. For PCA, we were capped by the number of original features (we could only use less than or equal to the number of original columns), while LDA enforced the much stricter imposition that caps the number of extracted features to the number of categories in the ground truth minus one.

The only restriction on the number of features RBMs are allowed to learn is that they are limited by the computation power of the computer running the network and human interpretation. RBMs can learn fewer or *more* features than we originally began with. The exact number of features to learn is up to the problem and can be gridsearched.

The graph of a Restricted Boltzmann Machine

So far, we have seen the visible and hidden layers of RBMs, but we have not yet seen how they learn features. Each of the visible layer's nodes take in a single feature from the dataset to be learned from. This data is then passed from the visible layer to the hidden layer through weights and biases:

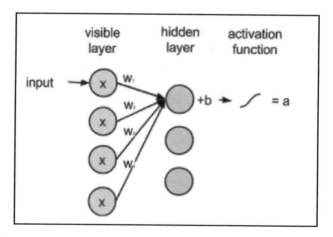

This visualization of an RBM shows the movement of a single data point through the graph through a single hidden node

The preceding visualization of an RBM shows the movement of a single data point through the graph and through a single hidden node. The visible layer has four nodes, representing the four columns of the original data. Each arrow represents a single feature of the data point moving through the four visible nodes in the first layer of the RBM. Each of the feature values is multiplied by a weight associated to that feature and are added up together. This calculation can also be summed up by a dot product between an input vector of data and a weight vector. The resulting weighted sum of the data is added to a bias variable and sent through an activation function (sigmoidal is popular). The result is stored in a variable called a.

As an example in Python, this code shows how a single data point (inputs) is multiplied by our weights vector and combined with the bias variable to create the activated variable, a:

```python
import numpy as np
import math

# sigmoidal function
def activation(x):
    return 1 / (1 + math.exp(-x))

inputs = np.array([1, 2, 3, 4])
weights = np.array([0.2, 0.324, 0.1, .001])
bias = 1.5

a = activation(np.dot(inputs.T, weights) + bias)

print a
0.9341341524806636
```

In a real RBM, each of the visible nodes is connected to each of the hidden nodes, and it looks something like this:

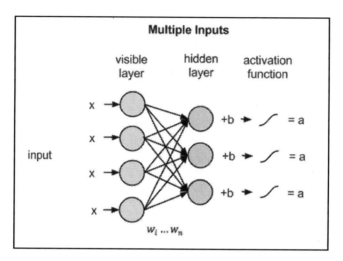

Because inputs from each visible node are passed to every single hidden node, an RBM can be defined as a **symmetrical bipartite graph**. The symmetrical part comes from the fact that the visible nodes are all connected with each hidden node. Bipartite means it has two parts (layers).

The restriction of a Boltzmann Machine

With our two layers of visible and hidden nodes, we have seen the connection between the layers (inter-layer connections), but we haven't seen any connections between nodes in the same layer (intra-layer connections). That is because there aren't any. The restriction in the RBM is that we do not allow for any intra-layer communication. This lets nodes independently create weights and biases that end up being (hopefully) independent features for our data.

Reconstructing the data

In this forward pass of the network, we can see how data goes forward through the network (from the visible layer to the hidden layer), but that doesn't explain how the RBM is able to learn new features from our data without ground truths. This is done through multiple forward and backward passes through the network between our visible and hidden layer.

In the reconstruction phase, we switch the network around and let the hidden layer become the input layer and let it feed our activation variables (a) backwards into the visible layer using the same weights, but a new set of biases. The activated variables that we calculated during the forward pass are then used to reconstruct the original input vectors. The following visualization shows us how activations are fed backwards through our graph using the same weights and different biases:

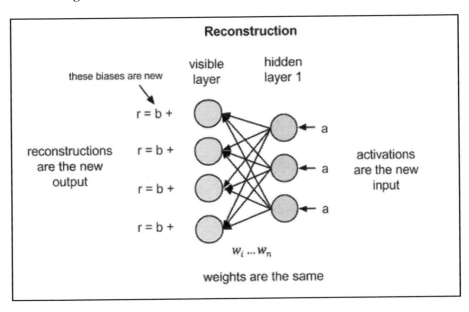

This becomes the network's way of evaluating itself. By passing the activations backwards through the network and obtaining an approximation of the original input, the network can adjust the weights in order to make the approximations closer to the original input. Towards the beginning of training, because the weights are randomly initialized (this is standard practice), the approximations will likely be very far off. Backpropagation through the network, which occurs in the same direction as our forward pass (confusing, we know), then adjusts the weights to minimize the distance between original input and approximations. This process is then repeated until the approximations are as close to the original input as possible. The number of times this back and forth process occurs is called the number of **iterations**.

The end result of this process is a network that has an *alter-ego* for each data point. To transform data, we simply pass it through the network and retrieve the activation variables and call those the new features. This process is a type of *generative learning* that attempts to learn a probability distribution that generated the original data and exploit knowledge to give us a new feature set of our raw data.

For example, if we were given an image of a digit and asked to classify which digit (0-9) the image was of, the forward pass of the network asks the question, given these pixels, what digit should I expect? On the backwards pass, the network is asking given a digit, what pixels should I expect? This is called a **joint probability** and it is the simultaneous probability of y given x and x given y, and it is expressed as the shared weights between the two layers of our network.

Let's introduce our new dataset and let it elucidate the usefulness of RBMs in feature learning.

MNIST dataset

The `MNIST` dataset consists of 6,000 images of handwritten digits between zero and nine and a ground-truth label to learn from. It is not unlike most of the other datasets that we have been working with in that we are attempting to fit a machine learning model to classify a response variable given a set of data points. The main difference here is that we are working with very low-level features as opposed to more interpretable features. Each data point will consist of 784 features (pixel values in a grey-scale image).

1. Let's begin with our imports:

   ```
   # import numpy and matplotlib
   import numpy as np
   import matplotlib.pyplot as plt
   %matplotlib inline

   from sklearn import linear_model, datasets, metrics
   # scikit-learn implementation of RBM
   from sklearn.neural_network import BernoulliRBM
   from sklearn.pipeline import Pipeline
   ```

2. The new import is the BernoulliRBM, which is the only RBM implementation in scikit-learn as of now. As the name suggests, we will have to do a small amount of preprocessing to ensure that our data complies with the assumptions required. Let's import our dataset directly into a NumPy array:

   ```
   # create numpy array from csv
   images = np.genfromtxt('../data/mnist_train.csv', delimiter=',')
   ```

3. We can verify the number of rows and columns that we are working with:

```
# 6000 images and 785 columns, 28X28 pixels + 1 response
images.shape

(6000, 785)
```

4. The 785 is comprised of 784 pixels and a single response column in the beginning (first column). Every column besides the response column holds a value between zero and 255 representing pixel intensity, where zero means a white background and 255 means a fully black pixel. We can extract the X and y variables from the data by separating the first column from the rest of the data:

```
# extract the X and y variable
images_X, images_y = images[:,1:], images[:,0]

# values are much larger than 0-1 but scikit-learn RBM version
assumes 0-1 scaling
np.min(images_X), np.max(images_X)
(0.0, 255.0)
```

5. If we take a look at the first image, we will see what we are working with:

```
plt.imshow(images_X[0].reshape(28, 28), cmap=plt.cm.gray_r)

images_y[0]
```

The plot is as follows:

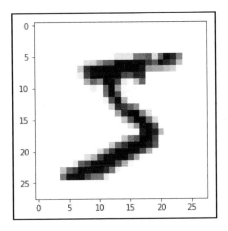

Looking good. Because the scikit-learn implementation of Restricted Boltzmann Machines will not allow for values outside of the range of 0-1, we will have to do a bit of preprocessing work.

The BernoulliRBM

The only scikit-learn implemented version of a Restricted Boltzmann Machine is called **BernoulliRBM** because it imposes a constraint on the type of probability distribution it can learn. The Bernoulli distribution allows for data values to be between zero and one. The scikit-learn documentation states that the model *assumes the inputs are either binary values or values between zero and one*. This is done to represent the fact that the node values represent a probability that the node is activated or not. It allows for quicker learning of feature sets. To account for this, we will alter our dataset to account for only hardcoded white/black pixel intensities. By doing so, every cell value will either be zero or one (white or black) to make learning more robust. We will accomplish this in two steps:

1. We will scale the values of the pixels to be between zero and one
2. We will change the pixel values in place to be true if the value is over 0.5, and false otherwise

Let's start by scaling the pixel values to be between 0 and 1:

```
# scale images_X to be between 0 and 1
images_X = images_X / 255.

# make pixels binary (either white or black)
images_X = (images_X > 0.5).astype(float)

np.min(images_X), np.max(images_X)
(0.0, 1.0)
```

Let's take a look at the same number five digit, as we did previously, with our newly altered pixels:

```
plt.imshow(images_X[0].reshape(28, 28), cmap=plt.cm.gray_r)

images_y[0]
```

The plot is as follows:

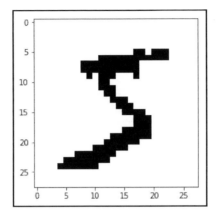

We can see that the fuzziness of the image has disappeared and we are left with a very crisp digit to classify with. Let's try now to extract features from our dataset of digits.

Extracting PCA components from MNIST

Before we move to our RBM, let's take a look at what happens when we apply a PCA to our dataset. Like we did in the last chapter, we will take our features (784 pixels that are either on or off) and apply an eigenvalue decomposition to the matrix to extract *eigendigits* from the dataset.

Let's take 100 components from the possible 784 and plot the components to see what the extracted features look like. We will do this by importing our PCA module, fitting it to our data with 100 components, and creating a matplotlib gallery to display the top 100 components available to us:

```
# import Principal Components Analysis module
from sklearn.decomposition import PCA

# extract 100 "eigen-digits"
pca = PCA(n_components=100)
pca.fit(images_X)

# graph the 100 components
plt.figure(figsize=(10, 10))
for i, comp in enumerate(pca.components_):
plt.subplot(10, 10, i + 1)
plt.imshow(comp.reshape((28, 28)), cmap=plt.cm.gray_r)
```

```
plt.xticks(())
plt.yticks(())
plt.suptitle('100 components extracted by PCA')

plt.show()
```

The following is the plot of the preceding code block:

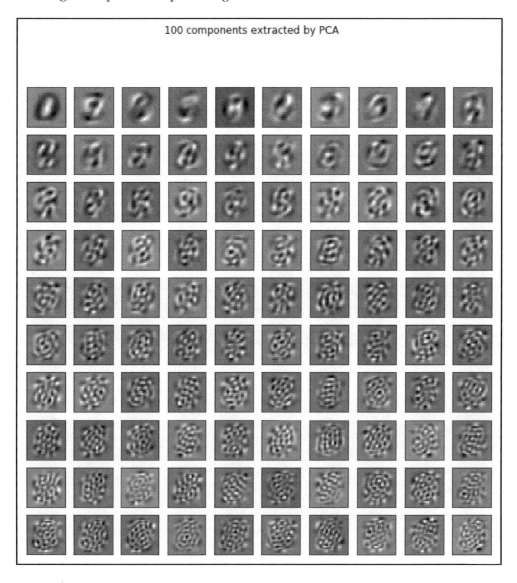

This gallery of images is showing us what the eigenvalues of the covariance matrix look like when reshaped to the same dimensions as the original images. This is an example of what extracted components look like when we focus our algorithms on a dataset of images. It is quite interesting to take a sneak peek into how the PCA components are attempting to grab linear transformations from the dataset. Each component is attempting to understand a certain "aspect" of the images that will translate into interpretable knowledge. For example, the first (and most important) eigen-image is likely capturing an images 0-quality that is, how like a 0 the digit looks.

It also is evident that the first ten components seem to retain some of the shape of the digits and after that, they appear to start devolving into what looks like nonsensical images. By the end of the gallery, we appear to be looking at random assortments of black and white pixels swirling around. This is probably because PCA (and also LDA) are parametric transformations and they are limited in the amount of information they can extract from complex datasets like images.

If we take a look to see how much variance the first 30 components are explaining, we would see that they are able to capture the majority of the information:

```
# first 30 components explain 64% of the variance

pca.explained_variance_ratio_[:30].sum()
.637414
```

This tells us that the first few dozen components are doing a good job at capturing the essence of the data, but after that, the components are likely not adding too much.

This can be further seen in a scree plot showing us the cumulative explained variance for our PCA components:

```
# Scree Plot

# extract all "eigen-digits"
full_pca = PCA(n_components=784)
full_pca.fit(images_X)

plt.plot(np.cumsum(full_pca.explained_variance_ratio_))

# 100 components captures about 90% of the variance
```

The following is the plot of the scree plot where the number of PCA components are on the *x* axis and the amount of cumulative variance explained lives on the *y* axis:

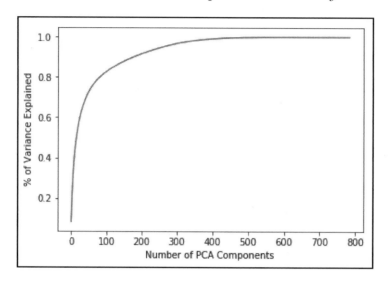

As we saw in the previous chapter, the transformations made by PCA are done through a single linear matrix operation by multiplying the components attribute of the PCA module with the data. We will show this again by taking the scikit-learn PCA object that we fit to 100 features and using it to transform a single MNIST image. We will take that transformed image and compare it the result of multiplying the original image with the `components_` attribute of the PCA module:

```
# Use the pca object, that we have already fitted, to transform the first
image in order to pull out the 100 new features
pca.transform(images_X[:1])

array([[ 0.61090568, 1.36377972, 0.42170385, -2.19662828, -0.45181077,
-1.320495 , 0.79434677, 0.30551126, 1.22978985, -0.72096767, ...

# reminder that transformation is a matrix multiplication away
np.dot(images_X[:1]-images_X.mean(axis=0), pca.components_.T)

array([[ 0.61090568, 1.36377972, 0.42170385, -2.19662828, -0.45181077,
-1.320495 , 0.79434677, 0.30551126, 1.22978985, -0.72096767,
```

Extracting RBM components from MNIST

Let's now create our first RBM in scikit-learn. We will start by instantiating a module to extract 100 components from our MNIST dataset.

We will also set the verbose parameter to True to allow us visibility into the training process as well as the random_state parameter to 0. The random_state parameter is an integer that allows for reproducibility in code. It fixes the random number generator and sets the weights and biases *randomly* at the same time, every time. We finally let n_iter be 20. This is the number of iterations we wish to do, or back and forth passes of the network:

```
# instantiate our BernoulliRBM
# we set a random_state to initialize our weights and biases to the same
starting point
# verbose is set to True to see the fitting period
# n_iter is the number of back and forth passes
# n_components (like PCA and LDA) represent the number of features to
create
# n_components can be any integer, less than , equal to, or greater than
the original number of features

rbm = BernoulliRBM(random_state=0, verbose=True, n_iter=20,
n_components=100)

rbm.fit(images_X)

[BernoulliRBM] Iteration 1, pseudo-likelihood = -138.59, time = 0.80s
[BernoulliRBM] Iteration 2, pseudo-likelihood = -120.25, time = 0.85s
[BernoulliRBM] Iteration 3, pseudo-likelihood = -116.46, time = 0.85s ...
[BernoulliRBM] Iteration 18, pseudo-likelihood = -101.90, time = 0.96s
[BernoulliRBM] Iteration 19, pseudo-likelihood = -109.99, time = 0.89s
[BernoulliRBM] Iteration 20, pseudo-likelihood = -103.00, time = 0.89s
```

Once training is complete; we can explore the end result of the process. RBM also has a components module, like PCA does:

```
# RBM also has components_ attribute
len(rbm.components_)

100
```

We can also plot the RBM components that were learned by the module to see how they differ from our eigendigits:

```
# plot the RBM components (representations of the new feature sets)
plt.figure(figsize=(10, 10))
```

```
for i, comp in enumerate(rbm.components_):
plt.subplot(10, 10, i + 1)
plt.imshow(comp.reshape((28, 28)), cmap=plt.cm.gray_r)
plt.xticks(())
plt.yticks(())
plt.suptitle('100 components extracted by RBM', fontsize=16)

plt.show()
```

The following is the result of the preceding code:

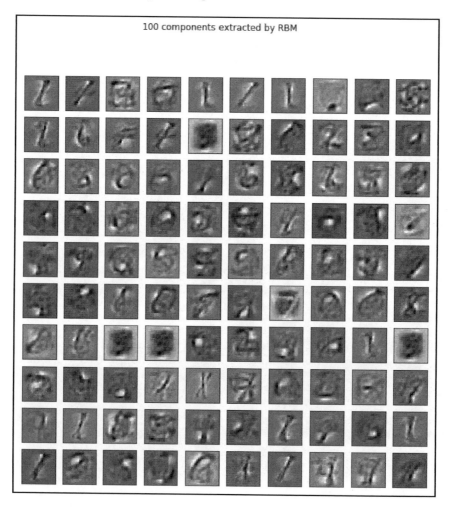

These features look very interesting. Where the PCA components became visual distortions after a while, the RBM components seem to be extracting various shapes and pen strokes with each component. At first glance, it looks like we have repeat features (for example, feature 15, 63, 64, and 70). We can do a quick NumPy check to see if any of the components are actually repeating, or if they are just very similar.

This code will check to see how many unique elements exist in `rbm.components_`. If the resulting shape has 100 elements in it, that means that every component of the RBM is in fact different:

```
# It looks like many of these components are exactly the same but

 # this shows that all components are actually different (albiet some very
slightly) from one another
 np.unique(rbm.components_.mean(axis=1)).shape

(100,)
```

This validates that our components are all unique from one another. We can use the RBM to transform data like we can with PCA by utilizing the `transform` method within the module:

```
# Use our Boltzman Machine to transform a single image of a 5
 image_new_features = rbm.transform(images_X[:1]).reshape(100,)

 image_new_features

 array([ 2.50169424e-16, 7.19295737e-16, 2.45862898e-09, 4.48783657e-01,
1.64530318e-16, 5.96184335e-15, 4.60051698e-20, 1.78646959e-08,
2.78104276e-23, ...
```

And we can also see that these components are **not** used in the same way as PCAs are, meaning that a simple matrix multiplication will not yield the same transformation as invoking the `transform` method embedded within the module:

```
# not the same as a simple matrix multiplication anymore
 # uses neural architecture (several matrix operations) to transform
features
 np.dot(images_X[:1]-images_X.mean(axis=0), rbm.components_.T)

 array([[ -3.60557365, -10.30403384, -6.94375031, 14.10772267, -6.68343281,
-5.72754674, -7.26618457, -26.32300164, ...
```

Now that we know that we have 100 new features to work with and we've seen them, let's see how they interact with our data.

Let's start by grabbing the 20 most represented features for the first image in our dataset, the digit 5:

```
# get the most represented features
top_features = image_new_features.argsort()[-20:][::-1]

print top_features

[56 63 62 14 69 83 82 49 92 29 21 45 15 34 28 94 18 3 79 58]

print image_new_features[top_features]

array([ 1. , 1. , 1. , 1. , 1. , 1. , 1. , 0.99999999, 0.99999996,
0.99999981, 0.99996997, 0.99994894, 0.99990515, 0.9996504 , 0.91615702,
0.86480507, 0.80646422, 0.44878366, 0.02906352, 0.01457827])
```

In this case, we actually have seven features in which the RBM has a full 100%. In our graph, this means that passing in these 784 pixels into our visible layers lights up nodes 56, 63, 62, 14, 69, 83, and 82 at full capacity. Let's isolate these features:

```
# plot the RBM components (representations of the new feature sets) for the
most represented features
plt.figure(figsize=(25, 25))
for i, comp in enumerate(top_features):
plt.subplot(5, 4, i + 1)
plt.imshow(rbm.components_[comp].reshape((28, 28)), cmap=plt.cm.gray_r)
plt.title("Component {}, feature value: {}".format(comp,
round(image_new_features[comp], 2)), fontsize=20)
plt.suptitle('Top 20 components extracted by RBM for first digit',
fontsize=30)

plt.show()
```

We get the following result for the preceding code:

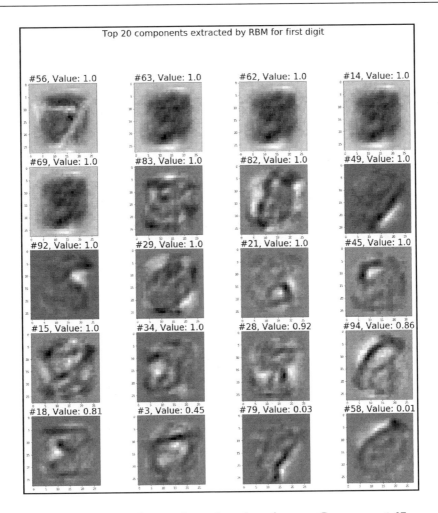

Top 20 components extracted by RBM for first digit

Taking a look at some of these, they make quite a lot of sense. **Component 45** seems to isolate the top-left corner of the digit **5**, while **Component 21** seems to grab the bottom loop of the digit. **Component 82** and **Component 34** seem to grab almost an entire 5 in one go. Let's see what the bottom of the barrel looks like for the number 5 by isolating the bottom 20 features that lit up in the RBM graph when these pixels were passed through:

```
# grab the least represented features
bottom_features = image_new_features.argsort()[:20]

plt.figure(figsize=(25, 25))
for i, comp in enumerate(bottom_features):
plt.subplot(5, 4, i + 1)
plt.imshow(rbm.components_[comp].reshape((28, 28)), cmap=plt.cm.gray_r)
```

```
plt.title("Component {}, feature value: {}".format(comp,
round(image_new_features[comp], 2)), fontsize=20)
    plt.suptitle('Bottom 20 components extracted by RBM for first digit',
fontsize=30)

    plt.show()
```

We get the following plot for the preceding code:

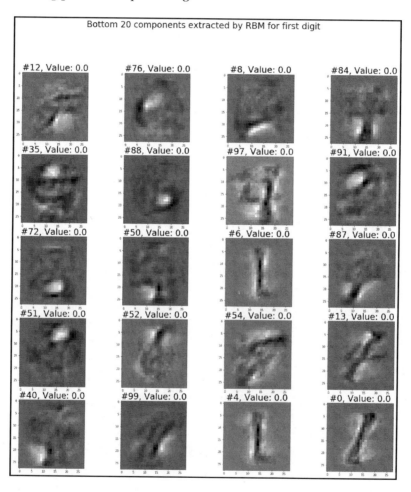

Component 13, **Component 4**, **Component 97**, and others seem to be trying to reveal different digits and not a 5, so it makes sense that these components are not being lit up by this combination of pixel strengths.

Using RBMs in a machine learning pipeline

Of course, we want to see how the RBM performs in our machine learning pipelines to not just visualize the workings of the model, but to see concrete results of the feature learning. To do this, we will create and run three pipelines:

- A logistic regression model by itself running on the raw pixel strengths
- A logistic regression running on extracted PCA components
- A logistic regression running on extracted RBM components

Each of these pipelines will be grid-searched across a number of components (for PCA and RBM) and the C parameter for logistic regression. Let's start with our simplest pipeline. We will run the raw pixel values through a logistic regression to see if the linear model is enough to separate out the digits.

Using a linear model on raw pixel values

To begin, we will run the raw pixel values through a logistic regression model in order to obtain something of a baseline model. We want to see if utilizing PCA or RBM components will allow the same linear classifier to perform better or worse. If we can find that the extracted latent features are performing better (in terms of accuracy of our linear model) then we can be sure it is the feature engineering that we are employing that is enhancing our pipeline, and nothing else.

First we will create our instantiated modules:

```
# import logistic regression and gridsearch module for some machine
learning

from sklearn.linear_model import LogisticRegression
from sklearn.model_selection import GridSearchCV

# create our logistic regression
lr = LogisticRegression()
params = {'C':[1e-2, 1e-1, 1e0, 1e1, 1e2]}

# instantiate a gridsearch class
grid = GridSearchCV(lr, params)
```

Once we done this, we can fit our module to our raw image data. This will give us a rough idea of how the raw pixel data performs in a machine learning pipeline:

```
# fit to our data
grid.fit(images_X, images_y)

# check the best params
grid.best_params_, grid.best_score_

({'C': 0.1}, 0.88749999999999996)
```

Logistic regression by itself does a decent job at using the raw pixel values to identify digits by giving about an **88.75% cross-validated accuracy**.

Using a linear model on extracted PCA components

Let's see if we can add in a PCA component to the pipeline to enhance this accuracy. We will begin again by setting up our variables. This time we will need to create a scikit-learn pipeline object to house the PCA module as well as our linear model. We will keep the same parameters that we used for the linear classifier and add new parameters for our PCA. We will attempt to find the optimal number of components between 10, 100, and 200 components. Try to take a moment and hypothesize which of three will end up being the best (hint, think back to the scree plot and explained variance):

```
# Use PCA to extract new features

lr = LogisticRegression()
pca = PCA()

# set the params for the pipeline
params = {'clf__C':[1e-1, 1e0, 1e1],
'pca__n_components': [10, 100, 200]}

# create our pipeline
pipeline = Pipeline([('pca', pca), ('clf', lr)])

# instantiate a gridsearh class
grid = GridSearchCV(pipeline, params)
```

We can now fit the gridsearch object to our raw image data. Note that the pipeline will take care of automatically extracting features from and transforming our raw pixel data:

```
# fit to our data
grid.fit(images_X, images_y)

# check the best params
grid.best_params_, grid.best_score_

({'clf__C': 1.0, 'pca__n_components': 100}, 0.88949999999999996)
```

We end up with a (slightly better) **88.95% cross-validated accuracy.** If we think about it, we should not be surprised that 100 was the best option out of 10, 100, and 200. From our brief analysis with the scree plot in a previous section, we found that 64% of the data was explained by a mere 30 components, so 10 components would definitely not be enough to explain the images well. The scree plot also started to level out at around 100 components, meaning that after the 100th component, the explained variance was truly not adding much, so 200 was too many components to use and would have started to lead to some overfitting. That leaves us with 100 as being the optimal number of PCA components to use. It should be noted that we could go further and attempt some hyper-parameter tuning to find an even more optimal number of components, but for now we will leave our pipeline as is and move to using RBM components.

Using a linear model on extracted RBM components

Even the optimal number of PCA components was unable to beat the logistic regression alone by much in terms of accuracy. Let's see how our RBM does. To make the following pipeline, we will keep the same parameters for the logistic regression model and find the optimal number of components between 10, 100, and 200 (like we did for the PCA pipeline). Note that we could try to expand the number of features past the number of raw pixels (784) but we will not attempt to.

We begin the same way by setting up our variables:

```
# Use the RBM to learn new features

rbm = BernoulliRBM(random_state=0)

# set up the params for our pipeline.
params = {'clf__C':[1e-1, 1e0, 1e1],
'rbm__n_components': [10, 100, 200]
}

# create our pipeline
pipeline = Pipeline([('rbm', rbm), ('clf', lr)])

# instantiate a gridsearch class
grid = GridSearchCV(pipeline, params)
```

Fitting this grid search to our raw pixels will reveal the optimal number of components:

```
# fit to our data
grid.fit(images_X, images_y)

# check the best params
grid.best_params_, grid.best_score_

({'clf__C': 1.0, 'rbm__n_components': 200}, 0.91766666666666663)
```

Our RBM module, with a **91.75% cross-validated accuracy**, was able to extract 200 new features from our digits and give us a boost of three percent in accuracy (which is a lot!) by not doing anything other than adding the BernoulliRBM module into our pipeline.

The fact that 200 was the optimal number of components suggests that we may even obtain a higher performance by trying to extract more than 200 components. We will leave this as an exercise to the reader.

This is evidence to the fact that feature learning algorithms work very well when dealing with very complex tasks such as image recognition, audio processing, and natural language processing. These large and interesting datasets have hidden components that are difficult for linear transformations like PCA or LDA to extract but non-parametric algorithms like RBM can.

Learning text features – word vectorizations

Our second example of feature learning will move away from images and towards text and natural language processing. When machines learn to read/write, they face a very large problem, context. In previous chapters, we have been able to vectorize documents by counting the number of words that appeared in each document and we fed those vectors into machine learning pipelines. By constructing new count-based features, we were able to use text in our supervised machine learning pipelines. This is very effective, up until a point. We are limited to only being to understand text as if they were only a **Bag of Words (BOW)**. This means that we regard documents as being nothing more than a collection of words out of order.

What's more is that each word on its own has no meaning. It is only in a collection of other words that a document can have meaning when using modules such as `CountVectorizer` and `TfidfVectorizer`. It is for this reason that we will turn our attention away from scikit-learn and onto a module called `gensim` for computing word embeddings.

Word embeddings

Up until this point, we have used scikit-learn to embed documents (tweets, reviews, URLs, and so on) into a vectorized format by regarding tokens (words, n-grams) as features and documents as having a certain amount of these tokens. For example, if we had 1,583 documents and we told our `CountVectorizer` to learn the top 1,000 tokens of `ngram_range` from one to five, we would end up with a matrix of shape (1583, 1000) where each row represented a single document and the 1,000 columns represented literal n-grams found in the corpus. But how do we achieve an even lower level of understanding? How do we start to teach the machine what words *mean* in context?

For example, if we were to ask you the following questions, you may give the following answers:

Q: What would you get if we took a king, removed the man aspect of it, and replaced it with a woman?

A: A queen

Q: London is to England as Paris is to _____.

A: France

You, a human, may find these questions simple, but how would a machine figure this out without knowing what the words by themselves mean in context? This is, in fact, one of the greatest challenges that we face in **natural language processing (NLP)** tasks.

Word embeddings are one approach to helping a machine understand context. A **word embedding** is a vectorization of a single word in a feature space of n dimensions, where *n* represents the number of latent characteristics that a word can have. This means that every word in our vocabulary is not longer, just a string, but a vector in and of itself. For example, if we extracted n=5 characteristics about each word, then each word in our vocabulary would correspond to a 1 x 5 vector. For example, we might have the following vectorizations:

```
# set some fake word embeddings
king = np.array([.2, -.5, .7, .2, -.9])
man = np.array([-.5, .2, -.2, .3, 0.])
woman = np.array([.7, -.3, .3, .6, .1])

queen = np.array([ 1.4, -1. , 1.2, 0.5, -0.8])
```

And with these vectorizations, we can tackle the question *What would you get if we took a king, removed the man aspect of it, and replaced it with a woman?* by performing the following operation:

$$king - man + woman$$

In code, this would look like:

```
np.array_equal((king - man + woman), queen)

True
```

This seems simple but it does some with a few caveats:

- Context (in the form of word embeddings) changes from corpus to corpus as does word meanings. This means that static word embeddings by themselves are not always the most useful
- Word embeddings are dependent on the corpus that they were learned from

Word embeddings allow us to perform very precise calculations on single words to achieve what we might consider context.

Two approaches to word embeddings - Word2vec and GloVe

There are two families of algorithms that dominate the space of word embeddings. They are called **Word2vec** and **GloVe**. Both methods are responsible for producing word embeddings by learning from very large corpus (collection of text documents). The main difference between these two algorithms is that the GloVe algorithm, out of Stanford, learns word embeddings through a series of matrix statistics while Word2vec, out of Google, learns them through a deep learning approach. Both algorithms have merits and our text will focus on using the Word2vec algorithm to learn word embeddings.

Word2Vec - another shallow neural network

In order to learn and extract word embeddings, Word2vec will implement another shallow neural network. This time, instead of generically throwing in new data into our visible layer, we will deliberately put in the correct data to give us the right word embeddings. Without going too into much detail, imagine a neural architecture with the following structure:

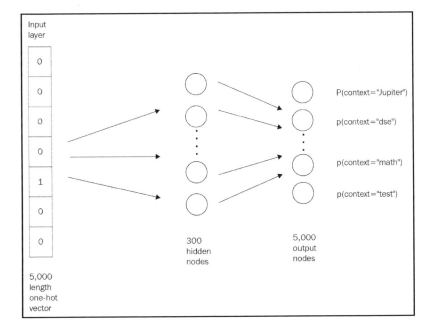

Like the RBM, we have a visible input layer and a hidden layer. In this case, our input layer has as many nodes as the length of vocabulary that we wish to learn from. This comes in handy if we have a corpus of millions of words but we wish to only learn a handful of them. In the preceding graph, we would be learning the context of 5,000 words. The hidden layer in this graph represents the number of features we wish to learn about each word. In this case, we will be embedding words into a 300-dimensional space.

The main difference between this neural network and the one we used for RBM is the existence of an output layer. Note that in our graph, the output layer has as many nodes as the input layer. This is not a coincidence. Word embedding models work by *predicting* nearby words based on the existence of a reference word. For example, if we were to predict the word *calculus*, we would want the final `math` node to light up the most. This gives the semblance of a supervised machine learning algorithm.

We then train the graph on this structure and eventually learn the 300-dimension word representations by passing in one-hot vectors of words and extracting the hidden layer's output vector and using that as our latent structure. In production, the previous diagram is extremely inefficient due to the very large number of output nodes. In order to make this process extremely more computationally efficient, different loss functions are utilized to capitalize on the text's structure.

The gensim package for creating Word2vec embeddings

We will not be implementing a full working neural network that performs the word embedding procedure, however we will be using a Python package called `gensim` to do this work for us:

```
# import the gensim package
import gensim
```

A `gensim` can take in a corpora of text and run the preceding neural network structure for us and obtain word embeddings with only a few lines of code. To see this in action, let's import a standard corpus to get started. Let's set a logger in our notebook so that we can see the training process in a bit more detail:

```
import logging

logging.basicConfig(format='%(asctime)s : %(levelname)s : %(message)s',
level=logging.INFO)
```

Now, let's create our corpus:

```
from gensim.models import word2vec, Word2Vec

sentences = word2vec.Text8Corpus('../data/text8')
```

Notice the term `word2vec`. This is a specific algorithm used to calculate word embeddings and the main algorithm used by `gensim`. It is one of the standards for word embeddings.

For gensim to do its job, sentences needs to be any iterable (list, generator, tuple, and so on) that holds sentences that are already tokenized. Once we have such a variable, we can put `gensim` to work by learning word embeddings:

```
# instantiate a gensim module on the sentences from above
# min_count allows us to ignore words that occur strictly less than this
value
# size is the dimension of words we wish to learn
model = gensim.models.Word2Vec(sentences, min_count=1, size=20)
```

```
2017-12-29 16:43:25,133 : INFO : collecting all words and their counts
2017-12-29 16:43:25,136 : INFO : PROGRESS: at sentence #0, processed 0
words, keeping 0 word types
2017-12-29 16:43:31,074 : INFO : collected 253854 word types from a corpus
of 17005207 raw words and 1701 sentences
2017-12-29 16:43:31,075 : INFO : Loading a fresh vocabulary
2017-12-29 16:43:31,990 : INFO : min_count=1 retains 253854 unique words
(100% of original 253854, drops 0)
2017-12-29 16:43:31,991 : INFO : min_count=1 leaves 17005207 word corpus
(100% of original 17005207, drops 0)
2017-12-29 16:43:32,668 : INFO : deleting the raw counts dictionary of
253854 items
2017-12-29 16:43:32,676 : INFO : sample=0.001 downsamples 36 most-common
words
2017-12-29 16:43:32,678 : INFO : downsampling leaves estimated 12819131
word corpus (75.4% of prior 17005207)
2017-12-29 16:43:32,679 : INFO : estimated required memory for 253854
words and 20 dimensions: 167543640 bytes
2017-12-29 16:43:33,431 : INFO : resetting layer weights
2017-12-29 16:43:36,097 : INFO : training model with 3 workers on 253854
vocabulary and 20 features, using sg=0 hs=0 sample=0.001 negative=5
window=5
2017-12-29 16:43:37,102 : INFO : PROGRESS: at 1.32% examples, 837067
words/s, in_qsize 5, out_qsize 0
2017-12-29 16:43:38,107 : INFO : PROGRESS: at 2.61% examples, 828701
words/s,
... 2017-12-29 16:44:53,508 : INFO : PROGRESS: at 98.21% examples, 813353
```

```
words/s, in_qsize 6, out_qsize 0 2017-12-29 16:44:54,513 : INFO : PROGRESS:
at 99.58% examples, 813962 words/s, in_qsize 4, out_qsize 0
... 2017-12-29 16:44:54,829 : INFO : training on 85026035 raw words
(64096185 effective words) took 78.7s, 814121 effective words/s
```

This line of code will start the learning process. If you are passing in a large corpus, it may take a while. Now that the `gensim` module is done fitting, we can use it. We can grab individual embeddings by passing strings into the `word2vec` object:

```
# get the vectorization of a word
model.wv['king']
```

```
array([-0.48768288, 0.66667134, 2.33743191, 2.71835423, 4.17330408,
2.30985498, 1.92848825, 1.43448424, 3.91518641, -0.01281452, 3.82612252,
0.60087812, 6.15167284, 4.70150518, -1.65476751, 4.85853577, 3.45778084,
5.02583361, -2.98040175, 2.37563372], dtype=float32)
```

The `gensim` has built-in methods to get the most out of our word embeddings. For example, to answer the question about the `king`, we can use the the `most_similar` method:

```
# woman + king - man = queen
 model.wv.most_similar(positive=['woman', 'king'], negative=['man'],
topn=10)
```

```
[(u'emperor', 0.8988120555877686), (u'prince', 0.87584388256073),
(u'consul', 0.8575721979141235), (u'tsar', 0.8558996319770813),
(u'constantine', 0.8515684604644775), (u'pope', 0.8496872782707214),
(u'throne', 0.8495982885360718), (u'elector', 0.8379884362220764),
(u'judah', 0.8376096487045288), (u'emperors', 0.8356839418411255)]
```

Hmm, unfortunately this isn't giving us the answer we'd expect: `queen`. Let's try the `Paris` word association:

```
# London is to England as Paris is to ____
 model.wv.most_similar(positive=['Paris', 'England'], negative=['London'],
topn=1)
```

```
KeyError: "word 'Paris' not in vocabulary"
```

It appears that the word `Paris` was never even learned as it did not appear in our corpus. We can start to see the limitations to this procedure. Our embeddings will only be as good as the corpus we are selecting and the machines we use to calculate these embeddings. In our data directory, we have provided a pre-trained vocabulary of words that spans across 3,000,000 words found on websites indexed by Google with 300 dimensions learned for each word.

Let's go ahead and import these pre-trained embeddings. We can do this by using built-in importer tools in `gensim`:

```
# use a pretrained vocabulary with 3,000,000 words
import gensim

model =
gensim.models.KeyedVectors.load_word2vec_format('../data/GoogleNews-
vectors-negative300.bin', binary=True)

# 3,000,000 words in our vocab
len(model.wv.vocab)

3000000
```

These embeddings have been trained using vastly more powerful machines than anything we have at home and for a much longer period of time. Let's try our word problems out now:

```
# woman + king - man = queen
model.wv.most_similar(positive=['woman', 'king'], negative=['man'],
topn=1)

[(u'queen', 0.7118192911148071)]

# London is to England as Paris is to _____
model.wv.most_similar(positive=['Paris', 'England'], negative=['London'],
topn=1)

[(u'France', 0.6676377654075623)]
```

Excellent! It seems as though these word embeddings were trained enough to allow us to answer these complex word puzzles. The `most_similar` method, as used previously, will return the token in the vocabulary that is most similar to the words provided. Words in the `positive` list are vectors added to one another, while words in the `negative` list are subtracted from the resulting vector. The following graph provides a visual representation of how we use word vectors to extract meaning:

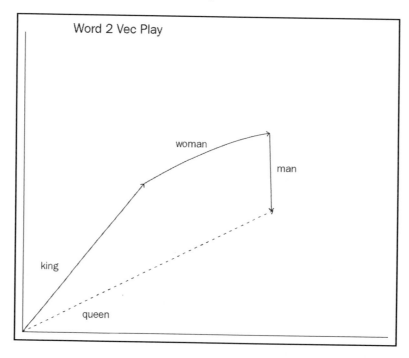

Here, we are starting with the vector representation for **king** and adding to it the concept (vector) for **woman**. From there, we subtract the **man** vector (by adding the negative of the vector) to obtain the dotted vector. This vector is the most similar to the vector representation for **queen**. This is how we obtain the formula:

king + woman - man = queen

The `gensim` has other methods that we may utilize such as `doesnt_match`. This method singles out words that do not belong to a list of words. It does so by isolating the word that is the most dissimilar on average to the rest of the words. For example, if we give the method four words, three of which are animals and the other is a plant, we hope it will figure out which of those doesn't belong:

```
# Pick out the oddball word in a sentence
model.wv.doesnt_match("duck bear cat tree".split())

'tree'
```

The package also includes methods to calculate a 0-1 score of similarity between single words that can be used to compare words on the fly:

```
# grab a similarity score between 0 and 1

# the similarity between the words woman and man, pretty similar
model.wv.similarity('woman', 'man')
0.766401223

# similarity between the words tree and man, not very similar
model.wv.similarity('tree', 'man')
0.229374587
```

Here, we can see that man is more similar to woman than man is to tree. We can use these helpful methods in order to implement some useful applications of word embeddings that would not be possible otherwise.

Application of word embeddings - information retrieval

There are countless applications for word embeddings; one of these is in the field of information retrieval. When humans input keywords and key phrases into search engines, search engines are able to recall and surface specific articles/stories that match those keywords exactly. For example, if we search for articles about dogs, we will get articles that mention the word dog. But what if we search for the word canine? We should still expect to see articles about dogs based on the fact that canines are dogs. Let's implement a simple information retrieval system to showcase the power of word embeddings.

Let's create a function that tries to grab embeddings of individual words from our gensim package and returns None if this lookup fails:

```
# helper function to try to grab embeddings for a word and returns None if
```

```
that word is not found
def get_embedding(string):
    try:
        return model.wv[string]
    except:
        return None
```

Now, let's create three article titles, one about a dog, one about a cat, and one about absolutely nothing at all for a distractor:

```
# very original article titles
sentences = [
"this is about a dog",
"this is about a cat",
"this is about nothing"
]
```

The goal is to input a reference word that is similar to dog or cat and be able to grab the more relevant title. To do this, we will first create a 3 x 300 matrix of vectorizations for each sentence. We will do this by taking the mean of every word in the sentence and using the resulting mean vector as an estimation of the vectorization of the entire sentence. Once we have a vectorization of every sentence, we can compare that against the embedding of the reference word by taking a dot product between them. The closest vector is the one with the largest dot product:

```
# Zero matrix of shape (3,300)
vectorized_sentences = np.zeros((len(sentences),300))
# for every sentence
for i, sentence in enumerate(sentences):
    # tokenize sentence into words
    words = sentence.split(' ')
    # embed whichever words that we can
    embedded_words = [get_embedding(w) for w in words]
    embedded_words = filter(lambda x:x is not None, embedded_words)
    # Take a mean of the vectors to get an estimate vectorization of the
sentence
    vectorized_sentence = reduce(lambda x,y:x+y,
embedded_words)/len(embedded_words)
    # change the ith row (in place) to be the ith vectorization
    vectorized_sentences[i:] = vectorized_sentence

vectorized_sentences.shape
(3, 300)
```

One thing to notice here is that we are creating a vectorization of documents (collection of words) and not considering the order of the words. How is this better than utilizing a `CountVectorizer` or a `TfidfVectorizer` to grab a count-based vectorization of text? The gensim method is attempting to project our text onto a latent structure learned by the context of individual words, while the scikit-learn vectorizers are only able to use the vocab at our disposal to create our vectorizations. In these three sentences, there are only seven unique words:

this, is, about, a, dog, cat, nothing

So, the maximum shape our `CountVectorizer` or `TfidfVectorizer` can project is (3, 7). Let's try to grab the most relevant sentence to the word dog:

```
# we want articles most similar to the reference word "dog"
reference_word = 'dog'

# take a dot product between the embedding of dof and our vectorized matrix
best_sentence_idx = np.dot(vectorized_sentences,
get_embedding(reference_word)).argsort()[-1]

# output the most relevant sentence
sentences[best_sentence_idx]

'this is about a dog'
```

That one was easy. Given the word dog, we should be able to retrieve the sentence about a dog. This should also hold true if we input the word cat:

```
reference_word = 'cat'
best_sentence_idx = np.dot(vectorized_sentences,
get_embedding(reference_word)).argsort()[-1]

sentences[best_sentence_idx]

'this is about a cat'
```

Now, let's try something harder. Let's input the words canine and tiger and see if we get the dog and cat sentences respectively:

```
reference_word = 'canine'
best_sentence_idx = np.dot(vectorized_sentences,
get_embedding(reference_word)).argsort()[-1]

print sentences[best_sentence_idx]

'this is about a dog'
```

```
reference_word = 'tiger'
best_sentence_idx = np.dot(vectorized_sentences,
get_embedding(reference_word)).argsort()[-1]

print sentences[best_sentence_idx]

'this is about a cat'
```

Let's try a slightly more interesting example. The following are chapter titles from Sinan's first book, *Principles of Data Science*:

```
# Chapter titles from Sinan's first book, "The Principles of Data Science

sentences = """How to Sound Like a Data Scientist
Types of Data
The Five Steps of Data Science
Basic Mathematics
A Gentle Introduction to Probability
Advanced Probability
Basic Statistics
Advanced Statistics
Communicating Data
Machine Learning Essentials
Beyond the Essentials
Case Studies """.split('\n')
```

This will give us a list of 12 different chapter titles to retrieve from. The goal then will be to use a reference word to sort and serve up the top three most relevant chapter titles to read, given the topic. For example, if we asked our algorithm to give us chapters relating to *math*, we might expect to be recommended the chapters about basic mathematics, statistics, and probability.

Let's try to see which chapters are the best to read, given human input. Before we do so, let's calculate a matrix of vectorized documents like we did with our previous three sentences:

```
# Zero matrix of shape (3,300)
vectorized_sentences = np.zeros((len(sentences),300))
# for every sentence
for i, sentence in enumerate(sentences):
    # tokenize sentence into words
    words = sentence.split(' ')
    # embed whichever words that we can
    embedded_words = [get_embedding(w) for w in words]
    embedded_words = filter(lambda x:x is not None, embedded_words)
    # Take a mean of the vectors to get an estimate vectorization of the
sentence
    vectorized_sentence = reduce(lambda x,y:x+y,
```

```
embedded_words)/len(embedded_words)
    # change the ith row (in place) to be the ith vectorization
    vectorized_sentences[i:] = vectorized_sentence

vectorized_sentences.shape
(12, 300)
```

Now, let's find the chapters that are most related to math:

```
# find chapters about math
reference_word = 'math'
best_sentence_idx = np.dot(vectorized_sentences,
get_embedding(reference_word)).argsort()[-3:][::-1]

[sentences[b] for b in best_sentence_idx]

['Basic Mathematics', 'Basic Statistics', 'Advanced Probability ']
```

Now, let's say we are giving a talk about data and want to know which chapters are going to be the most helpful in that area:

```
# which chapters are about giving talks about data
reference_word = 'talk'
best_sentence_idx = np.dot(vectorized_sentences,
get_embedding(reference_word)).argsort()[-3:][::-1]

[sentences[b] for b in best_sentence_idx]

['Communicating Data ', 'How to Sound Like a Data Scientist', 'Case Studies
']
```

And finally, which chapters are about AI:

```
# which chapters are about AI
reference_word = 'AI'
best_sentence_idx = np.dot(vectorized_sentences,
get_embedding(reference_word)).argsort()[-3:][::-1]

[sentences[b] for b in best_sentence_idx]

['Advanced Probability ', 'Advanced Statistics', 'Machine Learning
Essentials']
```

We can see how we can use word embeddings to retrieve information in the form of text given context learned from the universe of text.

Summary

This chapter focused on two feature learning tools: RBM and word embedding processes.

Both of these processes utilized deep learning architectures in order to learn new sets of features based on raw data. Both techniques took advantage of shallow networks in order to optimize for training times and used the weights and biases learned during the fitting phase to extract the latent structure of the data.

Our next chapter will showcase four examples of feature engineering on real data taken from the open internet and how the tools that we have learned in this book will help us create the optimal machine learning pipelines.

8
Case Studies

This book has gone through several different feature engineering algorithms and we have worked with many different datasets. In this chapter, we will go through a few case studies to help you deepen your understanding of the topics we have covered in the book. We will work through two full-length case studies from beginning to end to further understand how feature engineering tasks can help us create machine learning pipelines for real-life applications. For each case study, we will go through:

- The application that we are working towards
- The data in question that we are using
- A brief exploratory data analysis
- Setting up our machine learning pipelines and gathering metrics

Moreover, we will be going through the following cases:

- Facial recognition
- Predicting hotel reviews data

Let's get started!

Case study 1 - facial recognition

Our first case study will be to predict the labels for image data with a popular dataset called the **Labeled Faces** in the `Wild` dataset from the scikit-learn library. The dataset is called the `Olivetti Face` dataset and it comprises pictures of famous people's faces, with appropriate labels. Our task is that of **facial recognition**, a supervised machine learning model that is able to predict the name of the person given an image of their face.

Applications of facial recognition

Image processing and facial recognition are far-reaching. The ability to quickly discern people's faces from a crowd of people in video/images is vital for physical security as well as for giant social media companies. Search engines such as Google, with their image search capabilities, are using image recognition algorithms to match images and quantify similarities to a point where we can upload a photo of someone to get all other images of that same person.

The data

Let's start with loading in our dataset and several other import statements we will be using to plot our data. It is good practice to begin a Jupyter notebook (iPython) with all the import statements you will be using. Obviously, you may get partway through your work and realize that you need to import a new package; also, to stay organized, it is a good idea to keep them in the beginning of your work.

The following code block includes the `import` statements we will be using for this case study. We will utilize each import in the example and it will become clear to you what each of them is used for as we work out our example:

```
# the olivetti face dataset
from sklearn.datasets import fetch_lfw_people

# feature extraction modules
from sklearn.decomposition import PCA
from sklearn.discriminant_analysis import LinearDiscriminantAnalysis

# feature scaling module
from sklearn.preprocessing import StandardScaler

# standard python modules
from time import time
import numpy as np
import matplotlib.pyplot as plt

%matplotlib inline # this ensures that your plotting will show directly in
your jupyter notebook

# scikit-learn model selection modules from sklearn.model_selection import
train_test_split, GridSearchCV, cross_val_score

# metrics
from sklearn.metrics import classification_report, confusion_matrix,
```

```
accuracy_score

# machine learning modules
from sklearn.linear_model import LogisticRegression
from sklearn.pipeline import Pipeline
```

Now, we can get started! We proceed as follows:

1. First, let's load in our dataset and see what we are working with. We will use the `fetch_flw_people` function built in with scikit-learn:

```
lfw_people = fetch_lfw_people(min_faces_per_person=70, resize=0.4)
```

As you can see, we have a couple of optional parameters that we've invoked, specifically, `min_faces_per_person` and `resize`. The first parameter will only retain the pictures of people who are in the minimum number of different pictures that we specify. We have set this to be a minimum of 70 different pictures per person. The `resize` parameter is the ratio used to resize each face picture.

2. Let's inspect the image arrays to find shapes for plotting the images. We can do this with the following code:

```
n_samples, h, w = lfw_people.images.shape
n_samples, h, w

(1288, 50, 37)
```

We see that we have 1288 samples (images) and each image has a height of 50 pixels and a width of 37 pixels.

3. Now, let's set up the X and y for our machine learning pipeline. We will grab the `data` attribute of the `lfw_people` object:

```
# for machine learning we use the data directly (as relative pixel
positions info is ignored by this model)

X = lfw_people.data
y = lfw_people.target
n_features = X.shape[1]

n_features
1850
```

The fact that `n_features` ends up having $1,850$ columns comes from the fact that:

$$50 \times 37 = 1,850$$

We can now see the full shape of our data, as follows:

```
X.shape

(1288, 1850)
```

Some data exploration

We have 1,288 rows by 1,850 columns. To do some brief exploratory analysis, we can plot one of the images by using this code:

```
# plot one of the faces
plt.imshow(X[0].reshape((h, w)), cmap=plt.cm.gray)
lfw_people.target_names[y[0]]
```

This will give us the following label:

```
'Hugo Chavez'
```

The image is as follows:

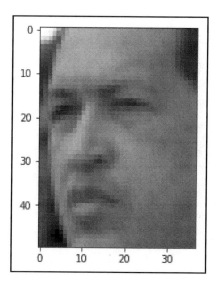

Now, let's plot the same image after applying a scaling module, as follows:

```
plt.imshow(StandardScaler().fit_transform(X)[0].reshape((h, w)),
cmap=plt.cm.gray)
lfw_people.target_names[y[0]]
```

Which gives us this output:

```
'Hugo Chavez'
```

We get the following image for the preceding code:

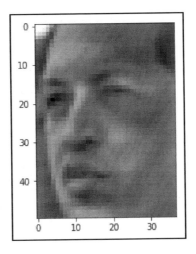

Here, you can see that the image is slightly different, with darker pixels around the face. Now, let's set up the label to predict:

```
# the label to predict is the id of the person
target_names = lfw_people.target_names
n_classes = target_names.shape[0]

print "Total dataset size:"
print "n_samples: %d" % n_samples
print "n_features: %d" % n_features
print "n_classes: %d" % n_classes
```

This gives us the following output:

```
Total dataset size:
n_samples: 1288
n_features: 1850
n_classes: 7
```

Applied facial recognition

Now, we can move on to the machine learning pipelines that will be used to create our facial recognition models:

1. We can start by creating `train`, `test`, and `split` in our dataset, as shown in the following code block:

```
# let's split our dataset into training and testing
X_train, X_test, y_train, y_test = train_test_split(X, y,
test_size=0.25, random_state=1)
```

2. We are ready to perform a **Principal Component Analysis (PCA)** on our dataset. We will want to instantiate a PCA first and ensure that we `scale` our data before applying PCA in our pipeline. This can be done as follows:

```
# instantiate the PCA module
pca = PCA(n_components=200, whiten=True)

# create a pipeline called preprocessing that will scale data and
then apply PCA
preprocessing = Pipeline([('scale', StandardScaler()), ('pca',
pca)])
```

3. Now, we can `fit` our pipeline:

```
print "Extracting the top %d eigenfaces from %d faces" % (200,
X_train.shape[0])

# fit the pipeline to the training set
preprocessing.fit(X_train)

# grab the PCA from the pipeline
extracted_pca = preprocessing.steps[1][1]
```

4. The output will be our print statement:

```
Extracting the top 200 eigenfaces from 966 faces
```

5. Let's look at the scree plot:

```
# Scree Plot

plt.plot(np.cumsum(extracted_pca.explained_variance_ratio_))
```

We can see that starting at 100 components captures over 90% of the variance, compared to the 1,850 original features.

6. We can create a function to plot our PCA components, like so:

```
comp = extracted_pca.components_
image_shape = (h, w)
def plot_gallery(title, images, n_col, n_row):
    plt.figure(figsize=(2. * n_col, 2.26 * n_row))
    plt.suptitle(title, size=16)
    for i, comp in enumerate(images):
        plt.subplot(n_row, n_col, i + 1)
        vmax = max(comp.max(), -comp.min())
        plt.imshow(comp.reshape(image_shape), cmap=plt.cm.gray,
                   vmin=-vmax, vmax=vmax)
        plt.xticks(())
        plt.yticks(())
    plt.subplots_adjust(0.01, 0.05, 0.99, 0.93, 0.04, 0.)
    plt.show()
```

7. We can now call our `plot_gallery` function, like so:

```
plot_gallery('PCA components', comp[:16], 4,4)
```

The output gives us these images:

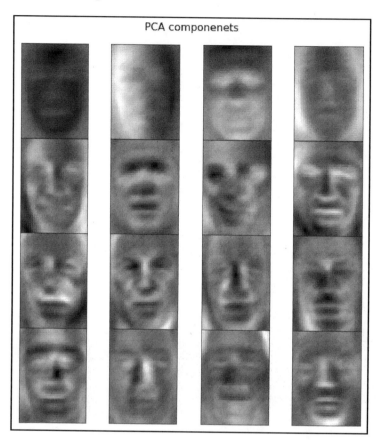

This lets us see our PCA components for a specific row and column! These **eigen-faces** are extracted features of humans that the PCA module is finding. Compare this to our result in Chapter 7, *Feature Learning*, where we used PCA to extract **eigen-digits**. Each of these components is meant to house vital information about faces that can be used to distinguish between different people. For example:

- The eigen-face in the third row, fourth column seems to be highlighting the moustache and beard areas in order to quantify how much facial hair would help in separating out our classes
- The eigen-face in the first row, fourth column seems to be showing a contrast between the background and the face, putting a number to the lighting situation of the image

Of course, these are interpretations by us, and different eigen-faces for different face datasets will output different images/components. We will move on to create a function that will allow us to clearly print a more readable confusion matrix with heat labels and options for normalization:

```
import itertools
def plot_confusion_matrix(cm, classes,
                          normalize=False,
                          title='Confusion matrix',
                          cmap=plt.cm.Blues):
    plt.imshow(cm, interpolation='nearest', cmap=cmap)
    plt.title(title)
    plt.colorbar()
    tick_marks = np.arange(len(classes))
    plt.xticks(tick_marks, classes, rotation=45)
    plt.yticks(tick_marks, classes)

    thresh = cm.max() / 2.
    for i, j in itertools.product(range(cm.shape[0]), range(cm.shape[1])):
        plt.text(j, i, cm[i, j],
                 horizontalalignment="center",
                 color="white" if cm[i, j] > thresh else "black")
    plt.ylabel('True label')
    plt.xlabel('Predicted label')
```

Now, we can fit without using PCA to see the difference. We will invoke our `plot_confusion_matrix` function so that we can visualize the accuracy of our model:

```
# fit without using PCA to see what the difference will be
t0 = time()

param_grid = {'C': [1e-2, 1e-1,1e0,1e1, 1e2]}
clf = GridSearchCV(logreg, param_grid)
clf = clf.fit(X_train, y_train)
best_clf = clf.best_estimator_

# Predicting people's names on the test set
y_pred = best_clf.predict(X_test)

print accuracy_score(y_pred, y_test), "Accuracy score for best estimator"
print(classification_report(y_test, y_pred, target_names=target_names))
print plot_confusion_matrix(confusion_matrix(y_test, y_pred,
labels=range(n_classes)), target_names)
print round((time() - t0), 1), "seconds to grid search and predict the test
set"
```

The output is as follows:

```
0.813664596273 Accuracy score for best estimator
                   precision     recall    f1-score    support

      Ariel Sharon     0.72        0.68       0.70          19
      Colin Powell     0.85        0.71       0.77          55
   Donald Rumsfeld     0.62        0.72       0.67          25
      George W Bush    0.88        0.91       0.89         142
 Gerhard Schroeder     0.79        0.84       0.81          31
       Hugo Chavez     0.87        0.81       0.84          16
        Tony Blair     0.71        0.71       0.71          34

       avg / total     0.82        0.81       0.81         322
```

```
None
39.9 seconds to grid search and predict the test set
```

We get the plot as follows:

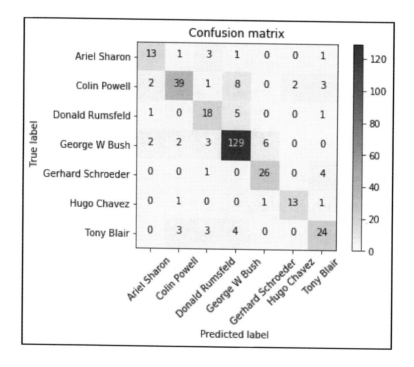

Using only raw pixels, our linear model was able to achieve **81.3%** accuracy. This time, let's apply PCA to see what the difference will be. We will hardcode the number of components to extract to 200 for now:

```
t0 = time()

face_pipeline = Pipeline(steps=[('PCA', PCA(n_components=200)),
('logistic', logreg)])

pipe_param_grid = {'logistic__C': [1e-2, 1e-1,1e0,1e1, 1e2]}
clf = GridSearchCV(face_pipeline, pipe_param_grid)
clf = clf.fit(X_train, y_train)
best_clf = clf.best_estimator_

# Predicting people's names on the test set
y_pred = best_clf.predict(X_test)

print accuracy_score(y_pred, y_test), "Accuracy score for best estimator"
print(classification_report(y_test, y_pred, target_names=target_names))
print plot_confusion_matrix(confusion_matrix(y_test, y_pred,
labels=range(n_classes)), target_names)
print round((time() - t0), 1), "seconds to grid search and predict the test
set"
```

The output with PCA looks like this:

```
0.739130434783 Accuracy score for best estimator
                   precision    recall  f1-score   support

      Ariel Sharon      0.67      0.63      0.65        19
      Colin Powell      0.69      0.60      0.64        55
   Donald Rumsfeld      0.74      0.68      0.71        25
     George W Bush      0.76      0.88      0.82       142
 Gerhard Schroeder      0.77      0.77      0.77        31
       Hugo Chavez      0.62      0.62      0.62        16
        Tony Blair      0.77      0.50      0.61        34

       avg / total      0.74      0.74      0.73       322

None
74.5 seconds to grid search and predict the test set
```

We get the plot as follows:

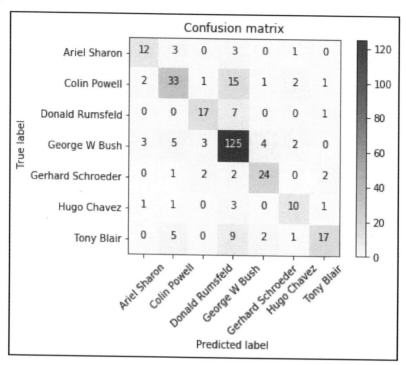

Interesting! We can see that our accuracy went down to **73.9%** and our time to predict went up by applying PCA. We should not get discouraged, however; this likely means that we have not found the optimal number of components to use yet.

Let's plot a few of the predicted names versus the true names within our test set to see some of the errors/correct labels that our models are producing:

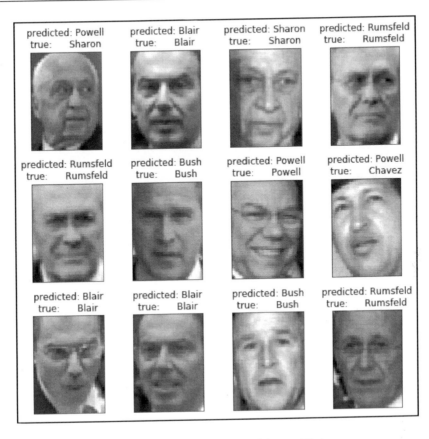

This is a great way to visualize our results when working with images.

Let's now implement a grid search to find the best model and accuracy for our data. First, we will create a function that will perform the grid search for us and print the accuracy, parameters, average time to fit, and average time to score neatly for us. This function is created like so:

```
def get_best_model_and_accuracy(model, params, X, y):
    grid = GridSearchCV(model,                  # the model to grid search
                        params,                  # the parameter set to try
                        error_score=0.)  # if a parameter set raises an
error, continue and set the performance as a big, fat 0
    grid.fit(X, y)                  # fit the model and parameters
    # our classical metric for performance
    print "Best Accuracy: {}".format(grid.best_score_)
    # the best parameters that caused the best accuracy
    print "Best Parameters: {}".format(grid.best_params_)
    # the average time it took a model to fit to the data (in seconds)
```

```
    print "Average Time to Fit (s):
{}".format(round(grid.cv_results_['mean_fit_time'].mean(), 3))
    # the average time it took a model to predict out of sample data (in
seconds)
    # this metric gives us insight into how this model will perform in
real-time analysis
    print "Average Time to Score (s):
{}".format(round(grid.cv_results_['mean_score_time'].mean(), 3))
```

Now, we can create a larger grid search pipeline that includes many more components, namely:

- A scaling module
- A PCA module to extract the best features that capture the variance in the data
- A **Linear Discriminat Analysis (LDA)** module to create features that best separate the faces from one another
- Our linear classifier, which will reap the benefits of our three feature engineering modules and attempt to distinguish between our faces

The code for creating large grid search pipeline is as follows:

```
# Create a larger pipeline to gridsearch
face_params = {'logistic__C':[1e-2, 1e-1, 1e0, 1e1, 1e2],
            'preprocessing__pca__n_components':[100, 150, 200, 250,
300],

            'preprocessing__pca__whiten':[True, False],
            'preprocessing__lda__n_components':range(1, 7)
            # [1, 2, 3, 4, 5, 6] recall the max allowed is n_classes-1
            }

pca = PCA()
lda = LinearDiscriminantAnalysis()

preprocessing = Pipeline([('scale', StandardScaler()), ('pca', pca),
('lda', lda)])

logreg = LogisticRegression()
face_pipeline = Pipeline(steps=[('preprocessing', preprocessing),
('logistic', logreg)])

get_best_model_and_accuracy(face_pipeline, face_params, X, y)
```

Here are the results:

```
Best Accuracy: 0.840062111801
Best Parameters: {'logistic__C': 0.1, 'preprocessing__pca__n_components':
```

```
150, 'preprocessing__lda__n_components': 5, 'preprocessing__pca__whiten':
False}
Average Time to Fit (s): 0.214
Average Time to Score (s): 0.009
```

We can see that our model accuracy has improved by a good amount, and also our time to predict and train is very fast!

Case study 2 - predicting topics of hotel reviews data

Our second case study will take a look at hotel reviews data and attempt to cluster the reviews into topics. We will be employing a **latent semantic analysis (LSA)**, which is a name given to the process of applying a PCA on sparse text document—term matrices. It is done to find latent structures in text for the purpose of classification and clustering.

Applications of text clustering

Text **clustering** is the act of assigning different topics to pieces of text for the purpose of understanding what documents are about. Imagine a large hotel chain that gets thousands of reviews a week from around the world. Employees of the hotel would like to know what people are saying in order to have a better idea of what they are doing well and what can be improved.

Of course, the limiting factor here is the ability for humans to read all of these texts quickly and correctly. We can train machines to identify the types of things that people are talking about and then predict the topics of new and incoming reviews in order to automate this process.

Hotel review data

The dataset that we will use to achieve this result comes from Kaggle and can be found here at: `https://www.kaggle.com/datafiniti/hotel-reviews`. It contains over 35,000 distinct reviews of 1,000 different hotels around the world. Our job will be to isolate the text of the reviews and identify *topics* (what people are talking about). Then, we'll create a machine learning model that can predict/identify the topics of incoming reviews:

First, let's organize our import statements, as follows:

```
# used for row normalization
from sklearn.preprocessing import Normalizer

# scikit-learn's KMeans clustering module
from sklearn.cluster import KMeans

# data manipulation tool
import pandas as pd

# import a sentence tokenizer from nltk
from nltk.tokenize import sent_tokenize

# feature extraction module (TruncatedSVD will be explained soon)
from sklearn.decomposition import PCA from sklearn.decomposition import
TruncatedSVD
```

Now, let's load in our data, as shown in the following code snippet:

```
hotel_reviews = pd.read_csv('../data/7282_1.csv')
```

Once we have imported our data, let's work to take a peek into what our raw text data looks like.

Exploration of the data

Let's look at the shape of our dataset:

```
hotel_reviews.shape
```

```
(35912, 19)
```

This is showing us that we are working with 35,912 rows and 19 columns. Eventually, we will be concerned only with the column that contains the text data, but for now, let's see what the first few rows look like to get a better sense of what is included in our data:

```
hotel_reviews.head()
```

This gives us the following table:

	address	categories	city	country	latitude	longitude	name	postalCode	province	reviews. date	reviews. dateAdded	reviews. doRecommend	reviews. id	reviews. rating	reviews. text	reviews. title	reviews. userCity	reviews. username	reviews. userProvince
0	Riviera San Nicol 11/a	Hotels	Mableton	US	45.421611	12.376187	Hotel Russo Palace	30126	GA	2013-09-22T00:00:00Z	2016-10-24T00:00:25Z	NaN	NaN	4.0	Pleasant 10 min walk along the sea front to th...	Good location away from the crouds	NaN	Russ (kent)	NaN

1	Riviera San Nicol 11/a	Hotels	Mableton	US	45.421611	12.376187	Hotel Russo Palace	30126	GA	2015-04-03T00:00:00Z	2016-10-24T00:00:25Z	NaN	NaN	5.0	Really lovely hotel. Stayed on the very top fl...	Great hotel with Jacuzzi bath!	NaN	A Traveler	NaN
2	Riviera San Nicol 11/a	Hotels	Mableton	US	45.421611	12.376187	Hotel Russo Palace	30126	GA	2014-05-13T00:00:00Z	2016-10-24T00:00:25Z	NaN	NaN	5.0	Ett mycket bra hotell. Det som drog ner betyge...	Lugnt l◆◆ge	NaN	Maud	NaN
3	Riviera San Nicol 11/a	Hotels	Mableton	US	45.421611	12.376187	Hotel Russo Palace	30126	GA	2013-10-27T00:00:00Z	2016-10-24T00:00:25Z	NaN	NaN	5.0	We stayed here for four nights in October. The...	Good location on the Lido.	NaN	Julie	NaN
4	Riviera San Nicol 11/a	Hotels	Mableton	US	45.421611	12.376187	Hotel Russo Palace	30126	GA	2015-03-05T00:00:00Z	2016-10-24T00:00:25Z	NaN	NaN	5.0	We stayed here for four nights in October. The...	◆◆◆◆◆◆ ◆◆◆◆◆◆◆◆◆◆◆◆◆◆	NaN	sungchul	NaN

Let's only include reviews from the United States in order to try and include only English reviews. First, let's plot our data, like so:

```
# plot the lats and longs of reviews
hotel_reviews.plot.scatter(x='longitude', y='latitude')
```

The output looks something like this:

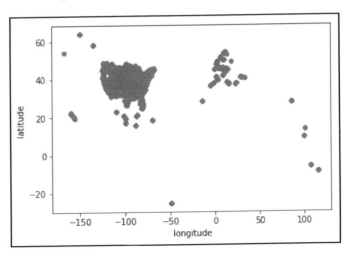

For the purpose of making our dataset a bit easier to work with, let's use pandas to subset the reviews and only include those that came from the United States:

```
# Filter to only include reviews within the US
hotel_reviews = hotel_reviews[((hotel_reviews['latitude']<=50.0) &
(hotel_reviews['latitude']>=24.0)) & ((hotel_reviews['longitude']<=-65.0) &
(hotel_reviews['longitude']>=-122.0))]
```

```
# Plot the lats and longs again
hotel_reviews.plot.scatter(x='longitude', y='latitude')
# Only looking at reviews that are coming from the US
```

The output is as follows:

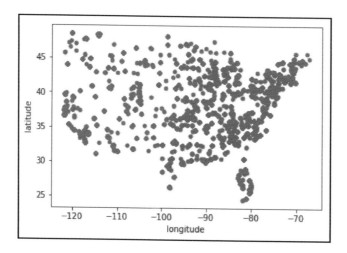

It looks like a map of the U.S.! Let's `shape` our filtered dataset now:

```
hotel_reviews.shape
```

We have 30,692 rows and 19 columns. When we write reviews for hotels, we usually write about different things in the same review. For this reason, we will attempt to assign topics to single sentences rather than to the entire review.

To do so, let's grab the text column from our data, like so:

```
texts = hotel_reviews['reviews.text']
```

The clustering model

We can tokenize the text into sentences so that we expand our dataset. We imported a function called `sent_tokenize` from the `nltk` package (natural language toolkit). This function will take in a single string and output the sentence as an ordered list of sentences separated by punctuation. For example:

```
sent_tokenize("hello! I am Sinan. How are you??? I am fine")

['hello!', 'I am Sinan.', 'How are you???', 'I am fine']
```

We will apply this function to our entire corpus using some reduce logic in Python. Essentially, we are applying the `sent_tokenize` function to each review and creating a single list called `sentences` that will hold all of our sentences:

```
sentences = reduce(lambda x, y:x+y, texts.apply(lambda x:
sent_tokenize(str(x).decode('utf-8'))))
```

We can now see how many sentences we have:

```
# the number of sentences
len(sentences)

118151
```

This gives us 118,151—the number of sentences we have to work with. To create a document-term matrix, let's use `TfidfVectorizer` on our sentences:

```
from sklearn.feature_extraction.text import TfidfVectorizer

tfidf = TfidfVectorizer(ngram_range=(1, 2), stop_words='english')

tfidf_transformed = tfidf.fit_transform(sentences)

tfidf_transformed
```

We get the following:

```
<118151x280901 sparse matrix of type '<type 'numpy.float64'>'
        with 1180273 stored elements in Compressed Sparse Row format>
```

Now, let's try to fit a PCA to this data, like so:

```
# try to fit PCA

PCA(n_components=1000).fit(tfidf_transformed)
```

Upon running this code, we get the following error:

```
TypeError: PCA does not support sparse input. See TruncatedSVD for a
possible alternative.
```

The is error tells us that for PCA, we cannot have a sparse input, and it suggests that we use **TruncatedSVD. singular value decomposition (SVD)** is a matrix *trick* for computing the same PCA components (when the data is centered) that allow us to work with sparse matrices. Let's take this suggestion and use the `TruncatedSVD` module.

SVD versus PCA components

Before we move on with our hotel data, let's do a quick experiment with our `iris` data to
see whether our SVD and PCA really give us the same components:

1. Let's start by grabbing our iris data and creating both a centered and a scaled
   version:

```
# import the Iris dataset from scikit-learn
from sklearn.datasets import load_iris

# load the Iris dataset
iris = load_iris()

# seperate the features and response variable
iris_X, iris_y = iris.data, iris.target

X_centered = StandardScaler(with_std=False).fit_transform(iris_X)
X_scaled = StandardScaler().fit_transform(iris_X)
```

2. Let's continue by instantiating an SVD and a PCA object:

```
# test if we get the same components by using PCA and SVD
svd = TruncatedSVD(n_components=2)
pca = PCA(n_components=2)
```

3. Now, let's apply both SVD and PCA to our raw `iris` data, centered version, and
   scaled version to compare:

```
# check if components of PCA and TruncatedSVD are same for a
dataset
# by substracting the two matrices and seeing if, on average, the
elements are very close to 0
print (pca.fit(iris_X).components_ -
svd.fit(iris_X).components_).mean()
```

```
0.130183123094  # not close to 0
# matrices are NOT the same
```

```
# check if components of PCA and TruncatedSVD are same for a
centered dataset
print (pca.fit(X_centered).components_ -
svd.fit(X_centered).components_).mean()
```

```
1.73472347598e-18  # close to 0
```

```
# matrices ARE the same


# check if components of PCA and TruncatedSVD are same for a scaled
dataset
print (pca.fit(X_scaled).components_ -
svd.fit(X_scaled).components_).mean()

-1.59160878921e-16  # close to 0
# matrices ARE the same
```

4. This shows us that the SVD module will return the same components as PCA if our data is scaled, but different components when using the raw unscaled data. Let's continue with our hotel data:

```
svd = TruncatedSVD(n_components=1000)
svd.fit(tfidf_transformed)
```

The output is as follows:

```
TruncatedSVD(algorithm='randomized', n_components=1000, n_iter=5,
        random_state=None, tol=0.0)
```

5. Let's make a scree plot as we would with our PCA module to see the explained variance of our SVD components:

```
# Scree Plot

plt.plot(np.cumsum(svd.explained_variance_ratio_))
```

This gives us the following plot:

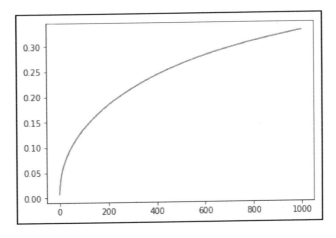

We can see that 1,000 components capture about 30% of the variance. Now, let's set up our LSA pipeline.

Latent semantic analysis

Latent semantic analysis (LSA) is a feature extraction tool. It is helpful for text that is a series of these three steps, which we have already learned in this book:

- A tfidf vectorization
- A PCA (SVD in this case to account for the sparsity of text)
- Row normalization

We can create a scikit-learn pipeline to perform LSA:

```
tfidf = TfidfVectorizer(ngram_range=(1, 2), stop_words='english')
svd = TruncatedSVD(n_components=10)  # will extract 10 "topics"
normalizer = Normalizer() # will give each document a unit norm

lsa = Pipeline(steps=[('tfidf', tfidf), ('svd', svd), ('normalizer',
normalizer)])
```

Now, we can fit and transform our sentences data, like so:

```
lsa_sentences = lsa.fit_transform(sentences)

lsa_sentences.shape

(118151, 10)
```

We have `118151` rows and 10 columns. These 10 columns come from the 10 extracted PCA/SVD components. We can now apply a `KMeans` clustering to our `lsa_sentences`, as follows:

```
cluster = KMeans(n_clusters=10)

cluster.fit(lsa_sentences)
```

 We are assuming that the reader has basic familiarity with clustering. For more information on clustering and how clustering works, please refer to *Principles of Data Science* by Packt: https://www.packtpub.com/big-data-and-business-intelligence/principles-data-science

It should be noted that we have chosen both 10 for the KMeans and our PCA. This is not necessary. Generally, you may extract more columns in the SVD module. With the 10 clusters, we are basically saying here, *I think there are 10 topics that people are talking about. Please assign each sentence to be one of those topics.*

The output is as follows:

```
KMeans(algorithm='auto', copy_x=True, init='k-means++', max_iter=300,
    n_clusters=10, n_init=10, n_jobs=1, precompute_distances='auto',
    random_state=None, tol=0.0001, verbose=0)
```

Let's time our fit and predict for our original document-term matrix of shape (118151, 280901) and then for our latent semantic analysis of shape (118151, 10) to see the differences:

1. First, the original dataset:

    ```
    %%timeit
    # time it takes to cluster on the original document-term matrix of
    shape (118151, 280901)
    cluster.fit(tfidf_transformed)
    ```

   This gives us:

    ```
    1 loop, best of 3: 4min 15s per loop
    ```

2. We will also time the prediction of Kmeans:

    ```
    %%timeit
    # also time the prediction phase of the Kmeans clustering
    cluster.predict(tfidf_transformed)
    ```

   This gives us:

    ```
    10 loops, best of 3: 120 ms per loop
    ```

3. Now, the LSA:

    ```
    %%timeit
    # time the time to cluster after latent semantic analysis of shape
    (118151, 10)
    cluster.fit(lsa_sentences)
    ```

This gives us:

```
1 loop, best of 3: 3.6 s per loop
```

4. We can see that the LSA is over 80 times faster than fitting on the original tfidf dataset. Suppose we time the prediction of the clustering with LSA, like so:

```
%%timeit
# also time the prediction phase of the Kmeans clustering after LSA
was performed
cluster.predict(lsa_sentences)
```

This gives us:

```
10 loops, best of 3: 34 ms per loop
```

We can see that the LSA dataset is over four times faster than predicting on the original `tfidf` dataset.

5. Now, let's transform the texts to a cluster distance space where each row represents an observation, like so:

```
cluster.transform(lsa_sentences).shape
(118151, 10)
predicted_cluster = cluster.predict(lsa_sentences)
predicted_cluster
```

The output gives us:

```
array([2, 2, 2, ..., 2, 2, 6], dtype=int32)
```

6. We can now get the distribution of topics, as follows:

```
# Distribution of "topics"
pd.Series(predicted_cluster).value_counts(normalize=True) # create
DataFrame of texts and predicted topics
texts_df = pd.DataFrame({'text':sentences,
'topic':predicted_cluster})

texts_df.head()

print "Top terms per cluster:"
original_space_centroids =
svd.inverse_transform(cluster.cluster_centers_)
order_centroids = original_space_centroids.argsort()[:, ::-1]
```

```
terms = lsa.steps[0][1].get_feature_names()
for i in range(10):
    print "Cluster %d:" % i
    print ', '.join([terms[ind] for ind in order_centroids[i, :5]])
    print
```

```
lsa.steps[0][1]
```

7. This gives us each topic with a list of the most *interesting* phrases (according to our TfidfVectorizer):

```
Top terms per cluster:
Cluster 0:
good, breakfast, breakfast good, room, great

Cluster 1:
hotel, recommend, good, recommend hotel, nice hotel

Cluster 2:
clean, room clean, rooms, clean comfortable, comfortable

Cluster 3:
room, room clean, hotel, nice, good

Cluster 4:
great, location, breakfast, hotel, stay

Cluster 5:
stay, hotel, good, enjoyed stay, enjoyed

Cluster 6:
comfortable, bed, clean comfortable, bed comfortable, room

Cluster 7:
nice, room, hotel, staff, nice hotel

Cluster 8:
hotel, room, good, great, stay

Cluster 9:
staff, friendly, staff friendly, helpful, friendly helpful
```

We can see the top terms by cluster, and some of them make a lot of sense. For example, cluster 1 seems to be about how people would recommend this hotel to their family and friends, while cluster 9 is about the staff and how they are friendly and helpful. In order to complete this application, we want to be able to predict new reviews with topics.

Now, we can try to predict the cluster of a new review, like so:

```
# topic prediction
print cluster.predict(lsa.transform(['I definitely recommend this hotel']))

print cluster.predict(lsa.transform(['super friendly staff. Love it!']))
```

The output gives us cluster 1 for the first prediction and cluster 9 for the second prediction, as follows:

```
[1]
[9]
```

Cool! `Cluster 1` corresponds to the following:

```
Cluster 1:
hotel, recommend, good, recommend hotel, nice hotel
```

`Cluster 9` corresponds to the following:

```
Cluster 9:
staff, friendly, staff friendly, helpful, friendly helpful
```

Looks like `Cluster 1` is recommending a hotel and `Cluster 9` is more staff-centered. Our predictions appear to be fairly accurate!

Summary

In this chapter, we saw two different case studies from two vastly different domains using many of the feature engineering methods learned in this book.

We do hope that you have found the contents of this book interesting and that you'll continue your learning! We leave it to you to keep exploring the world of feature engineering, machine learning, and data science. It is hoped that this book has been a catalyst for you to go out and learn even more about the subject.

For further reading past this book, I highly recommend looking into well-known data science books and blogs, such as:

- *Principles of Data Science* by Sinan Ozdemir, available through Packt at: https://www.packtpub.com/big-data-and-business-intelligence/principles-data-science
- *Machine Learning* and *AI* blog, KD-nuggets (https://www.kdnuggets.com/)

Other Books You May Enjoy

If you enjoyed this book, you may be interested in these other books by Packt:

Statistics for Machine Learning

Pratap Dangeti

ISBN: 978-1-78829-575-8

- Learn how to clean your data and ready it for analysis
- Understand the Statistical and Machine Learning fundamentals necessary to build models
- Understand the major differences and parallels between the statistical way and the Machine Learning way to solve problems
- Learn how to prepare data and feed models by using the appropriate Machine Learning algorithms from the more-than-adequate R and Python packages
- Analyze the results and tune the model appropriately to your own predictive goals
- Understand the concepts of required statistics for Machine Learning
- Introduce yourself to necessary fundamentals required for building supervised & unsupervised deep learning models
- Learn reinforcement learning and its application in the field of artificial intelligence domain

Machine Learning Algorithms

Giuseppe Bonaccorso

ISBN: 978-1-78588-962-2

- Acquaint yourself with important elements of Machine Learning
- Understand the feature selection and feature engineering process
- Assess performance and error trade-offs for Linear Regression
- Build a data model and understand how it works by using different types of algorithm
- Learn to tune the parameters of Support Vector machines
- Implement clusters to a dataset
- Explore the concept of Natural Processing Language and Recommendation Systems
- Create a ML architecture from scratch

Leave a review - let other readers know what you think

Please share your thoughts on this book with others by leaving a review on the site that you bought it from. If you purchased the book from Amazon, please leave us an honest review on this book's Amazon page. This is vital so that other potential readers can see and use your unbiased opinion to make purchasing decisions, we can understand what our customers think about our products, and our authors can see your feedback on the title that they have worked with Packt to create. It will only take a few minutes of your time, but is valuable to other potential customers, our authors, and Packt. Thank you!

Index

M

machine learning algorithms
  evaluation 21
machine learning pipeline
  RBMs, using in 251
  text, using in 137
  values, imputing in 87
machine learning
  used, for feature selection 171
mean squared error (MSE) 23
meta metrics 143
min-max scaling method 100, 101
missing values
  dealing with 74, 75, 76, 77
  identifying, in data 66
  imputing, in data 83, 85, 86
MNIST dataset
  about 238, 239
  PCA components, extracting from 241, 243, 244
  RBM components, extracting from 245, 247, 249
model-based feature selection 168

N

natural language processing (NLP) 7, 130, 168, 169
nominal level, of data
  mathematical operations 45, 47
non-parametric fallacy 232
normalization
  about 95
  min-max scaling method 100, 101
  row normalization method 102, 103
  z-score standardization 95, 96, 97, 98, 99, 100
numerical features
  extending 121

O

ordinal level, of data
  about 47
  mathematical operations 47, 49, 50

P

parametric assumptions
  of data 230
PCA components
  extracting, from MNIST 241, 243, 244
Pearson correlation
  using, for feature selection 153, 156, 158, 160
Pima Indian Diabetes Prediction dataset
  about 66, 67
  reference 66
pipelines
  in machine learning 87, 89, 90, 91
polynomial features
  about 124
  exploratory data analysis 126, 127, 129
  parameters 125
predictive analytics 25
Principal Component Analysis (PCA)
  about 185, 274
  data centering, effects 200
  data scaling, effects 202
  versus Linear Discriminant Analysis (LDA) 224
  with Iris dataset 187
  working 187
principal components
  about 185
  exploring 205, 207, 208
Principles of Data Science
  reference 230

Q

qualitative data 38
quantitative data 38
quantitative, versus qualitative data
  salary range, by job classification 39, 40, 43

R

ratio level, of data
  about 59
  mathematical operations 59
raw pixel values
  linear model, using on 251
RBM components
  extracting, from MNIST 245, 247, 249

Made in the USA
San Bernardino, CA
31 May 2018